new in town	coffee time	the friendliest thing	new sun in the sky	fine and dandy	love is wonderful ev'rywhere	my silent love
soft as spring	l'affaire	I know that you know	I understand	you are my sunshine	cocoanut sweet	summer in your eyes
everything I have is yours	let's get away from it all	you smell so good	I'll always be with you	little bird	make love to me	face to face

Selected Standards _ Euan Macdonald

back in your own back yard	just for now	draw me a circle	always in my heart	it's a good day	it's a big wide wonderful world	falling leaves
december	snowfall	through a long and sleepless night	the starlit hour	moonlight mood	how beautiful is night	there are such things
I never knew	all through the night	deep night	the bad and the beautiful	please be kind	where, I wonder	where are you?

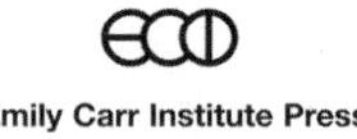

Emily Carr Institute Press

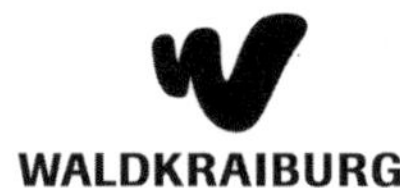

WALDKRAIBURG

jrp|ringier

deep night	where are you now	there's no you	easy come, easy go lover	if I should lose you	that's the beginning of the end	possesion
everything happens to me	deep in a dream	land of dreams	far away places	almost paradise	where flamingos fly	blue orchids
compared to you	imagination	ev'rywhere	all of me	fogbound	you're everywhere	more then you know

Selected Standards _ **Euan Macdonald**

call me	tenderly	as years go by	love	that tired routine called love	you only want it 'cos you haven't got it	love for sale
let's take a walk around the block	there will never be another you	ghost of yesterday	a hundred years from to-day	time alone will tell	show me the way to get out of this world	ev'rything's been done before
ev'rybody has the right to be wrong!	adios	we'll be together again	soon	live for life	never less then yesterday	again

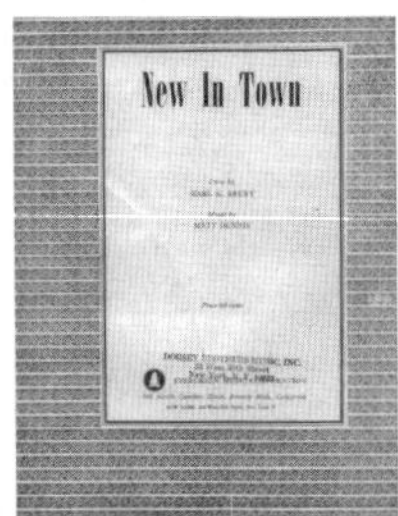
New In Town
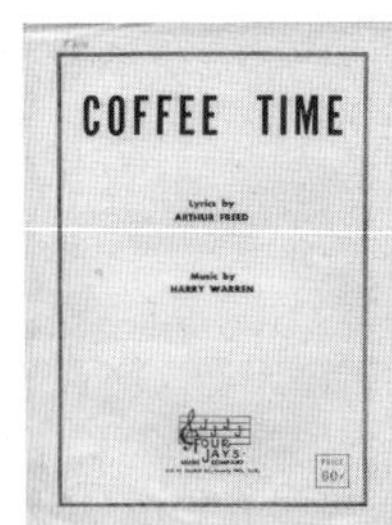
COFFEE TIME
Lyrics by
ARTHUR FREED
Music by
HARRY WARREN
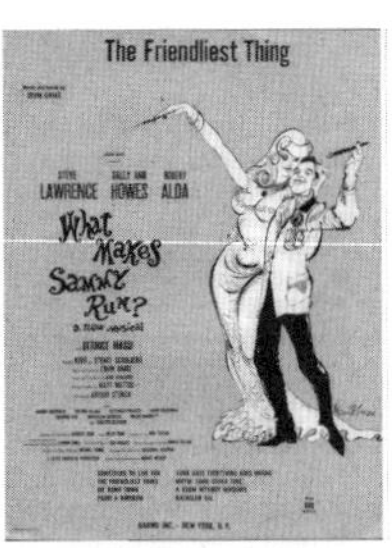
The Friendliest Thing
What Makes Sammy Run?
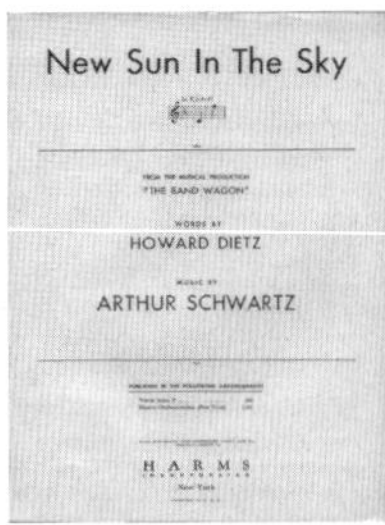
New Sun In The Sky
HOWARD DIETZ
ARTHUR SCHWARTZ
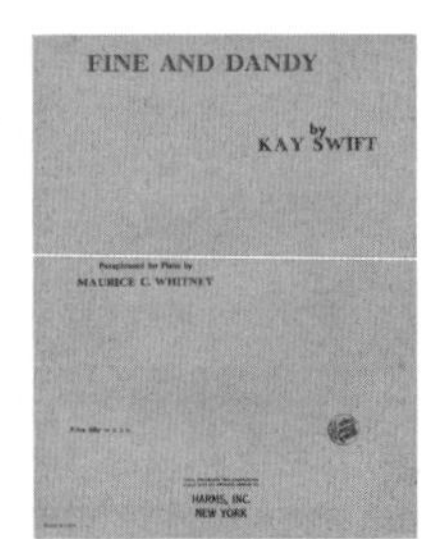
FINE AND DANDY
KAY SWIFT
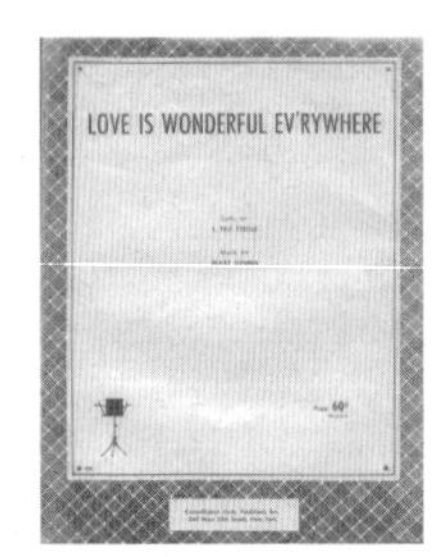
LOVE IS WONDERFUL EV'RYWHERE
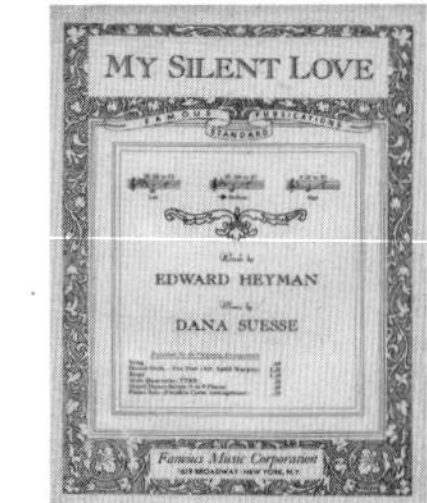
MY SILENT LOVE
EDWARD HEYMAN
DANA SUESSE
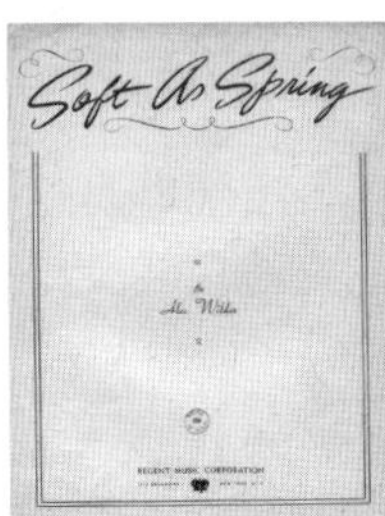
Soft As Spring
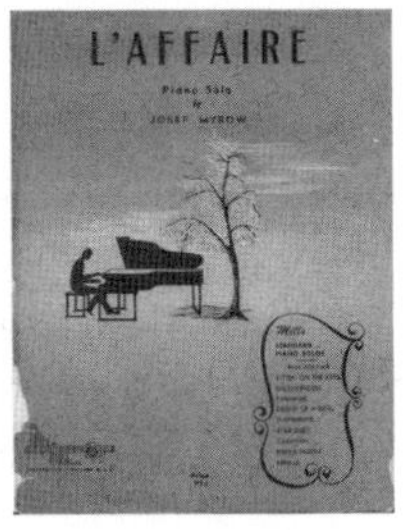
L'AFFAIRE
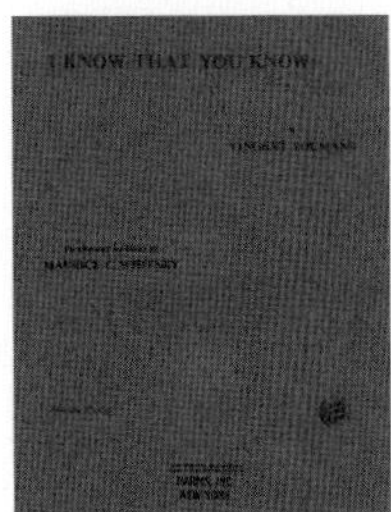
I KNOW THAT YOU KNOW
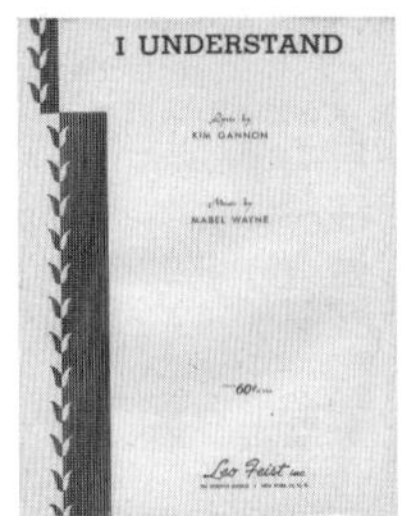
I UNDERSTAND
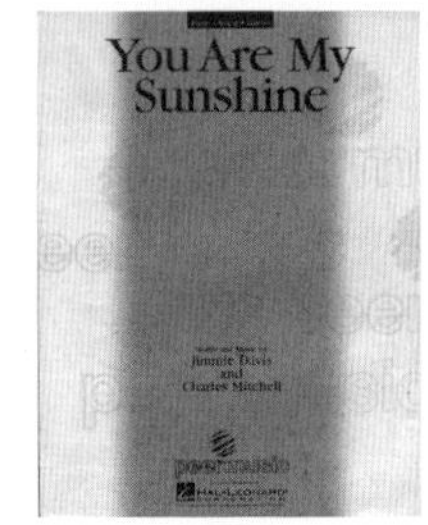
You Are My Sunshine
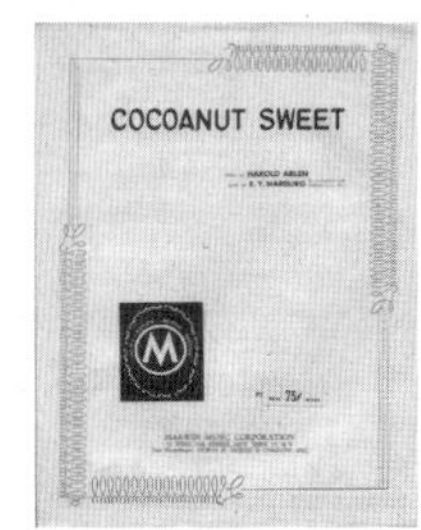
COCOANUT SWEET
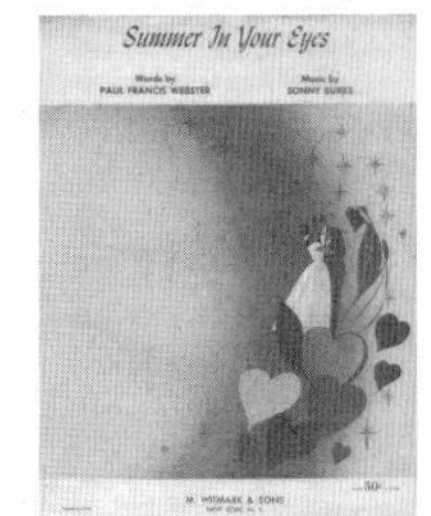
Summer In Your Eyes
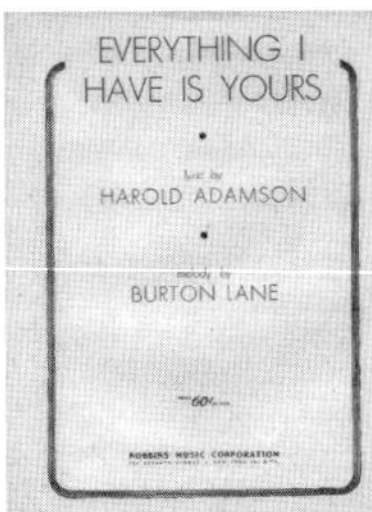
EVERYTHING I HAVE IS YOURS
HAROLD ADAMSON
BURTON LANE
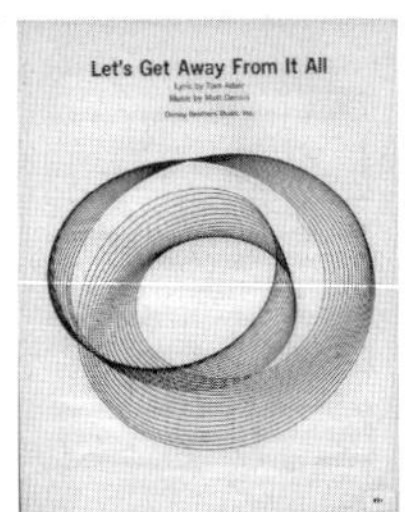
Let's Get Away From It All
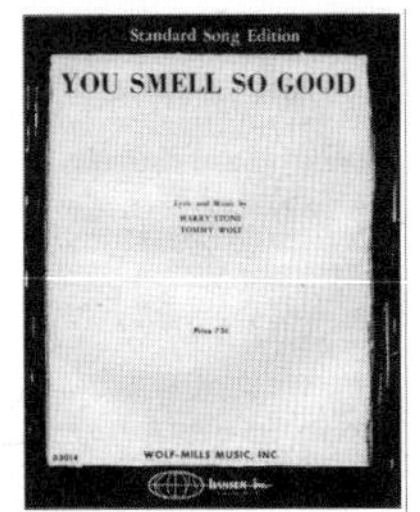
Standard Song Edition
YOU SMELL SO GOOD
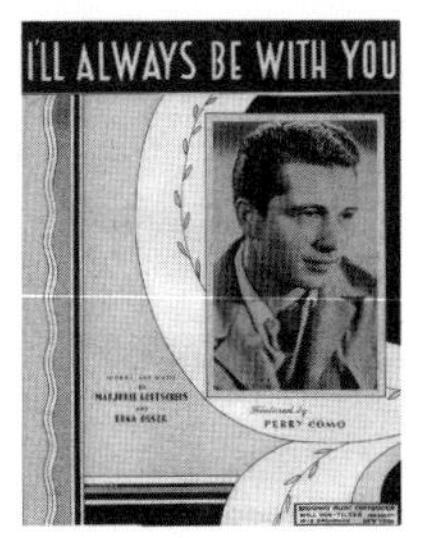
I'LL ALWAYS BE WITH YOU
PERRY COMO
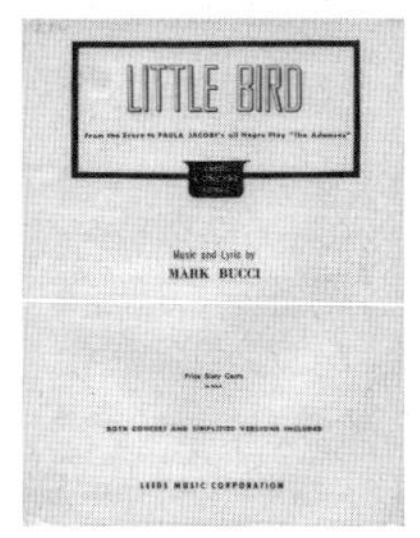
LITTLE BIRD
MARK BUCCI
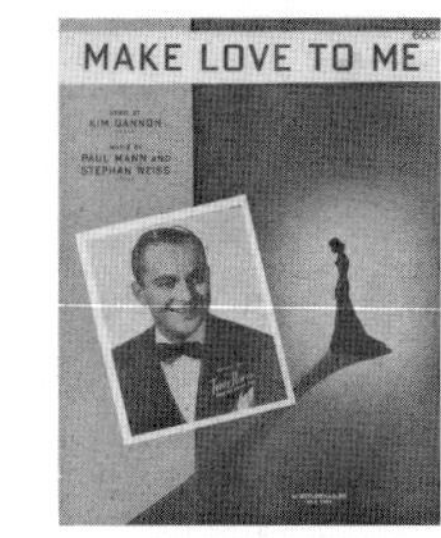
MAKE LOVE TO ME
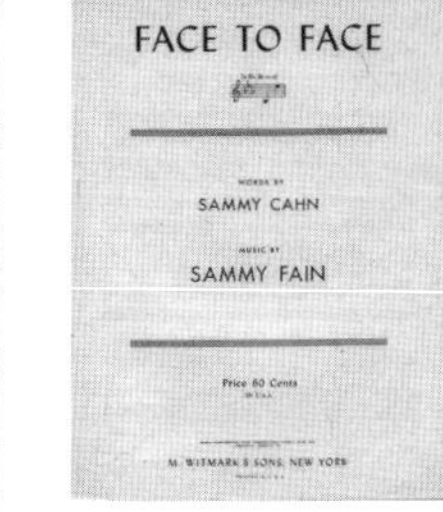
FACE TO FACE
SAMMY CAHN
SAMMY FAIN
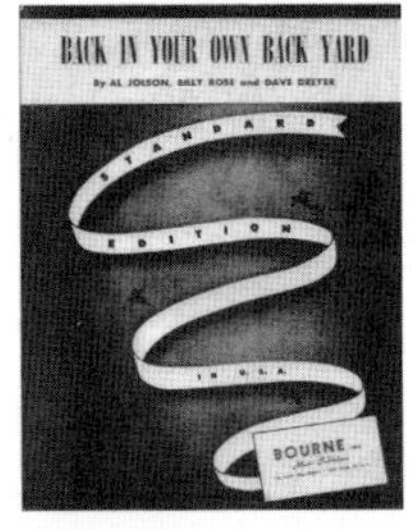
BACK IN YOUR OWN BACK YARD
BOURNE
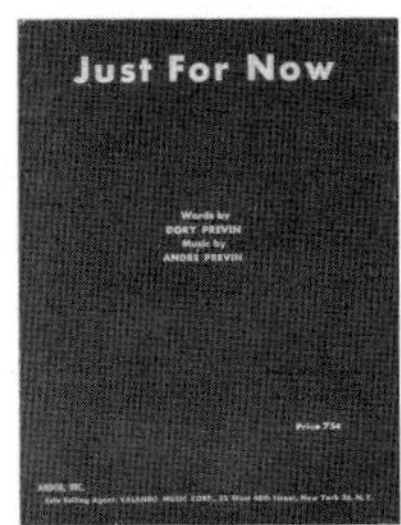
Just For Now
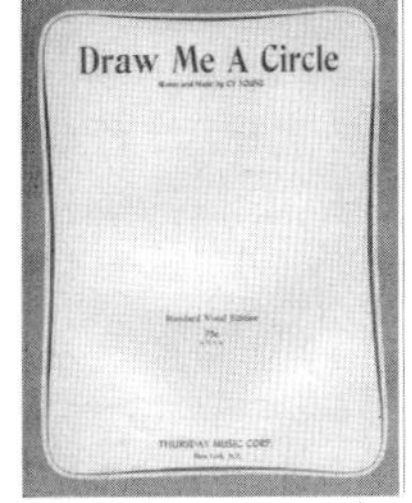
Draw Me A Circle
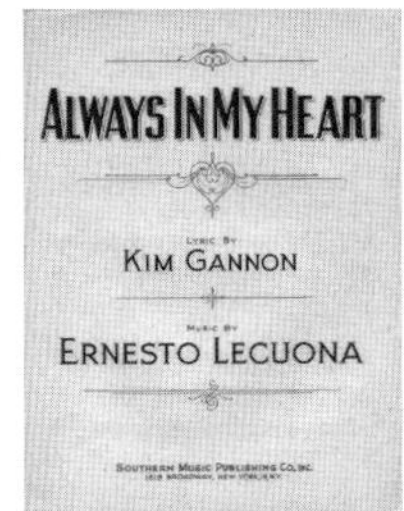
ALWAYS IN MY HEART
KIM GANNON
ERNESTO LECUONA
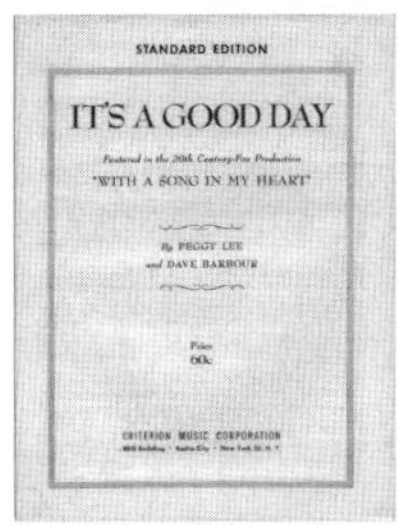
STANDARD EDITION
IT'S A GOOD DAY
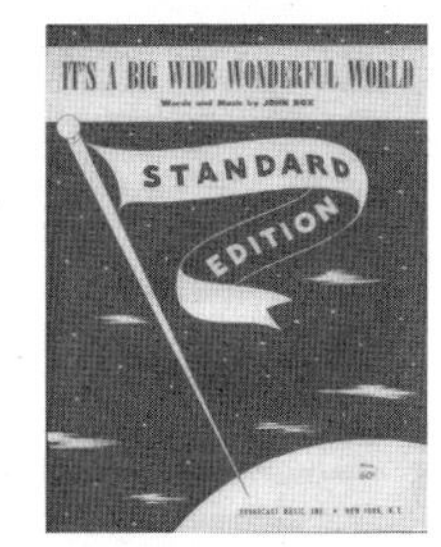
IT'S A BIG WIDE WONDERFUL WORLD
STANDARD EDITION
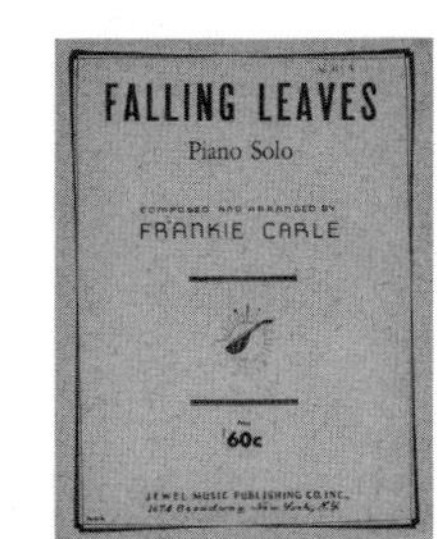
FALLING LEAVES
Piano Solo
FRANKIE CARLE
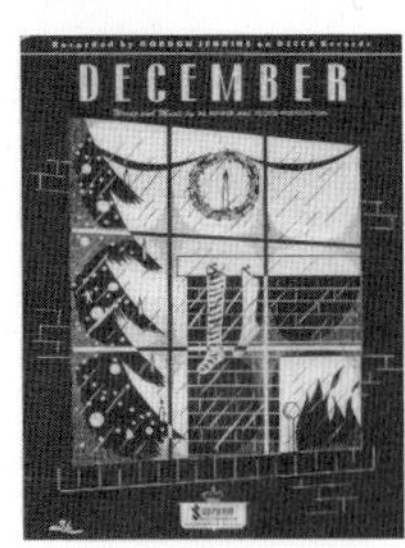
DECEMBER
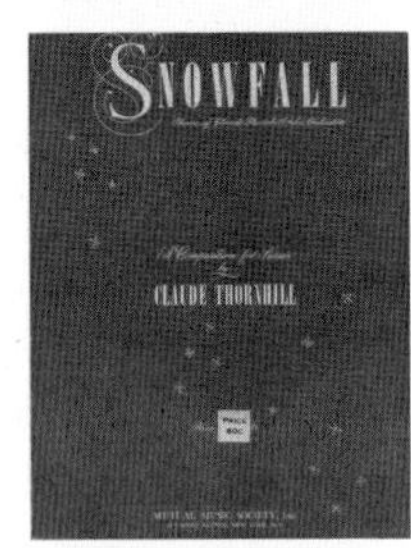
SNOWFALL
CLAUDE THORNHILL
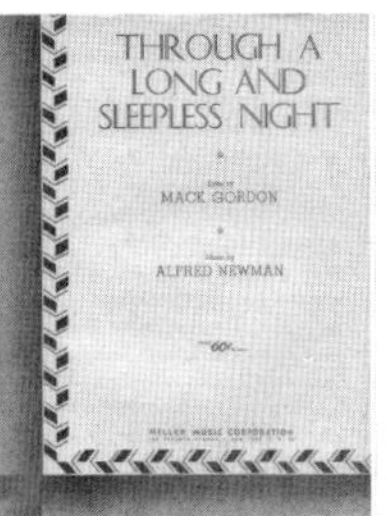
THROUGH A LONG AND SLEEPLESS NIGHT
MACK GORDON
ALFRED NEWMAN
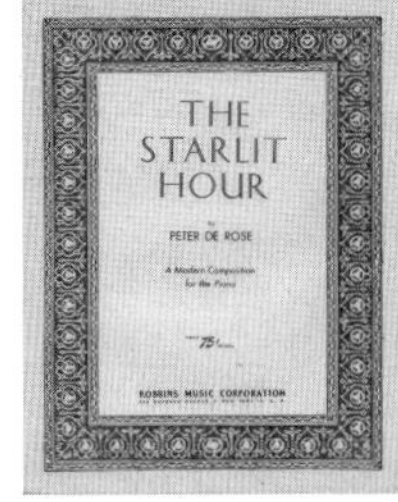
THE STARLIT HOUR
PETER DE ROSE
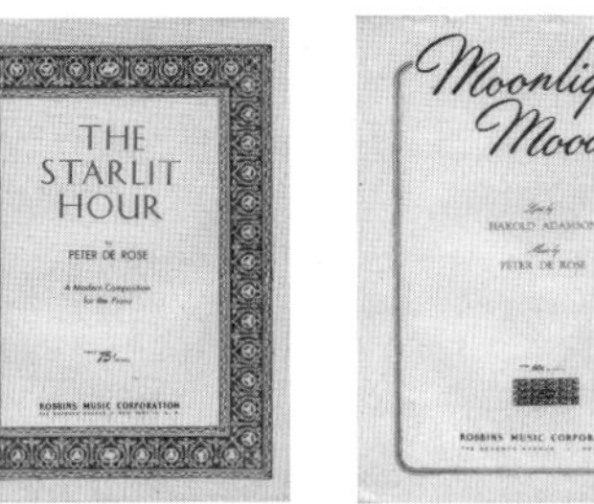
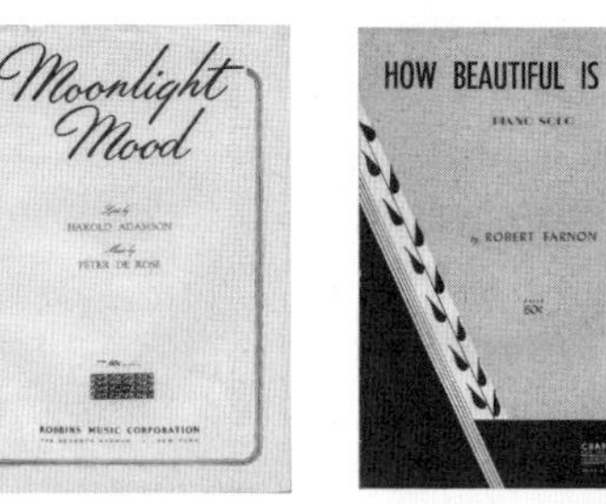
Moonlight Mood
PETER DE ROSE
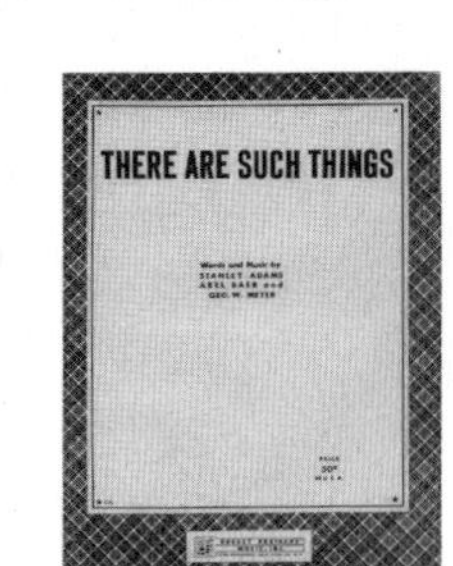
HOW BEAUTIFUL IS NIGHT
ROBERT FARNON
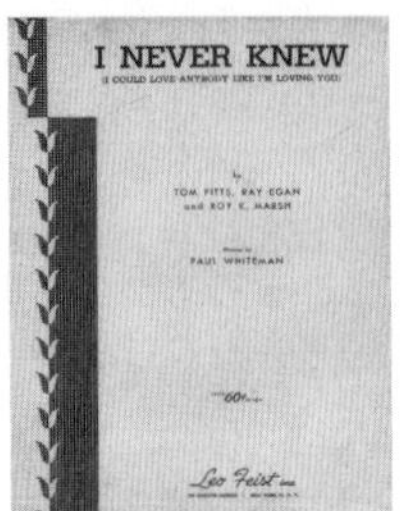
THERE ARE SUCH THINGS
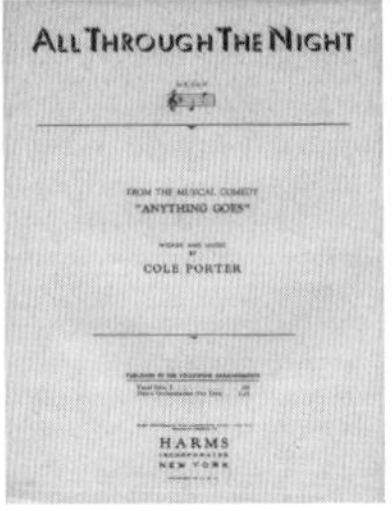
I NEVER KNEW
PAUL WHITEMAN
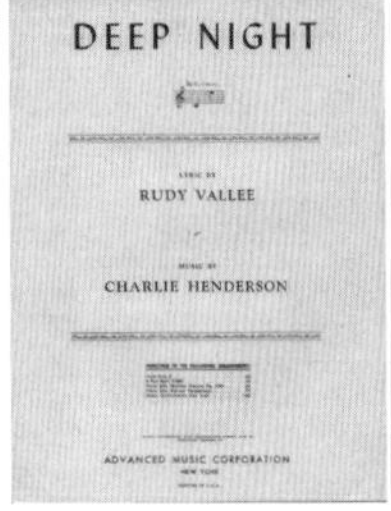
ALL THROUGH THE NIGHT
COLE PORTER
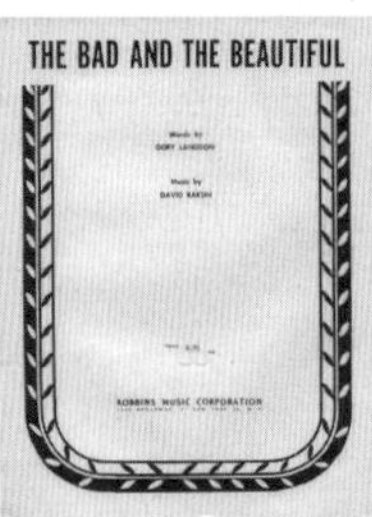
DEEP NIGHT
RUDY VALLEE
CHARLIE HENDERSON
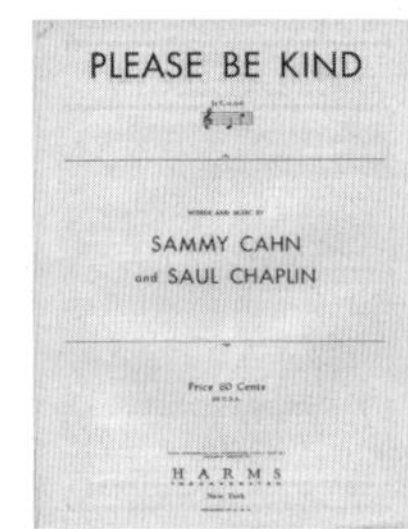
THE BAD AND THE BEAUTIFUL
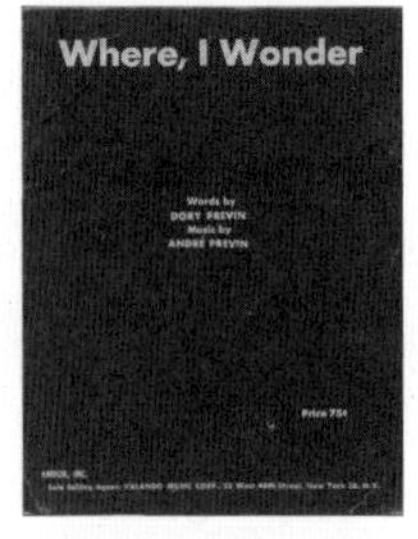
PLEASE BE KIND
SAMMY CAHN
SAUL CHAPLIN
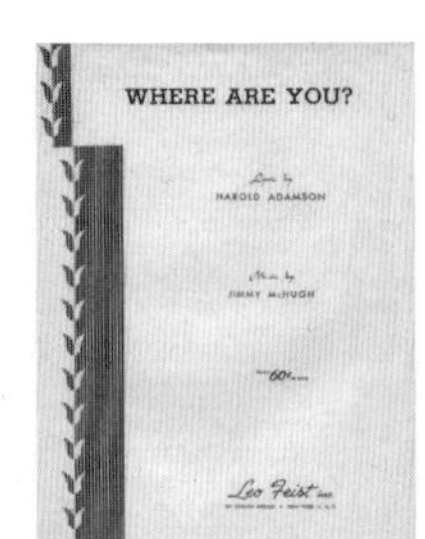
Where, I Wonder
ANDRE PREVIN

WHERE ARE YOU?
HAROLD ADAMSON

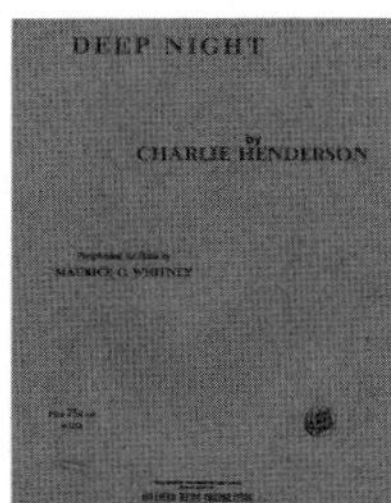
DEEP NIGHT
CHARLIE HENDERSON
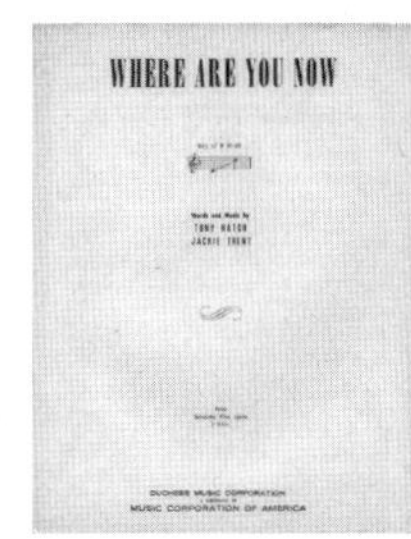
WHERE ARE YOU NOW
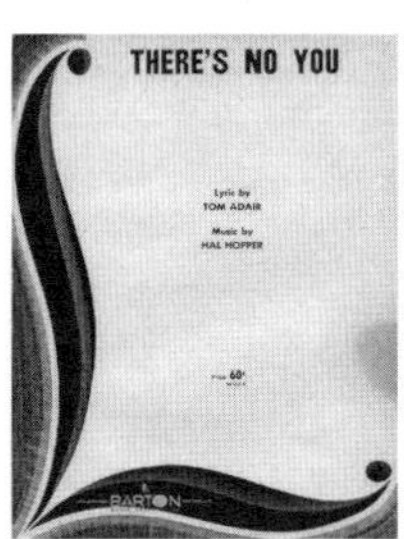
THERE'S NO YOU
Lyric by
TOM ADAIR
Music by
HAL HOPPER
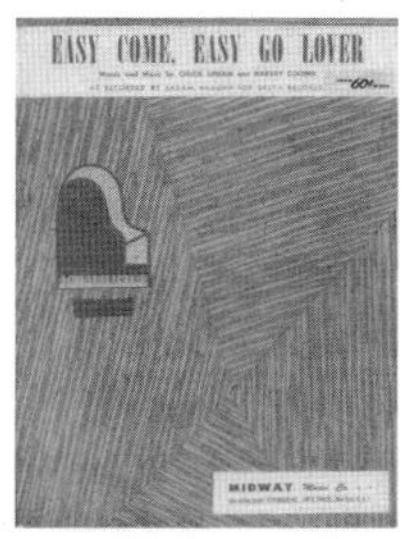
EASY COME, EASY GO LOVER
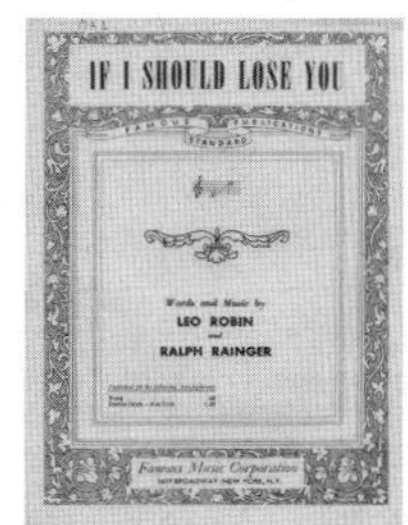
IF I SHOULD LOSE YOU
Words and Music by
LEO ROBIN
and
RALPH RAINGER
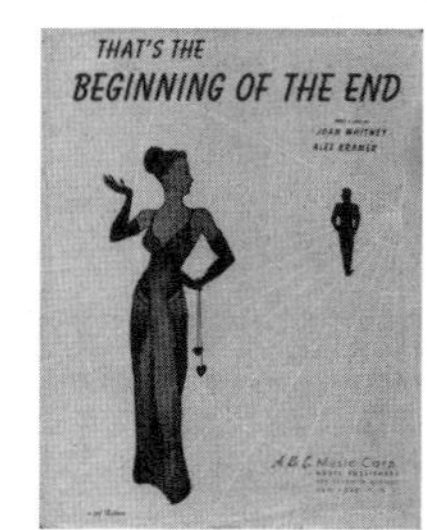
THAT'S THE
BEGINNING OF THE END
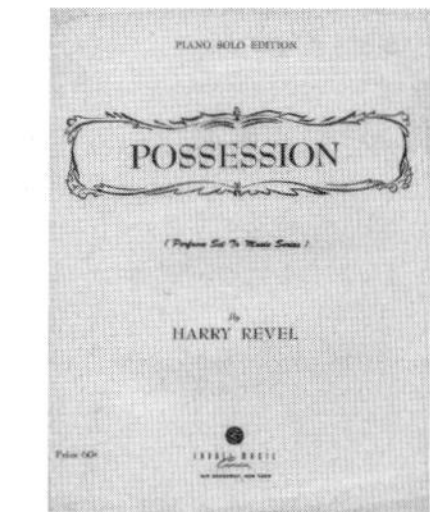
POSSESSION
by
HARRY REVEL
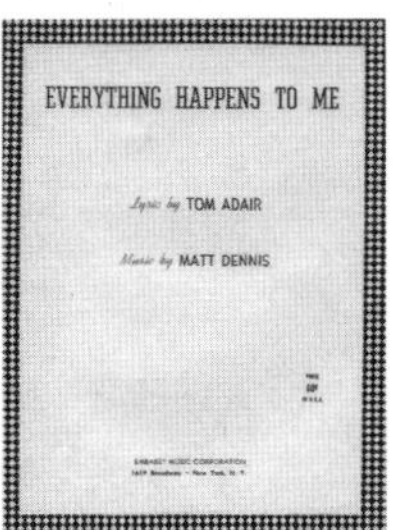
EVERYTHING HAPPENS TO ME
Lyric by TOM ADAIR
Music by MATT DENNIS
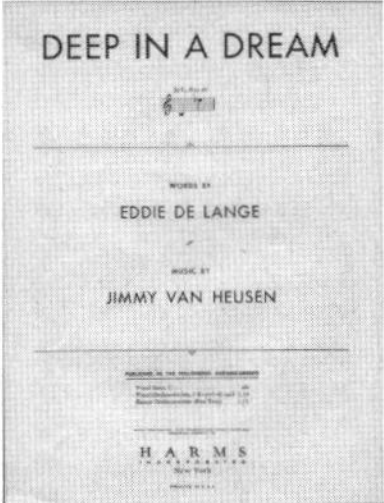
DEEP IN A DREAM
WORDS BY
EDDIE DE LANGE
MUSIC BY
JIMMY VAN HEUSEN
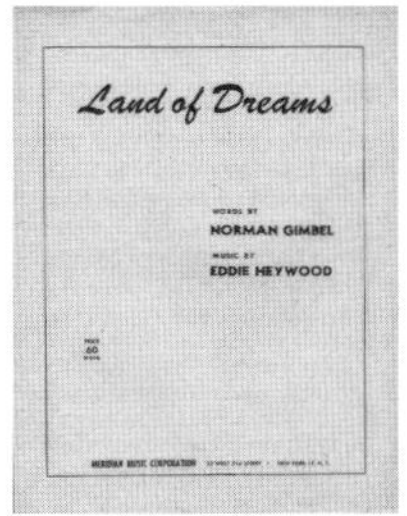
Land of Dreams
WORDS BY
NORMAN GIMBEL
MUSIC BY
EDDIE HEYWOOD
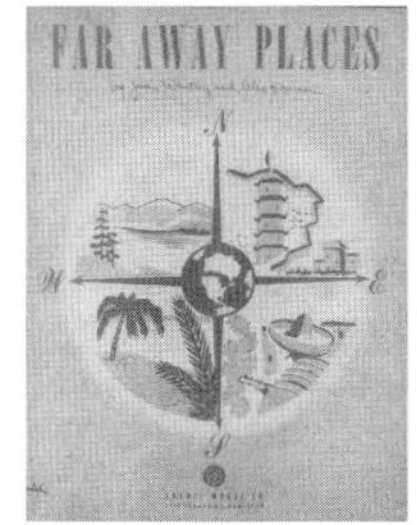
FAR AWAY PLACES
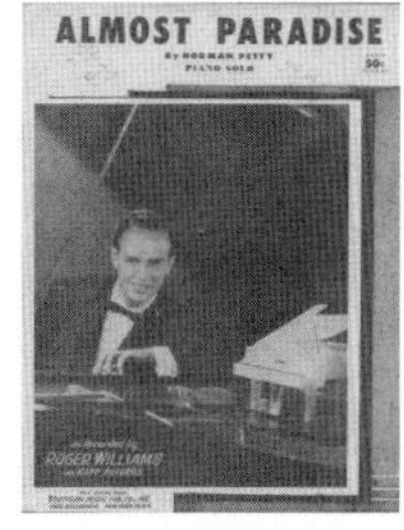
ALMOST PARADISE
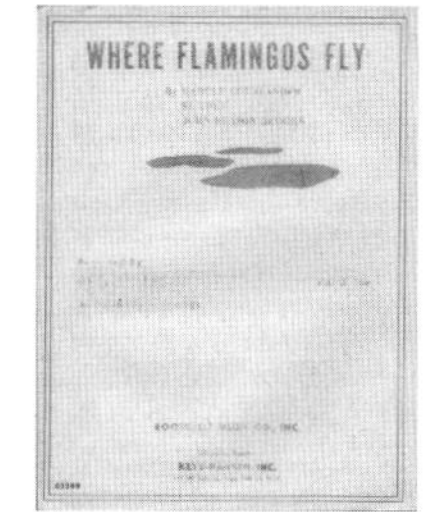
WHERE FLAMINGOS FLY
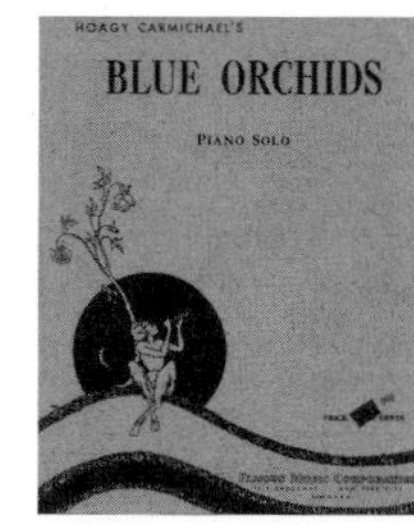
HOAGY CARMICHAEL'S
BLUE ORCHIDS
PIANO SOLO
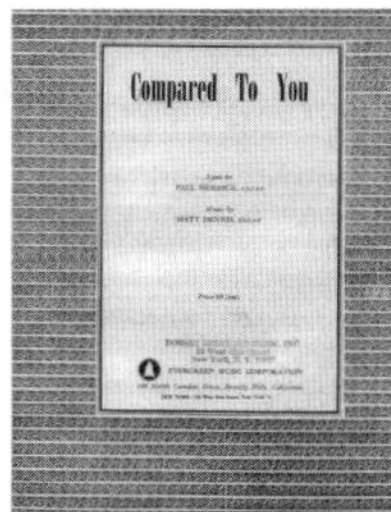
Compared To You
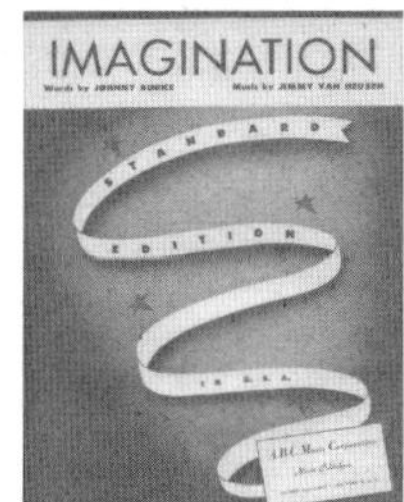
IMAGINATION
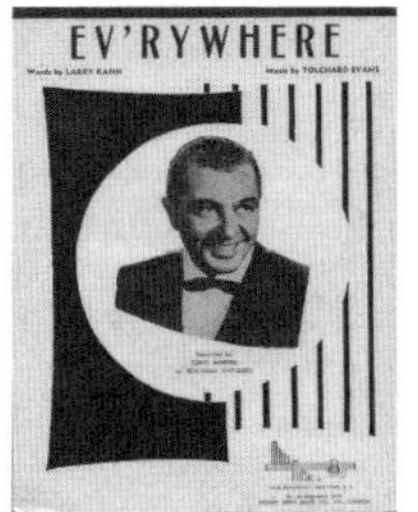
EV'RYWHERE
Words by LARRY KAHN
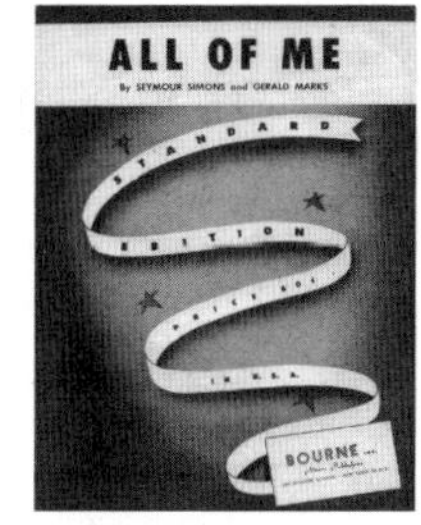
ALL OF ME
By SEYMOUR SIMONS and GERALD MARKS
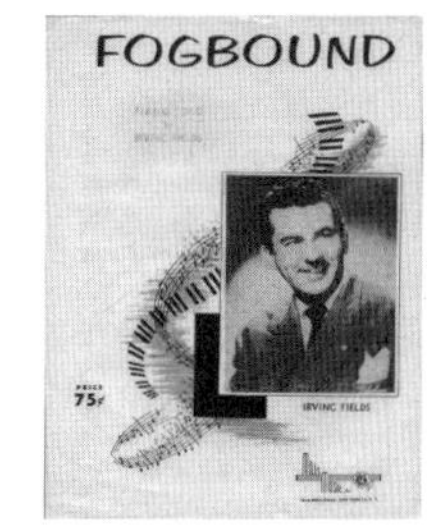
FOGBOUND
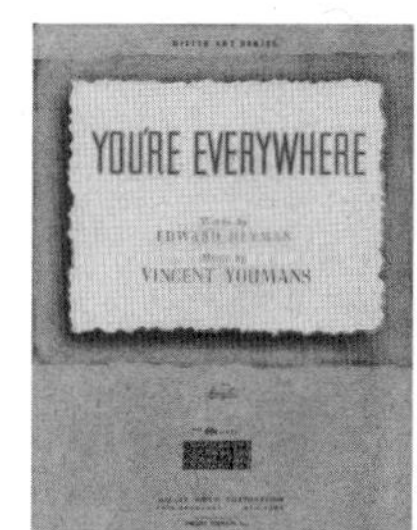
YOU'RE EVERYWHERE
Words by EDWARD HEYMAN
Music by VINCENT YOUMANS
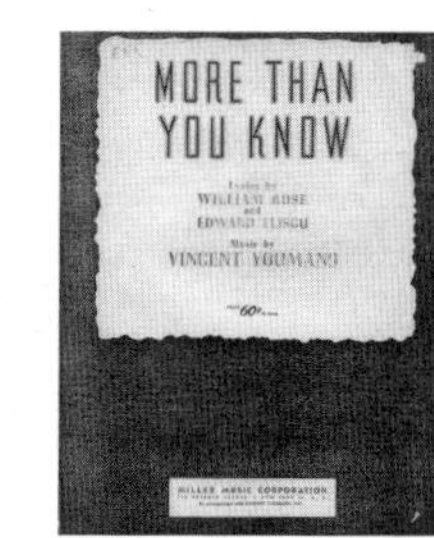
MORE THAN
YOU KNOW
Music by
VINCENT YOUMANS
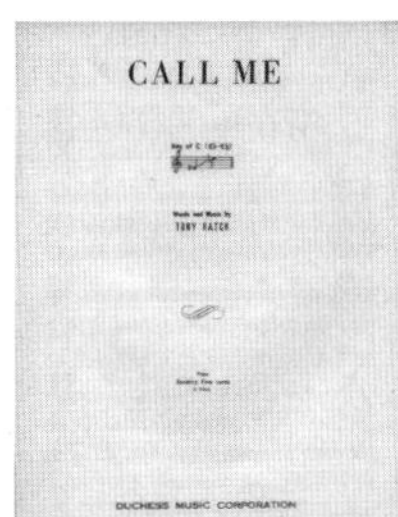
CALL ME
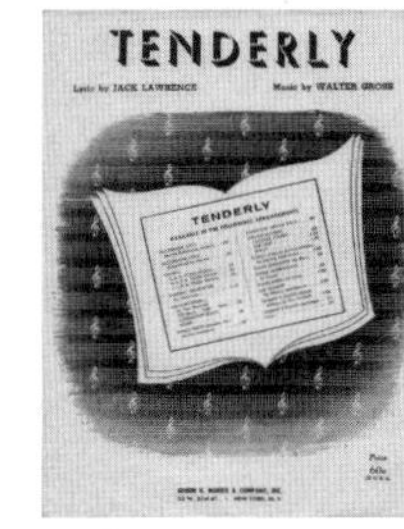
TENDERLY
Lyric by JACK LAWRENCE
Music by WALTER GROSS
TENDERLY
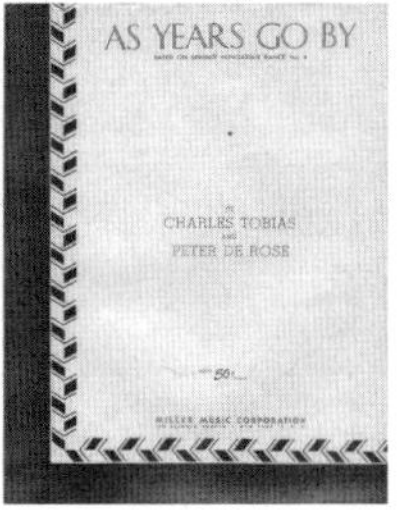
AS YEARS GO BY
CHARLES TOBIAS
PETER DE ROSE
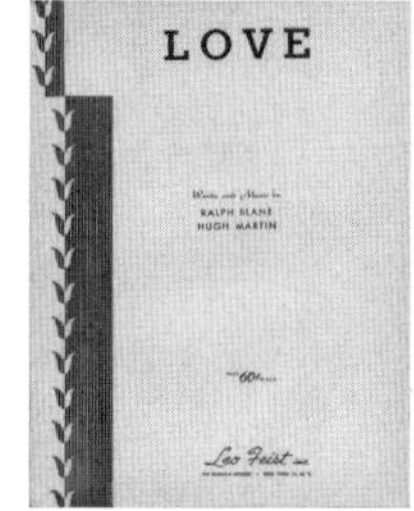
LOVE
Words and Music by
RALPH BLANE
HUGH MARTIN
Leo Feist Inc.
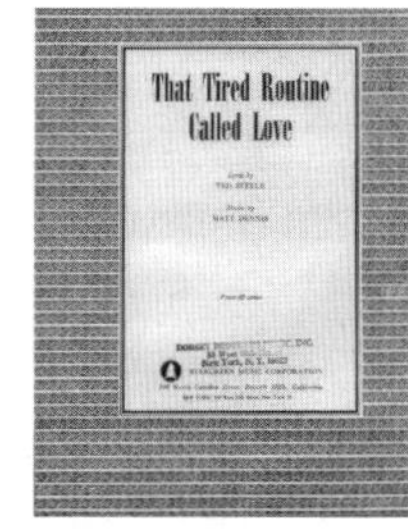
That Tired Routine
Called Love
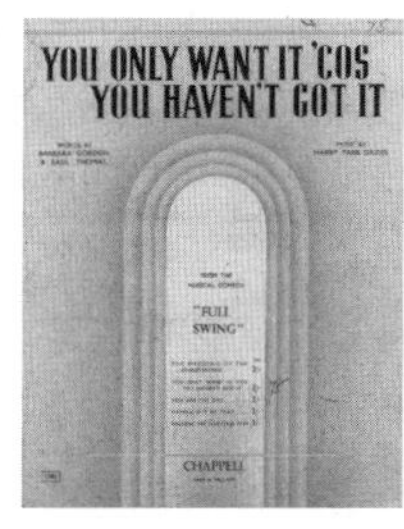
YOU ONLY WANT IT 'COS
YOU HAVEN'T GOT IT
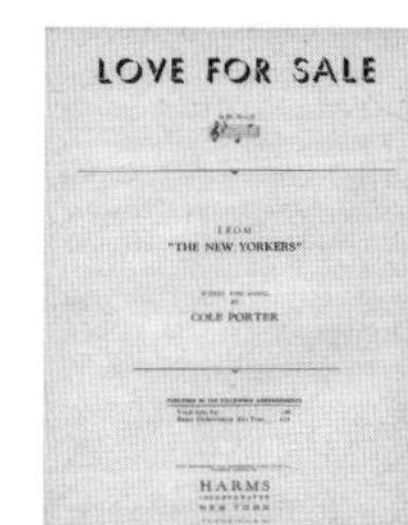
LOVE FOR SALE
FROM
"THE NEW YORKERS"
COLE PORTER
HARMS
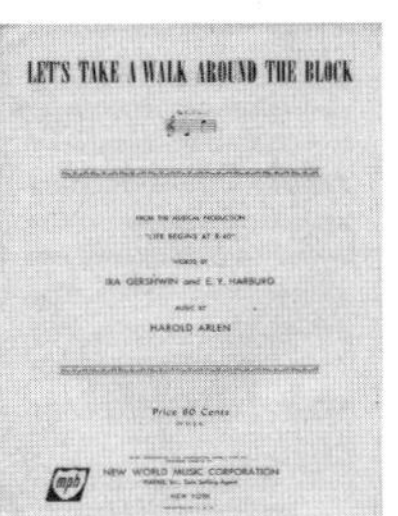
LET'S TAKE A WALK AROUND THE BLOCK
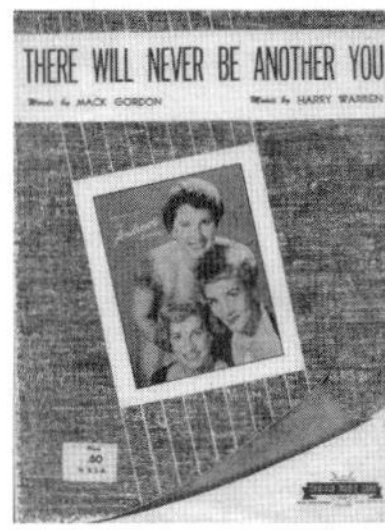
THERE WILL NEVER BE ANOTHER YOU
Words by MACK GORDON
Music by HARRY WARREN
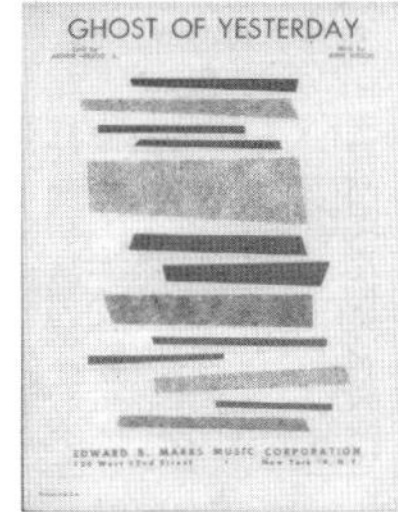
GHOST OF YESTERDAY
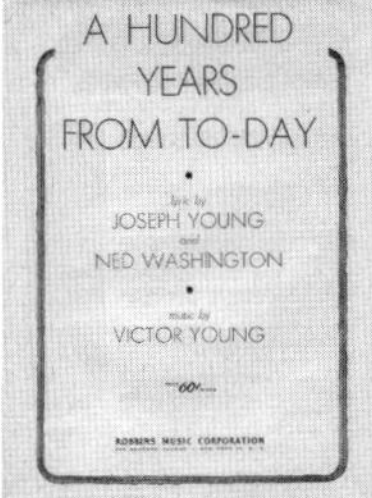
A HUNDRED
YEARS
FROM TO-DAY
Lyric by
JOSEPH YOUNG
and
NED WASHINGTON
Music by
VICTOR YOUNG
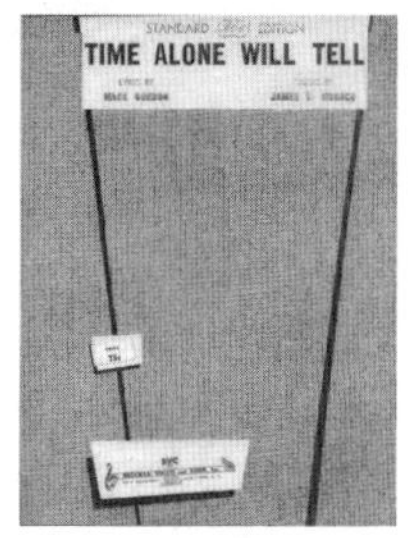
TIME ALONE WILL TELL
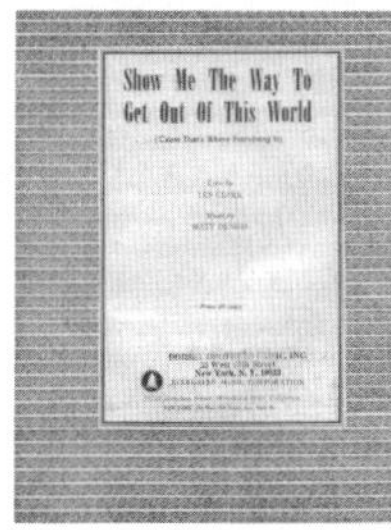
Show Me The Way To
Get Out Of This World
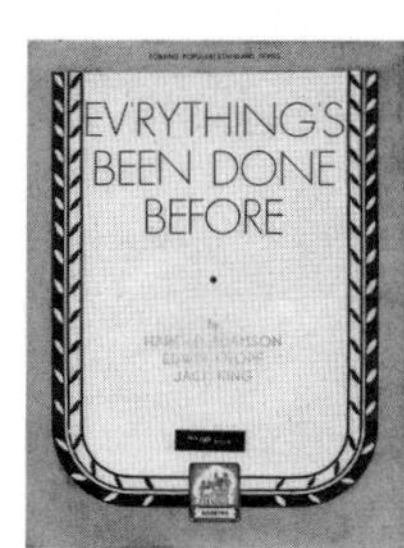
EV'RYTHING'S
BEEN DONE
BEFORE
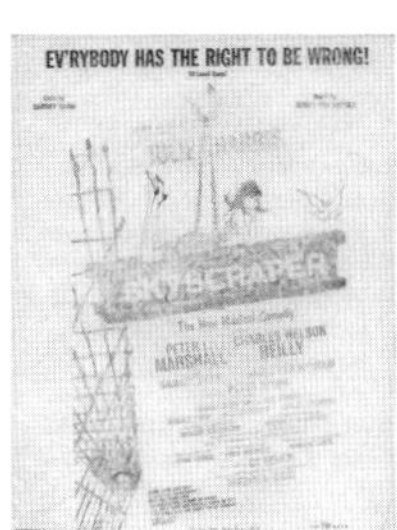
EV'RYBODY HAS THE RIGHT TO BE WRONG!
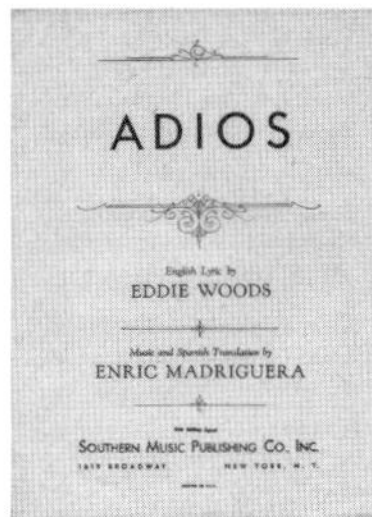
ADIOS
English Lyric by
EDDIE WOODS
Music and Spanish Translation by
ENRIC MADRIGUERA
SOUTHERN MUSIC PUBLISHING CO., INC.
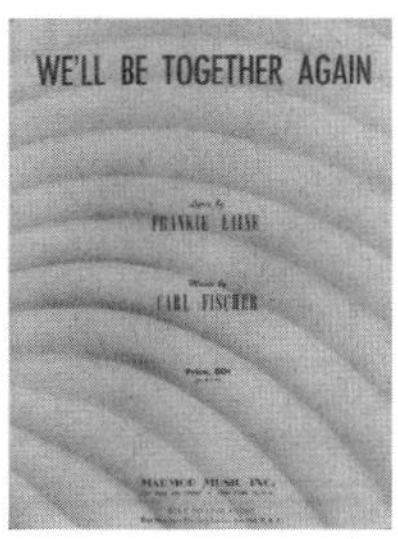
WE'LL BE TOGETHER AGAIN
Lyric by
FRANKIE LAINE
Music by
CARL FISCHER
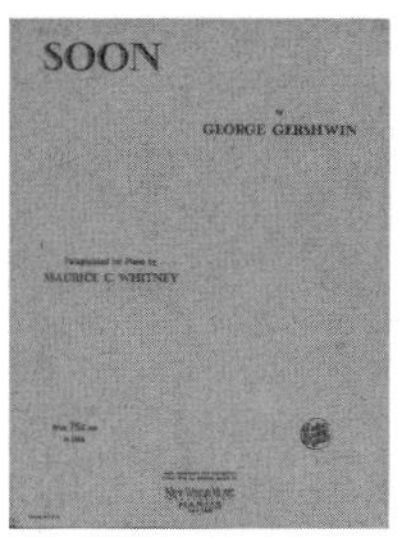
SOON
GEORGE GERSHWIN
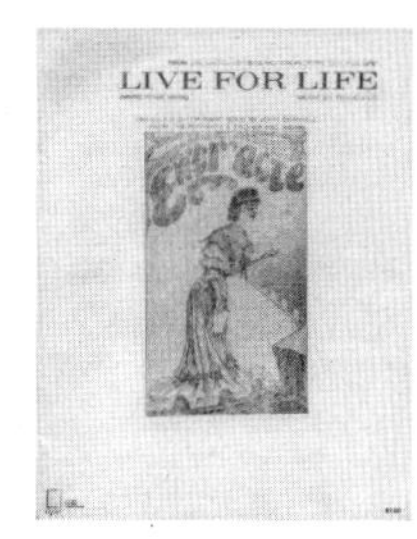
LIVE FOR LIFE
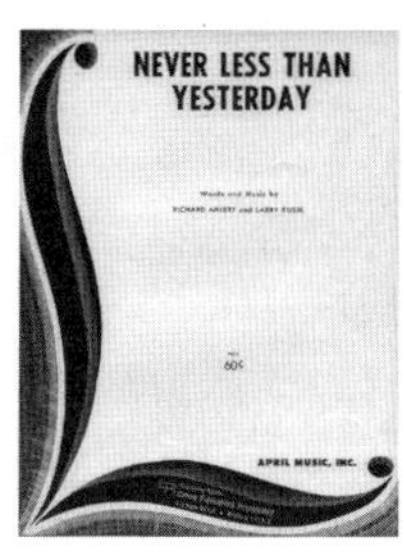
NEVER LESS THAN
YESTERDAY
Words and Music by
RICHARD AHLERT and LARRY WAGE
APRIL MUSIC, INC.
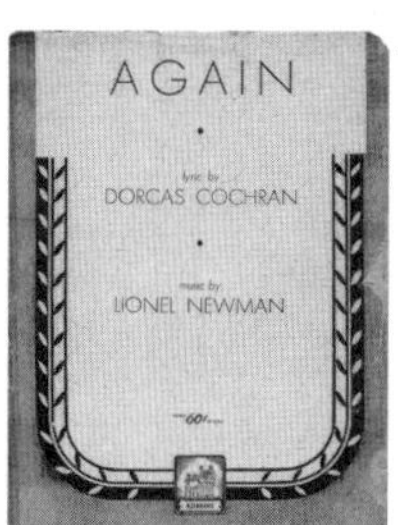
AGAIN
Lyric by
DORCAS COCHRAN
Music by
LIONEL NEWMAN

New In Town

Lyric by

EARL K. BRENT

Music by

MATT DENNIS

Price 60 cents

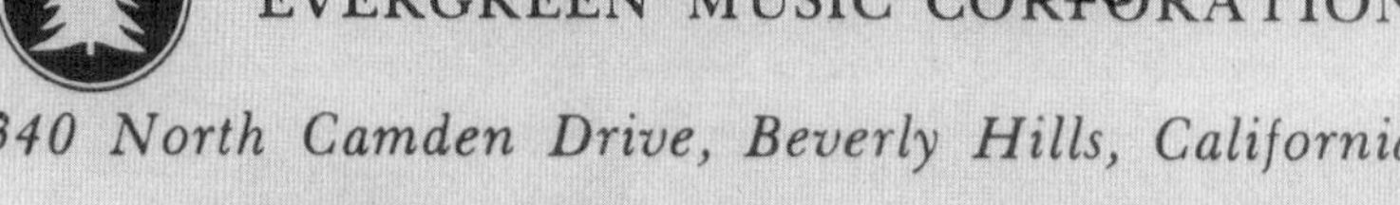

DORSEY BROTHERS MUSIC, INC.
33 West 60th Street
New York, N.Y. 10023
EVERGREEN MUSIC CORPORATION

340 North Camden Drive, Beverly Hills, California

NEW YORK: 240 West 55th Street, New York 19.

COFFEE TIME

Lyrics by
ARTHUR FREED

Music by
HARRY WARREN

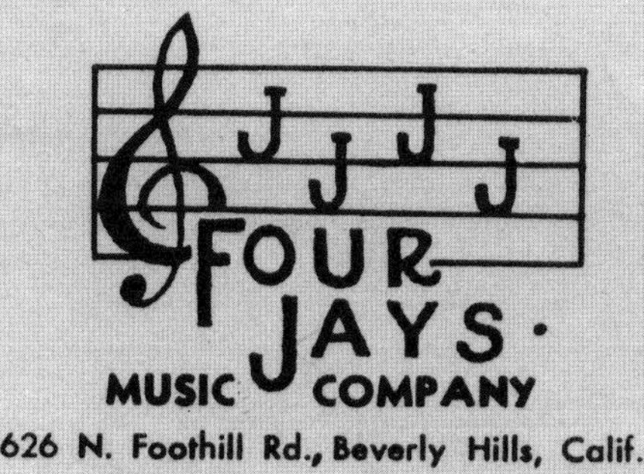

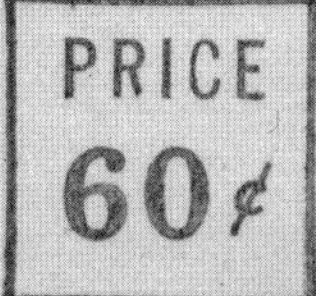

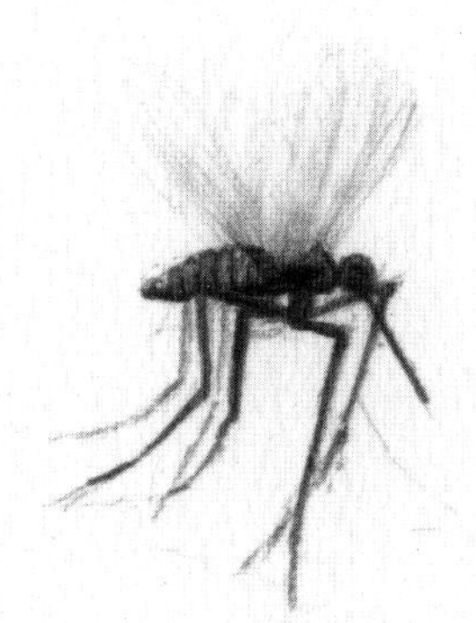

The Friendliest Thing

Words and music by
ERVIN DRAKE

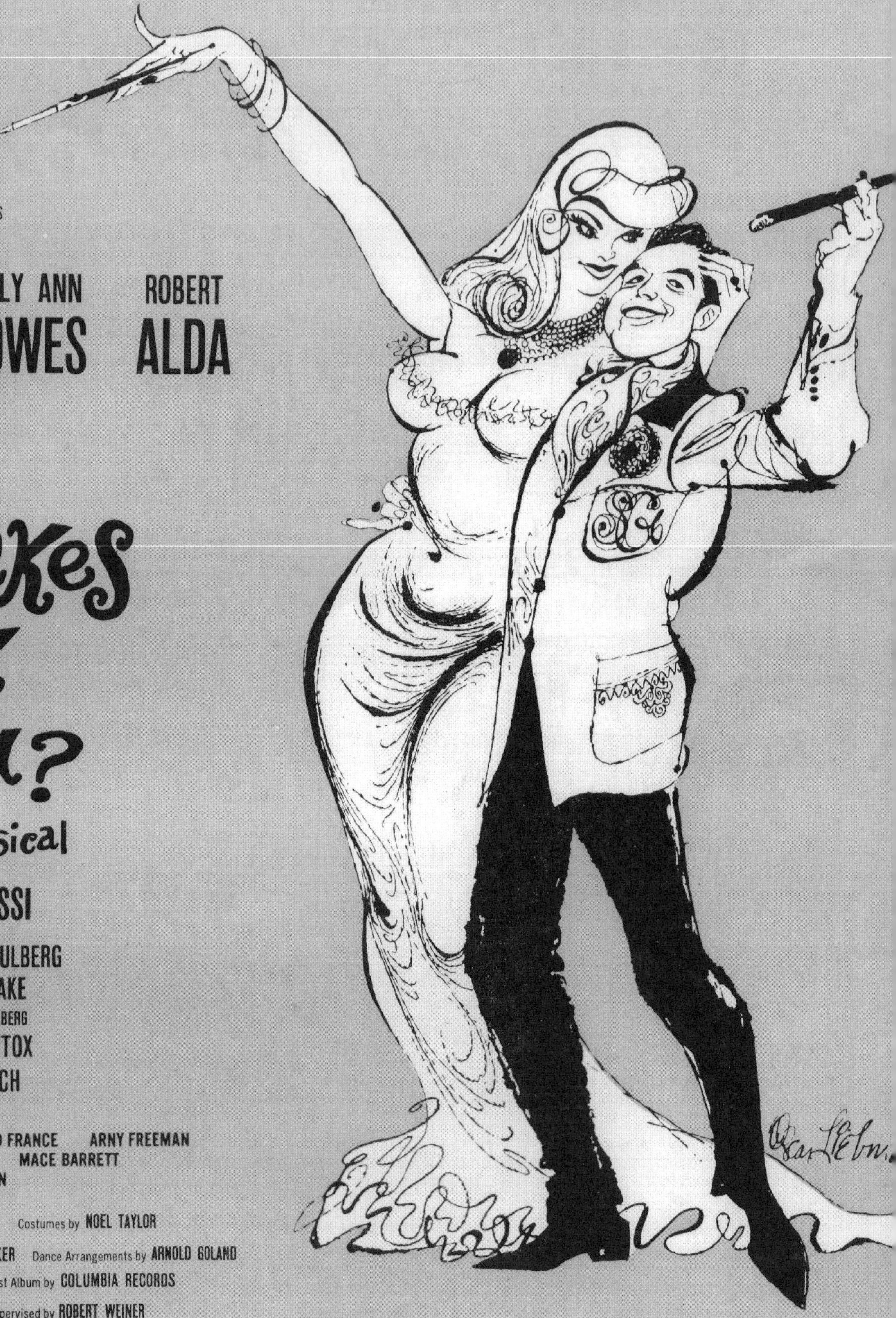

Printed in U.S.A.

HARMS INC. • NEW YORK, N. Y.

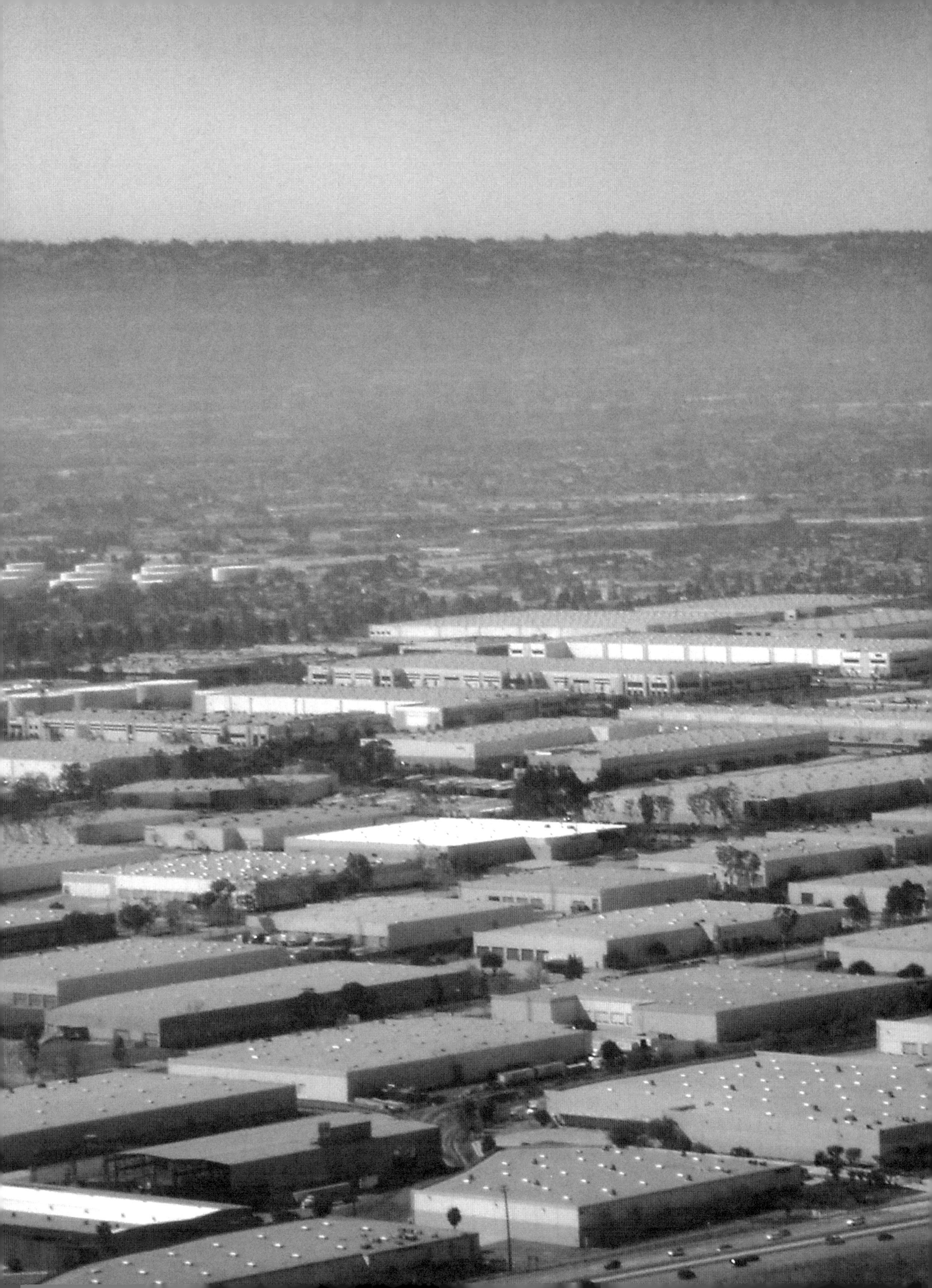

New Sun In The Sky

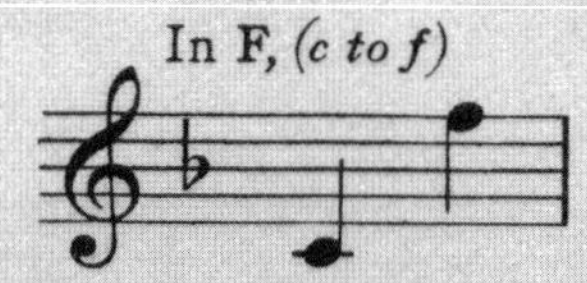

FROM THE MUSICAL PRODUCTION
"THE BAND WAGON"

WORDS BY

HOWARD DIETZ

MUSIC BY

ARTHUR SCHWARTZ

PUBLISHED IN THE FOLLOWING ARRANGEMENTS

Vocal Solo, F 60
Dance Orchestration (Fox Trot) 1.00

WHEN PERFORMING THIS COMPOSITION KINDLY GIVE ALL
PROGRAM CREDITS TO

HARMS
INCORPORATED

New York

PRINTED IN U. S. A.

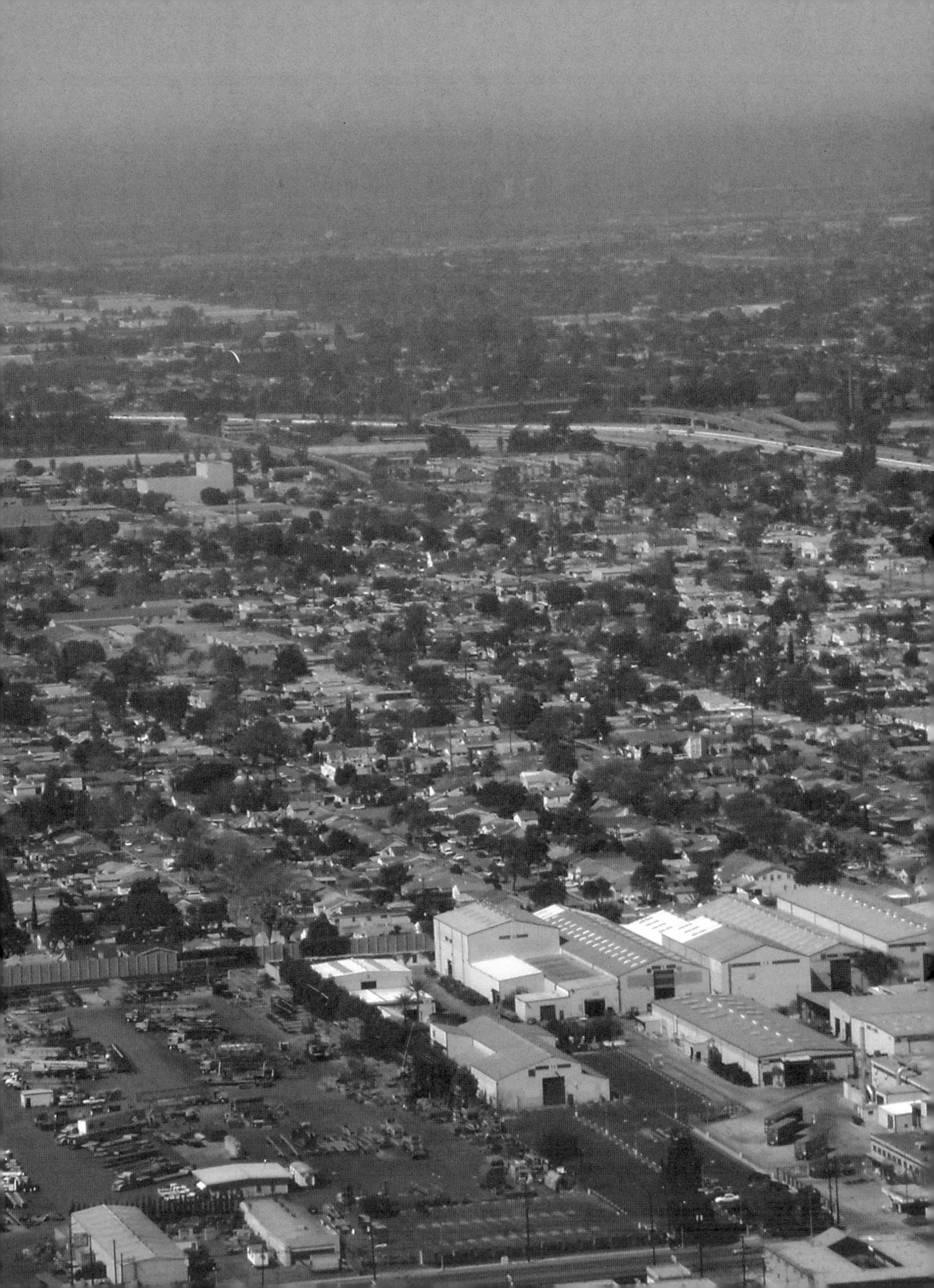

FINE AND DANDY

by
KAY SWIFT

Paraphrased for Piano by
MAURICE C. WHITNEY

Price 60¢ in U.S.A.

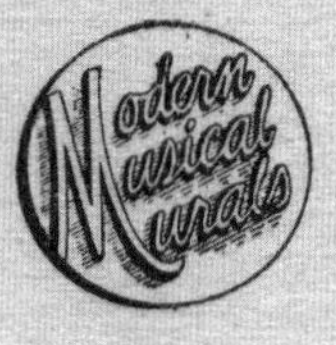

WHEN PERFORMING THIS COMPOSITION
KINDLY GIVE ALL PROGRAM CREDITS TO

HARMS, INC.
NEW YORK

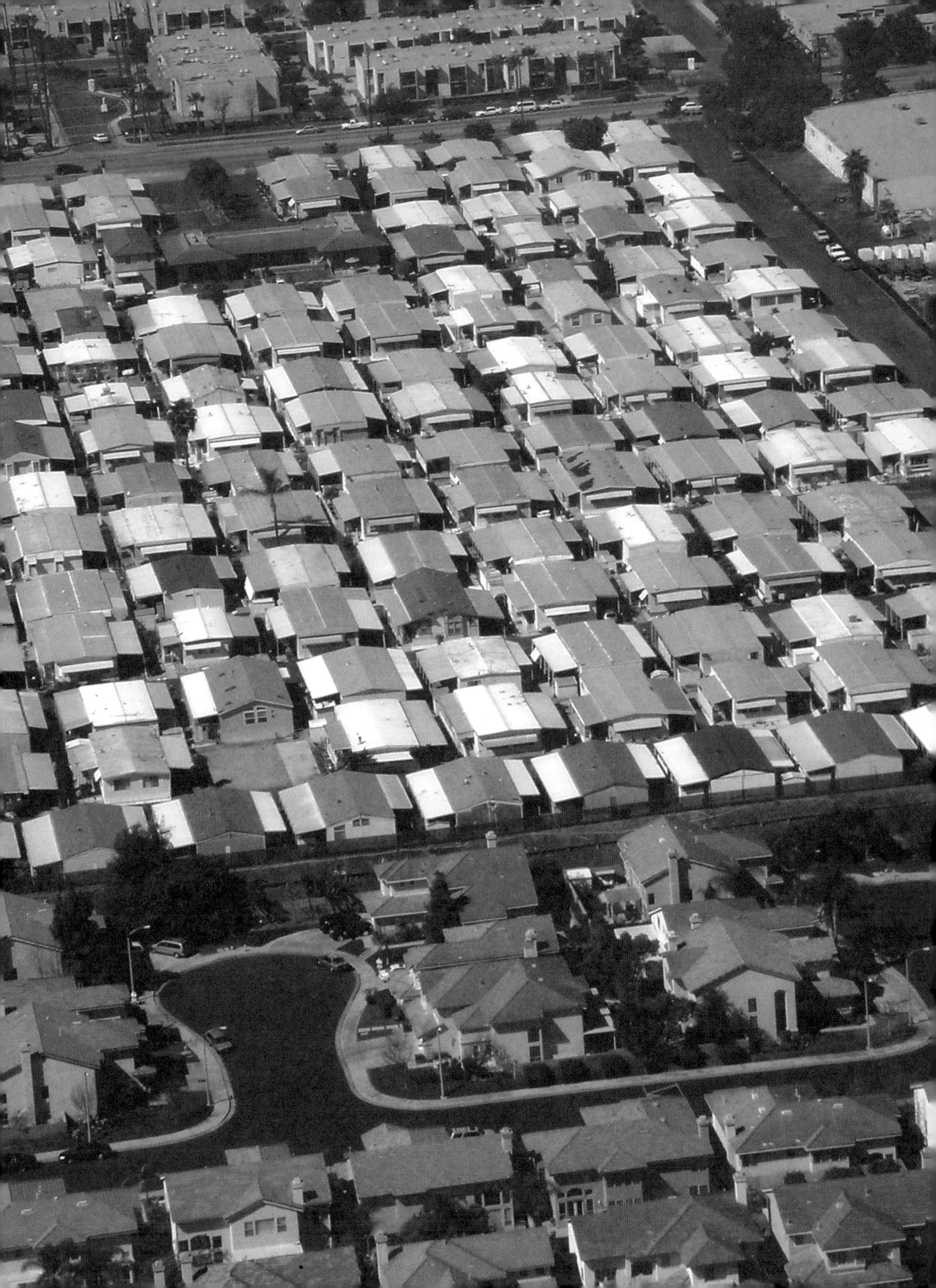

LOVE IS WONDERFUL EV'RYWHERE

Lyric by
L. TED STEELE

Music by
MATT DENNIS

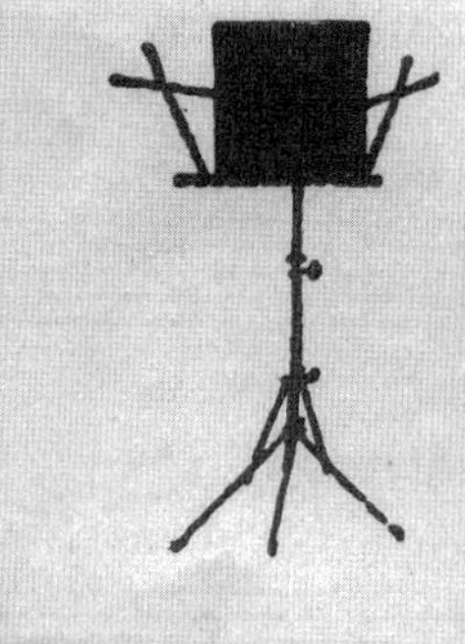

Price **60¢**
IN U.S.A.

Consolidated Music Publishers, Inc.
240 West 55th Street, New York

MY SILENT LOVE

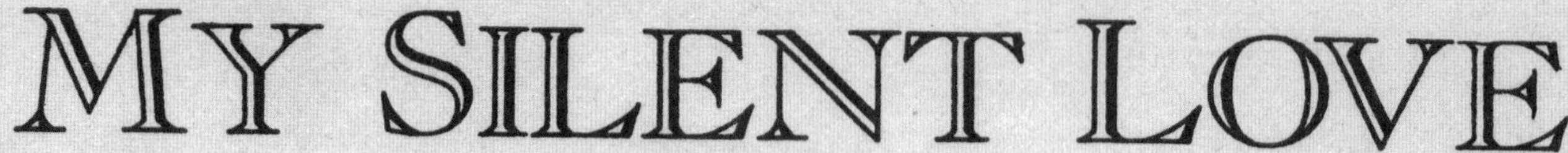

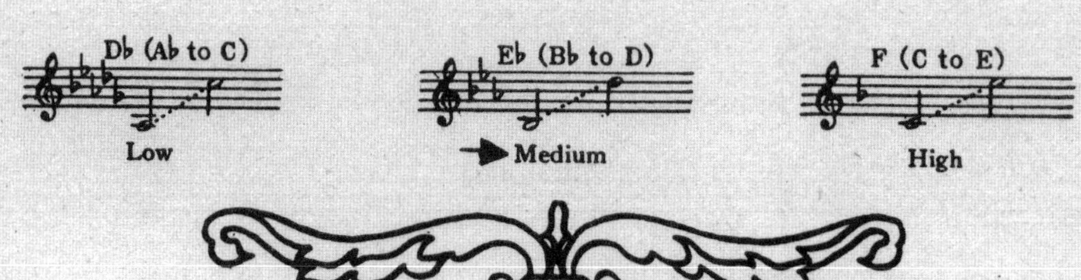

Words by

EDWARD HEYMAN

Music by

DANA SUESSE

Published for the Following Arrangements

Song	.60
Dance Orch.—Fox Trot (Arr. Spud Murphy)	1.25
Band	1.25
Male Quartette (TTBB)	.20
Small Dance Series (3 to 9 Pieces)	.60
Piano Solo (Frankie Carle Arrangement)	.75

Famous Music Corporation
1619 BROADWAY · NEW YORK, N.Y.

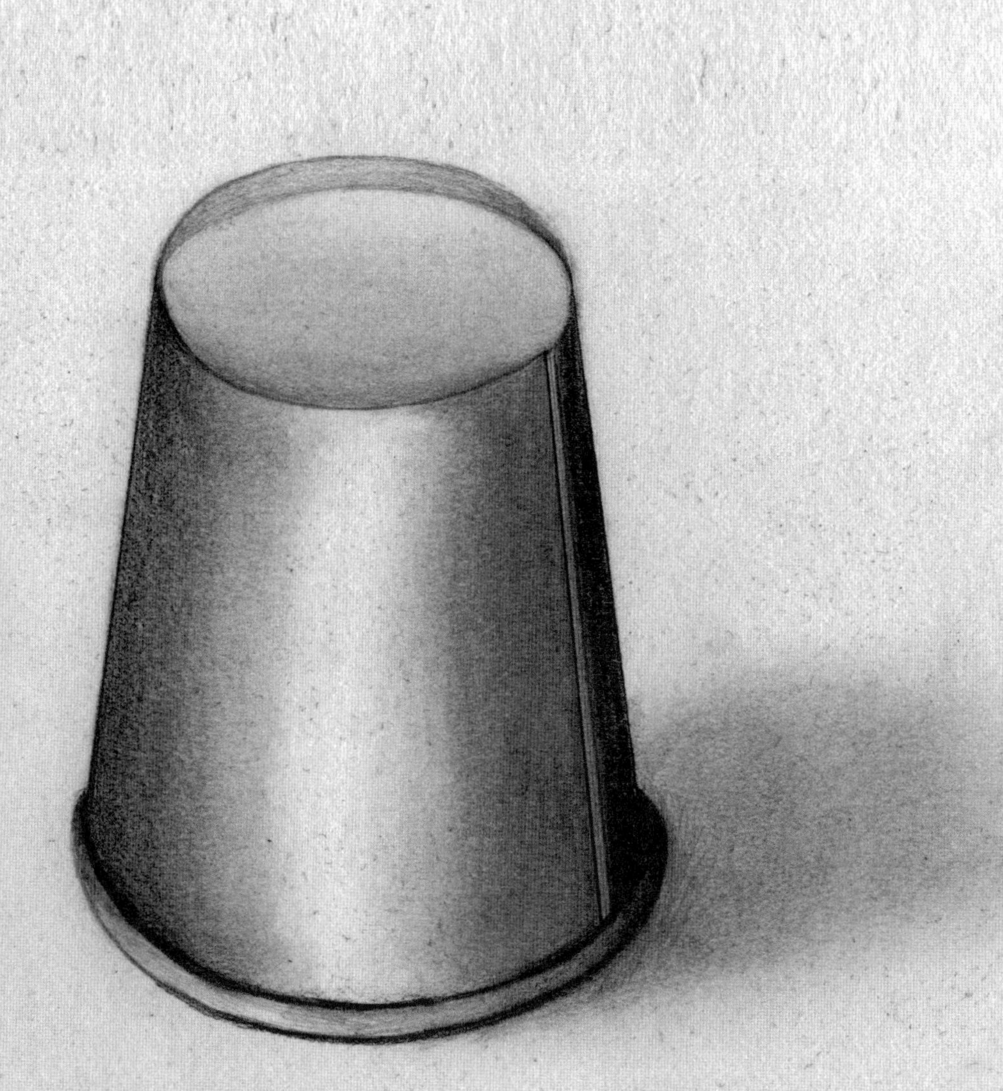

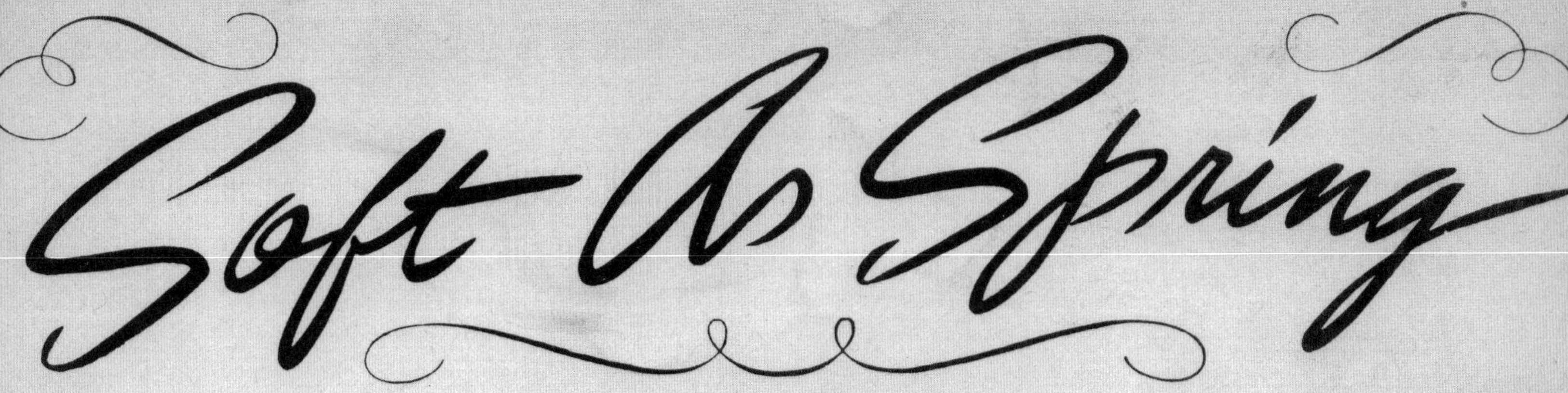

☆

By

Alec Wilder

☆

REGENT MUSIC CORPORATION

1619 BROADWAY   NEW YORK, N. Y.

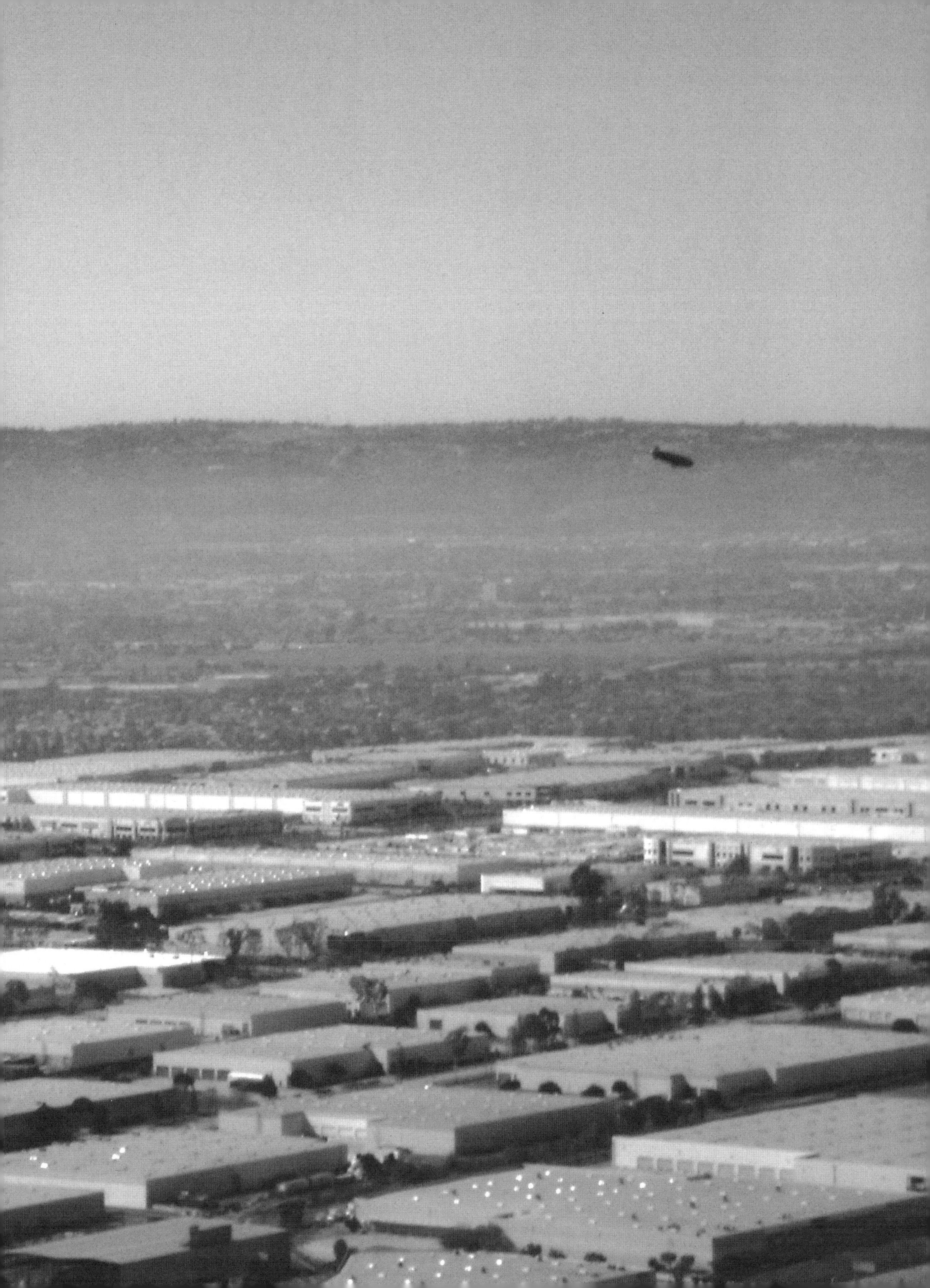

L'AFFAIRE

Piano Solo
by
JOSEF MYROW

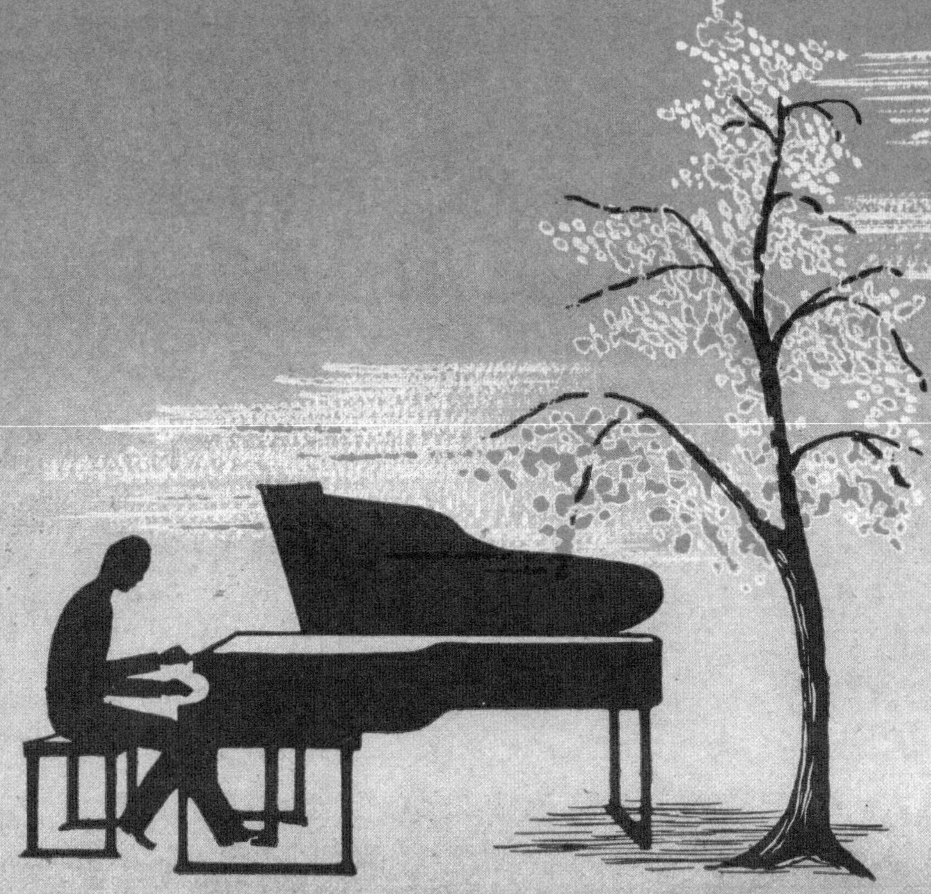

Mills Music, Inc.
1619 BROADWAY, NEW YORK 19, N. Y

Price
75¢

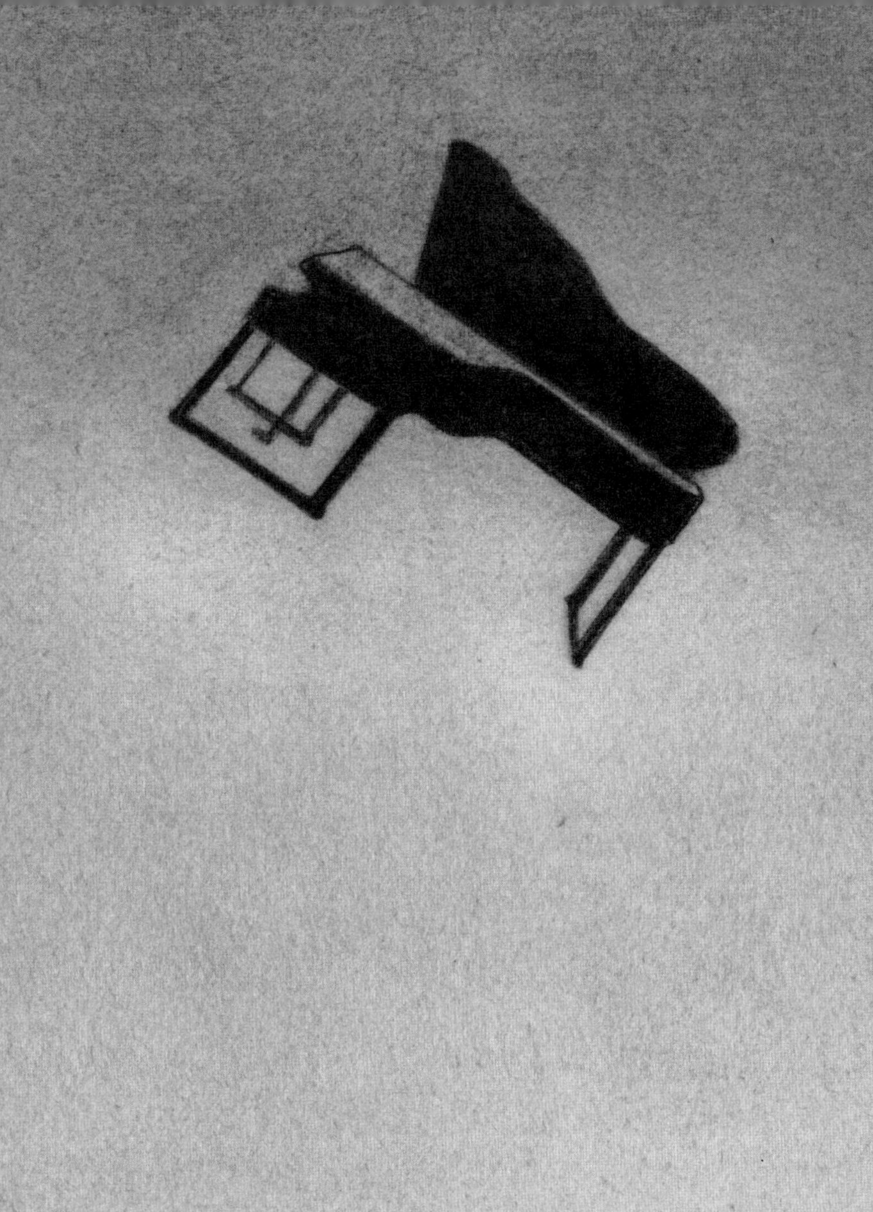

I KNOW THAT YOU KNOW

by

VINCENT YOUMANS

Paraphrased for Piano by

MAURICE C. WHITNEY

Price 60¢ in U.S.A.

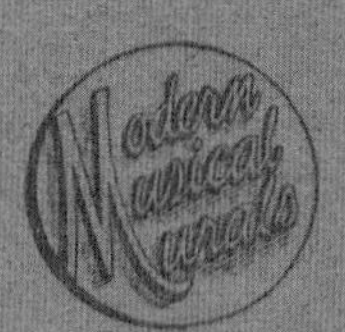

HARMS, INC.
NEW YORK

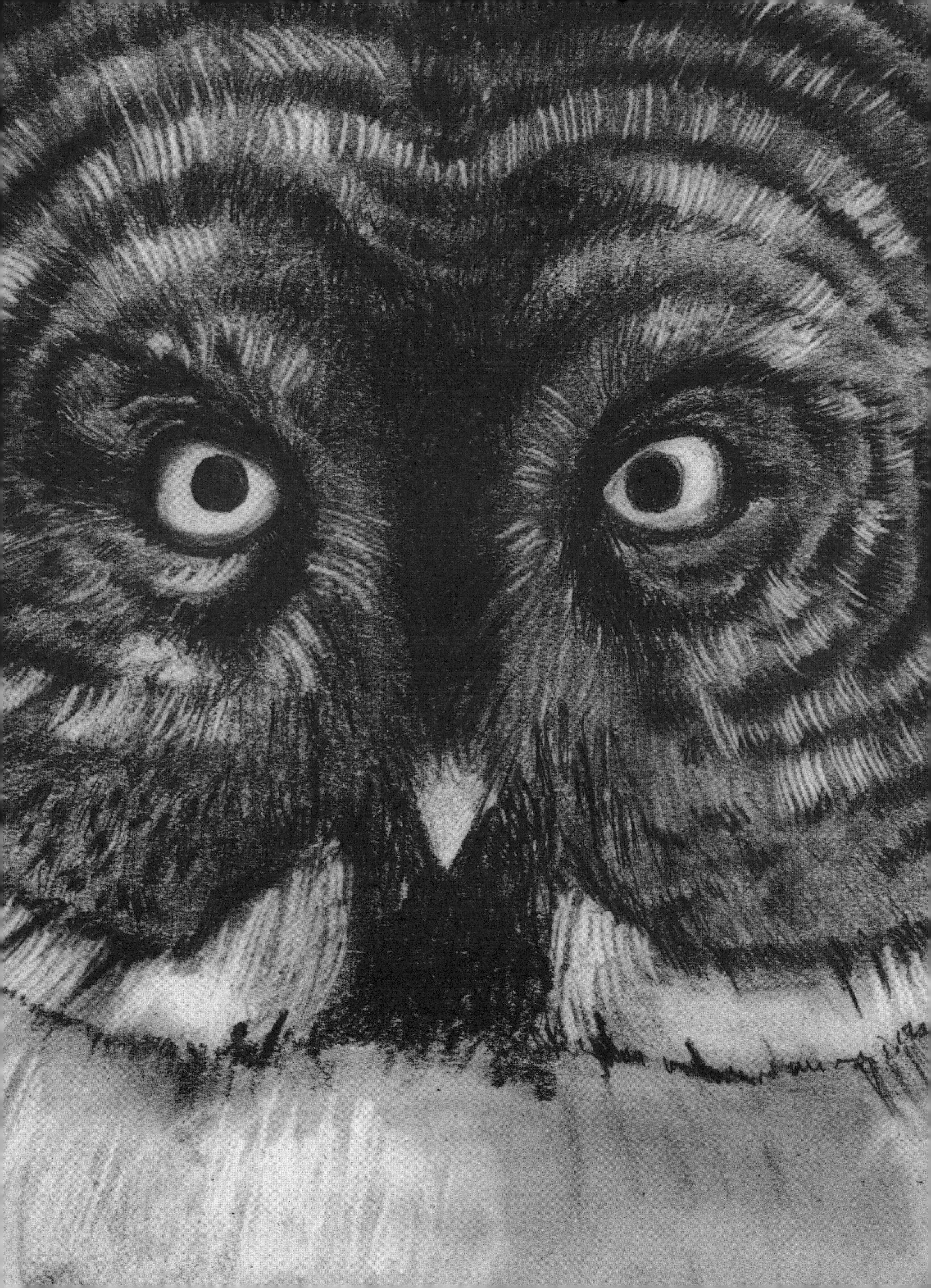

I UNDERSTAND

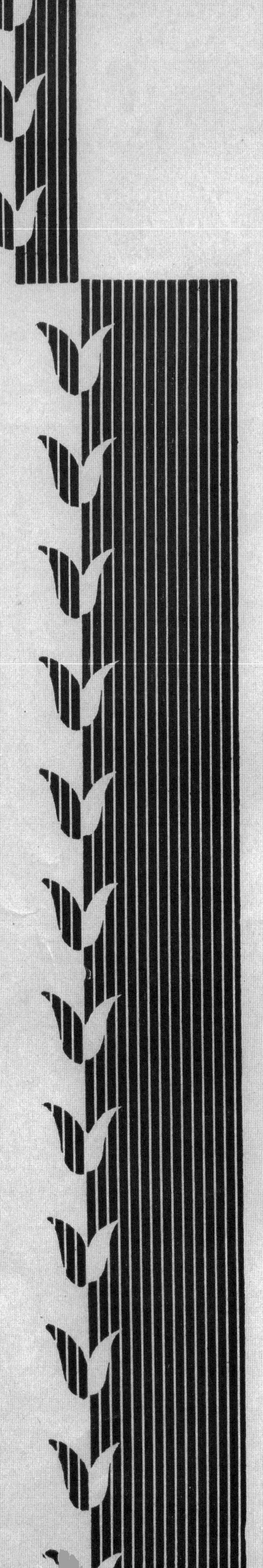

Lyric by
KIM GANNON

Music by
MABEL WAYNE

PRICE **60¢** IN U.S.A.

Leo Feist inc.

799 SEVENTH AVENUE • NEW YORK 19, N. Y.

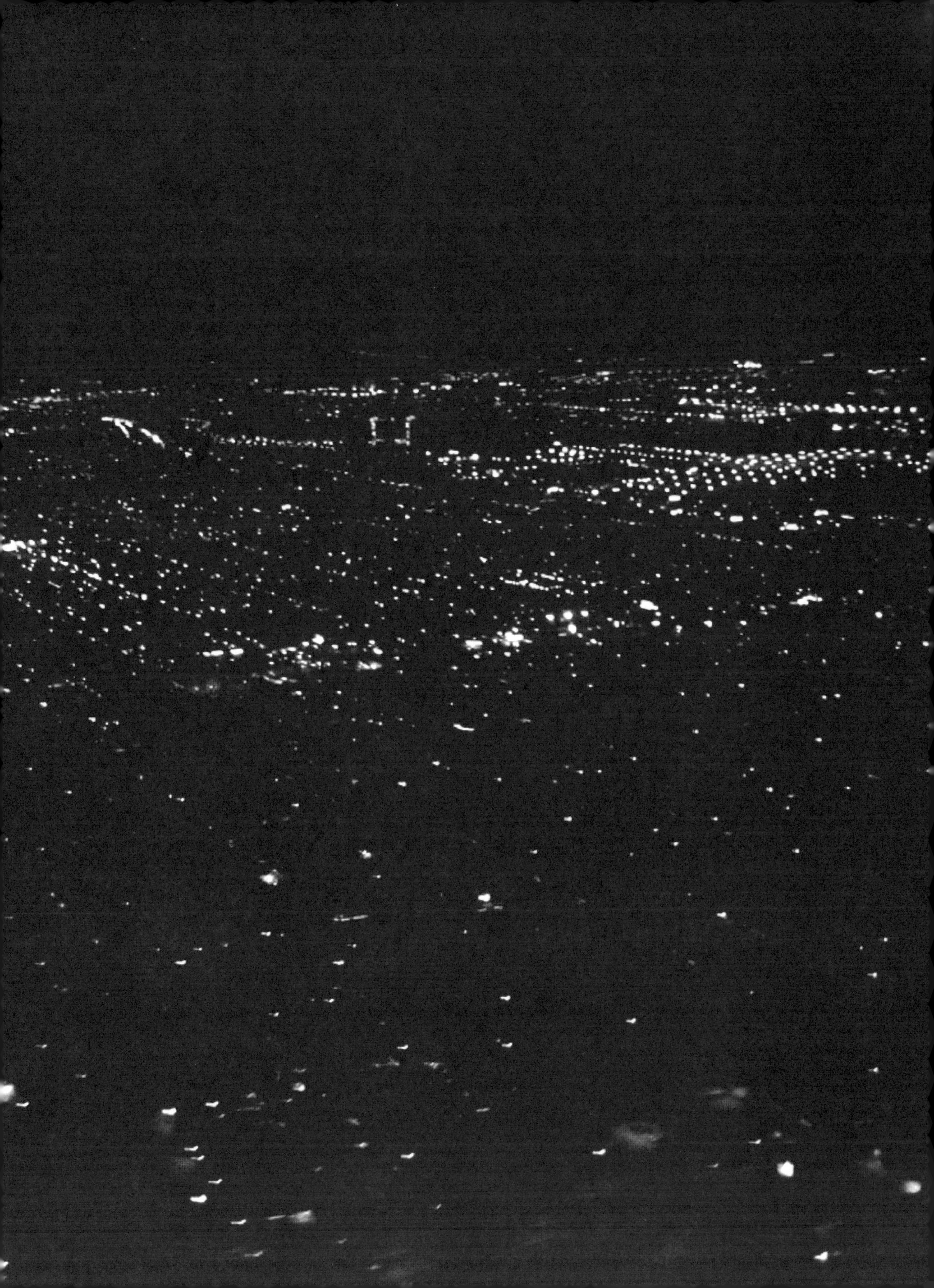

Piano • Vocal • Guitar

You Are My Sunshine

Words and Music by
Jimmie Davis
and
Charles Mitchell

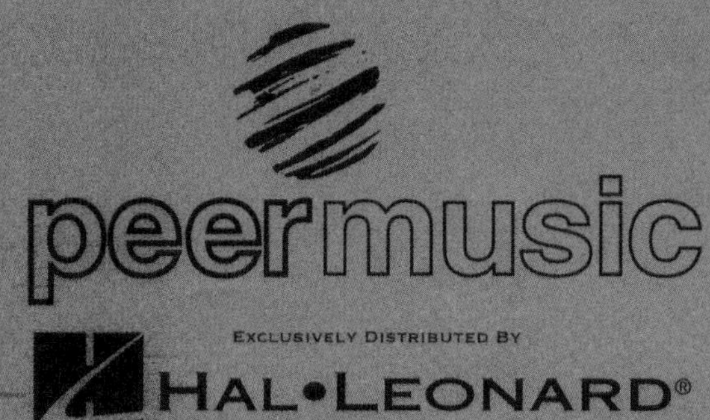

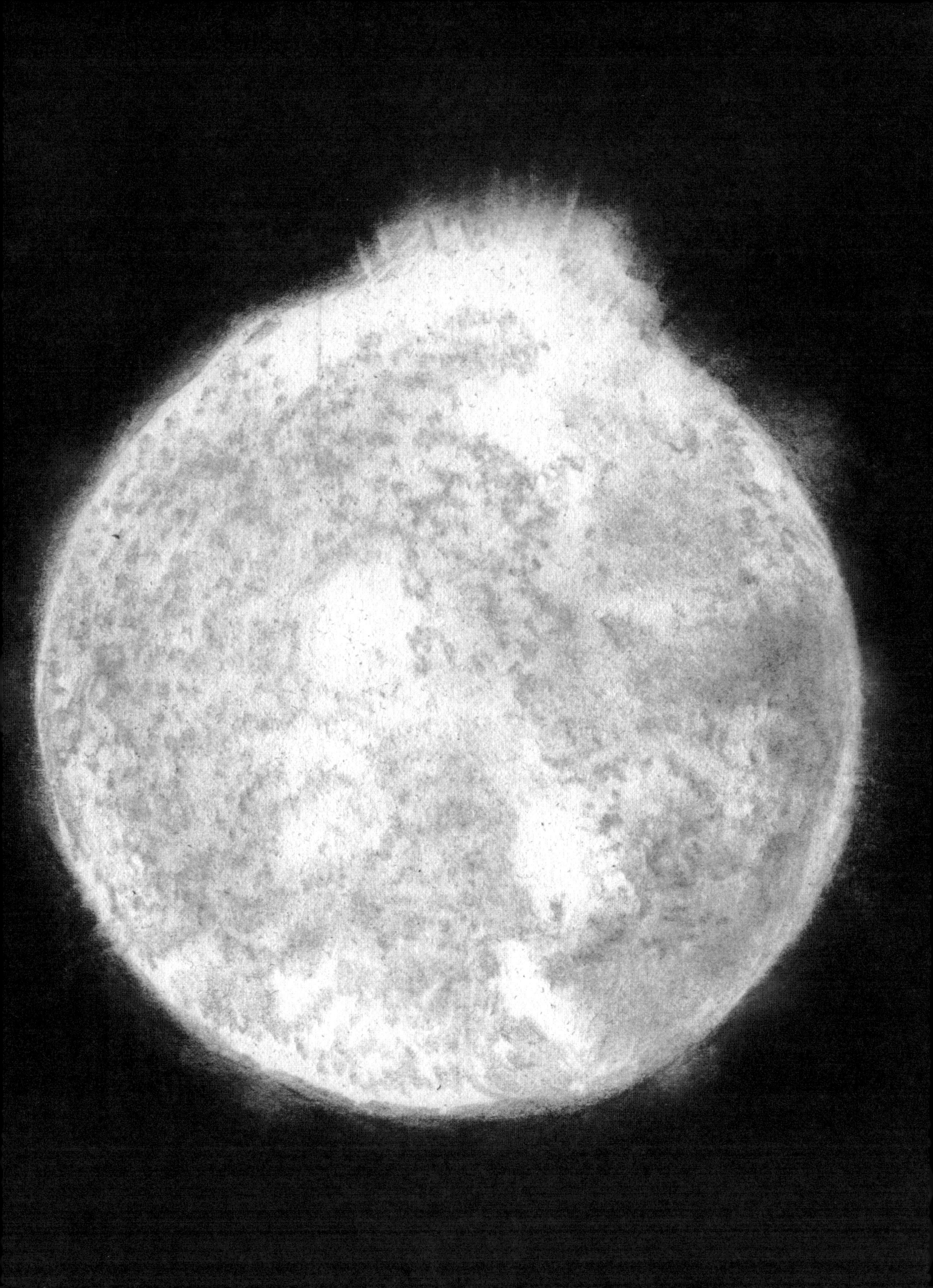

COCOANUT SWEET

Music by **HAROLD ARLEN**
Lyrics by **E. Y. HARBURG** (By arrangement with Chappell & Co., Inc.)

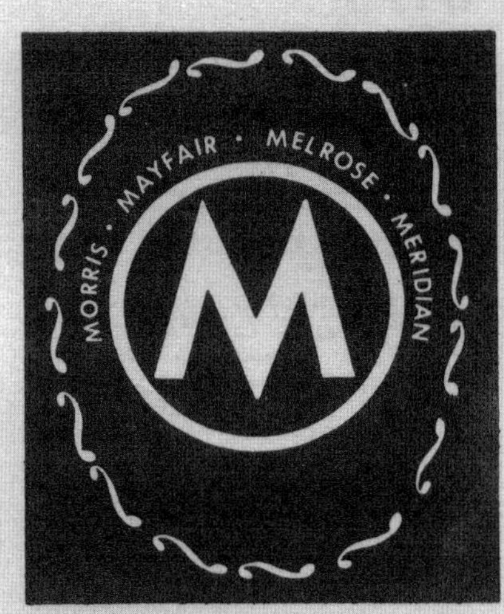

PRICE 75¢ IN U.S.A.

HARWIN MUSIC CORPORATION
31 WEST 54th STREET, NEW YORK 19, N.Y.
Sole Distributor: EDWIN H. MORRIS & COMPANY, INC.

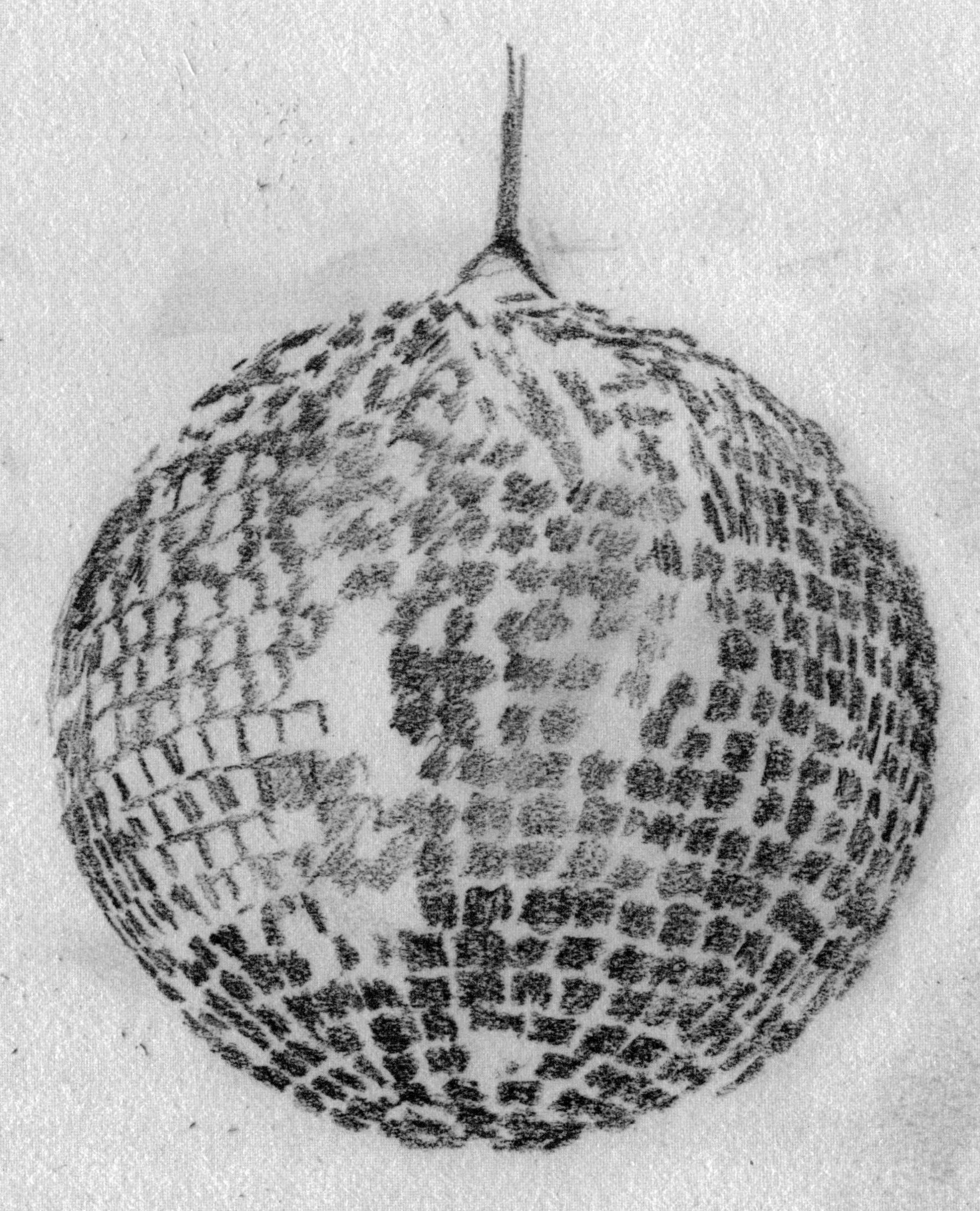

you are my disco ball —

Summer In Your Eyes

Words by
PAUL FRANCIS WEBSTER

Music by
SONNY BURKE

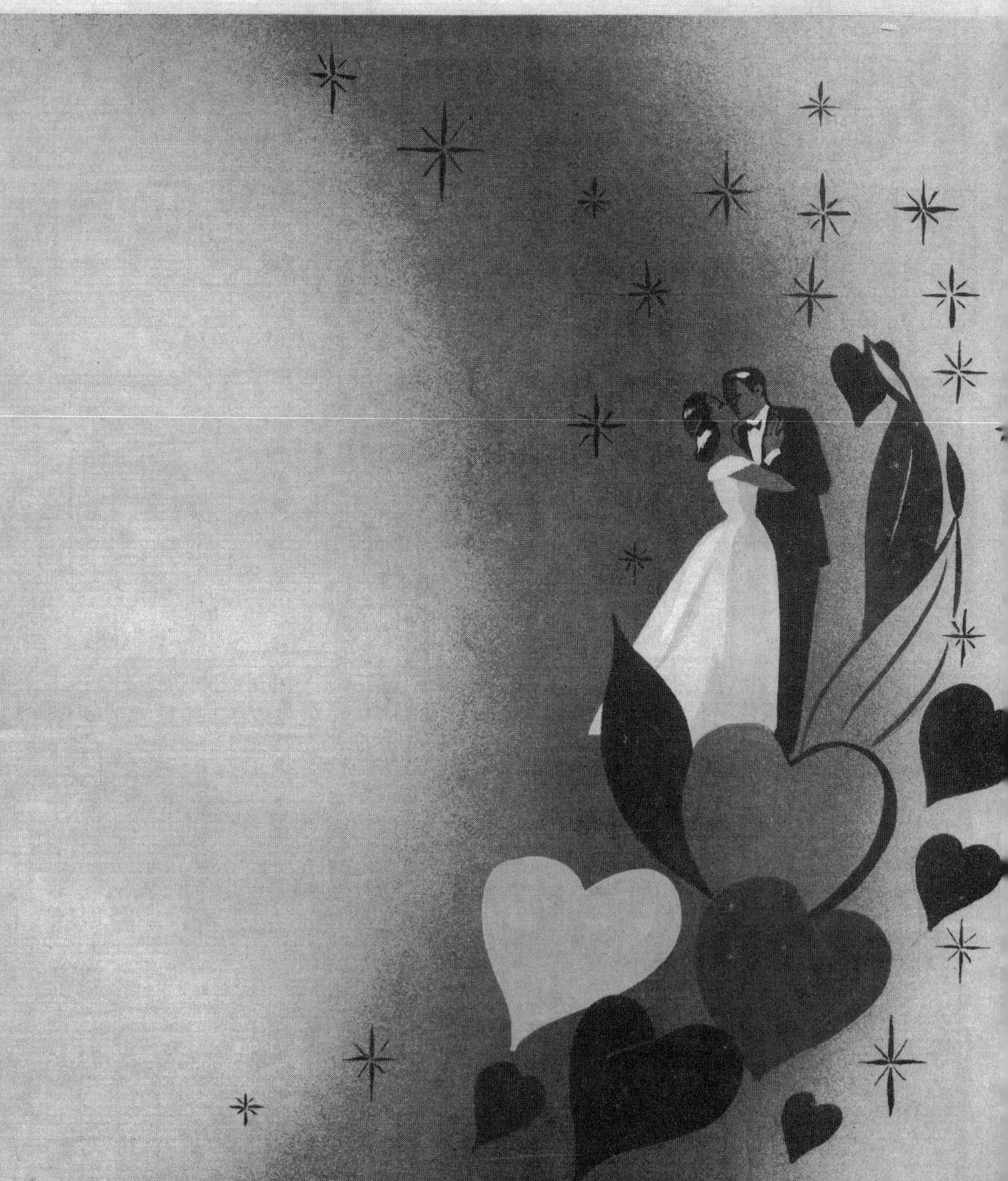

PRICE **50¢** IN U.S.A.

M. WITMARK & SONS
NEW YORK, N. Y.

Printed in U.S.A.

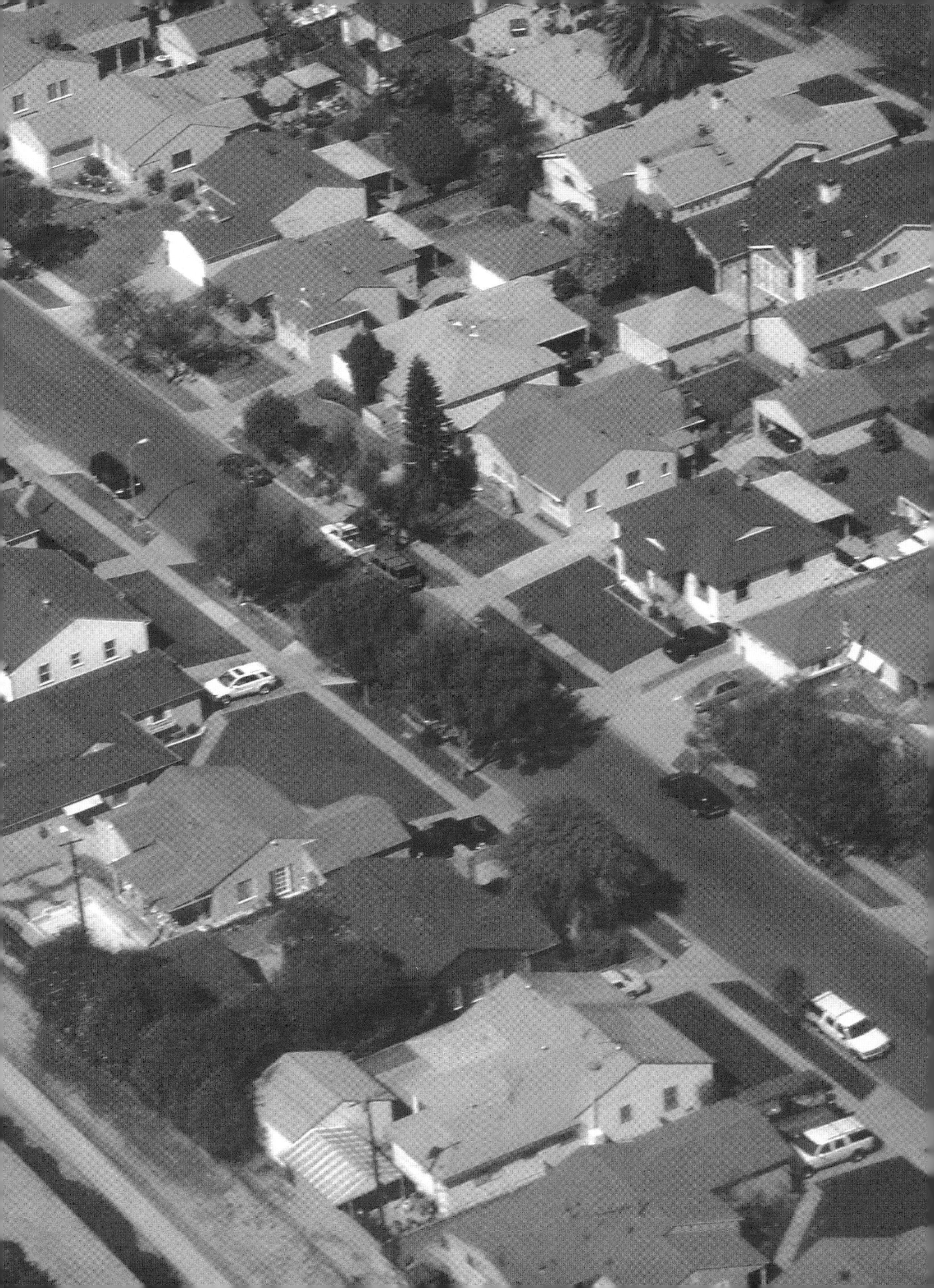

EVERYTHING I HAVE IS YOURS

•

lyric by

HAROLD ADAMSON

•

melody by

BURTON LANE

PRICE **60¢** IN U.S.A.

ROBBINS MUSIC CORPORATION
799 SEVENTH AVENUE • NEW YORK 19, N. Y.

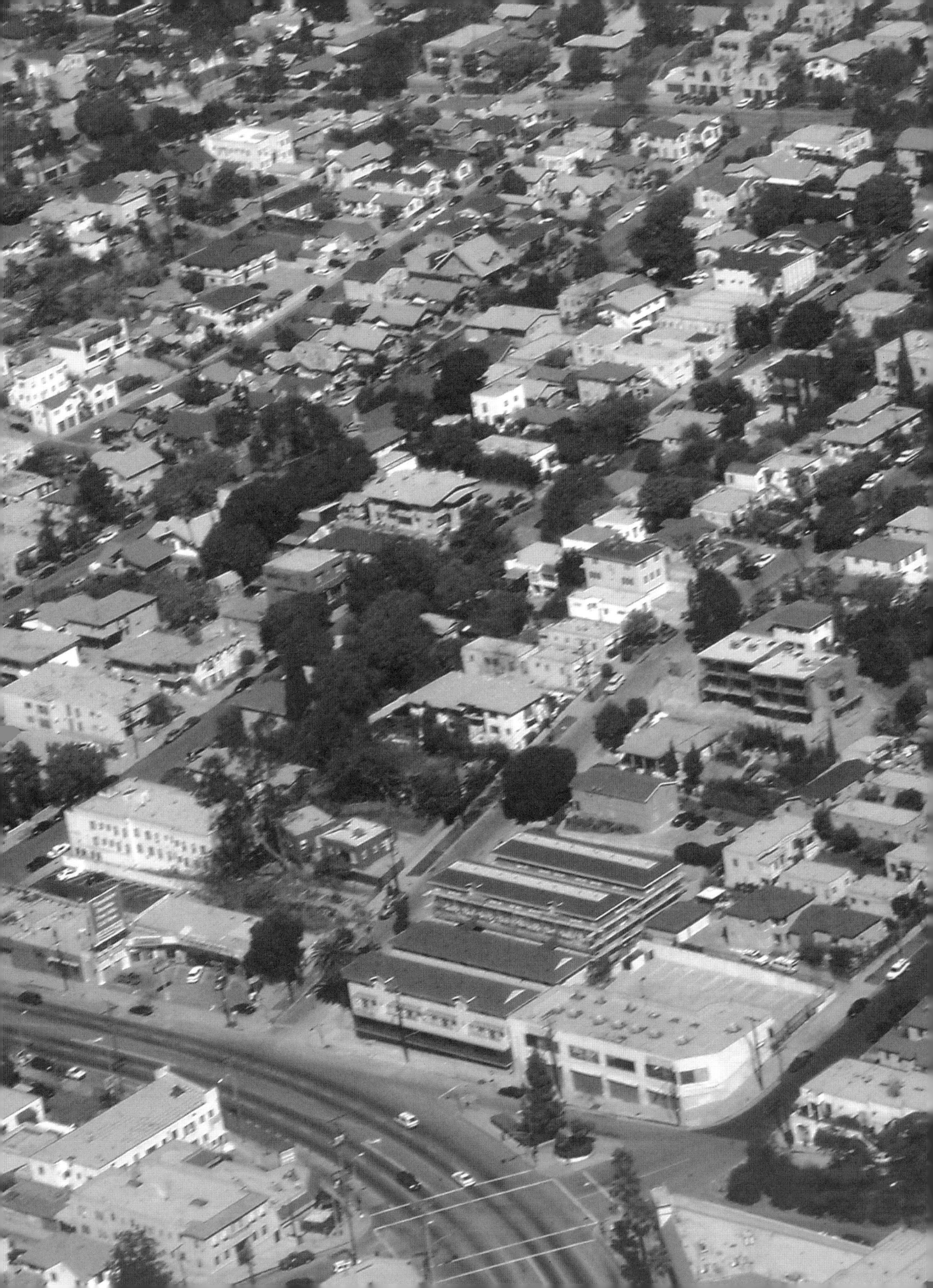

Let's Get Away From It All

Lyric by Tom Adair
Music by Matt Dennis

Dorsey Brothers Music, Inc.

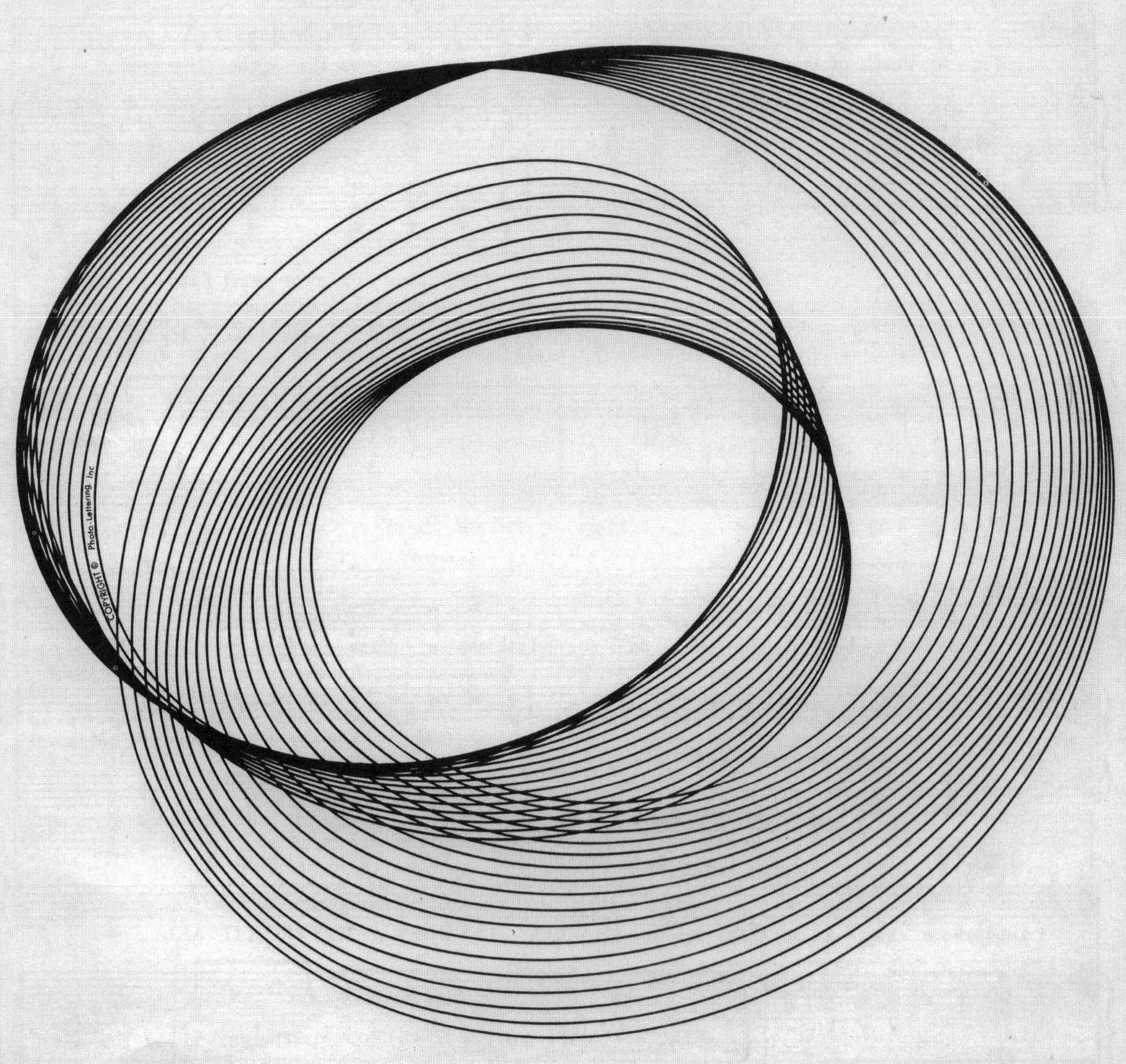

85¢

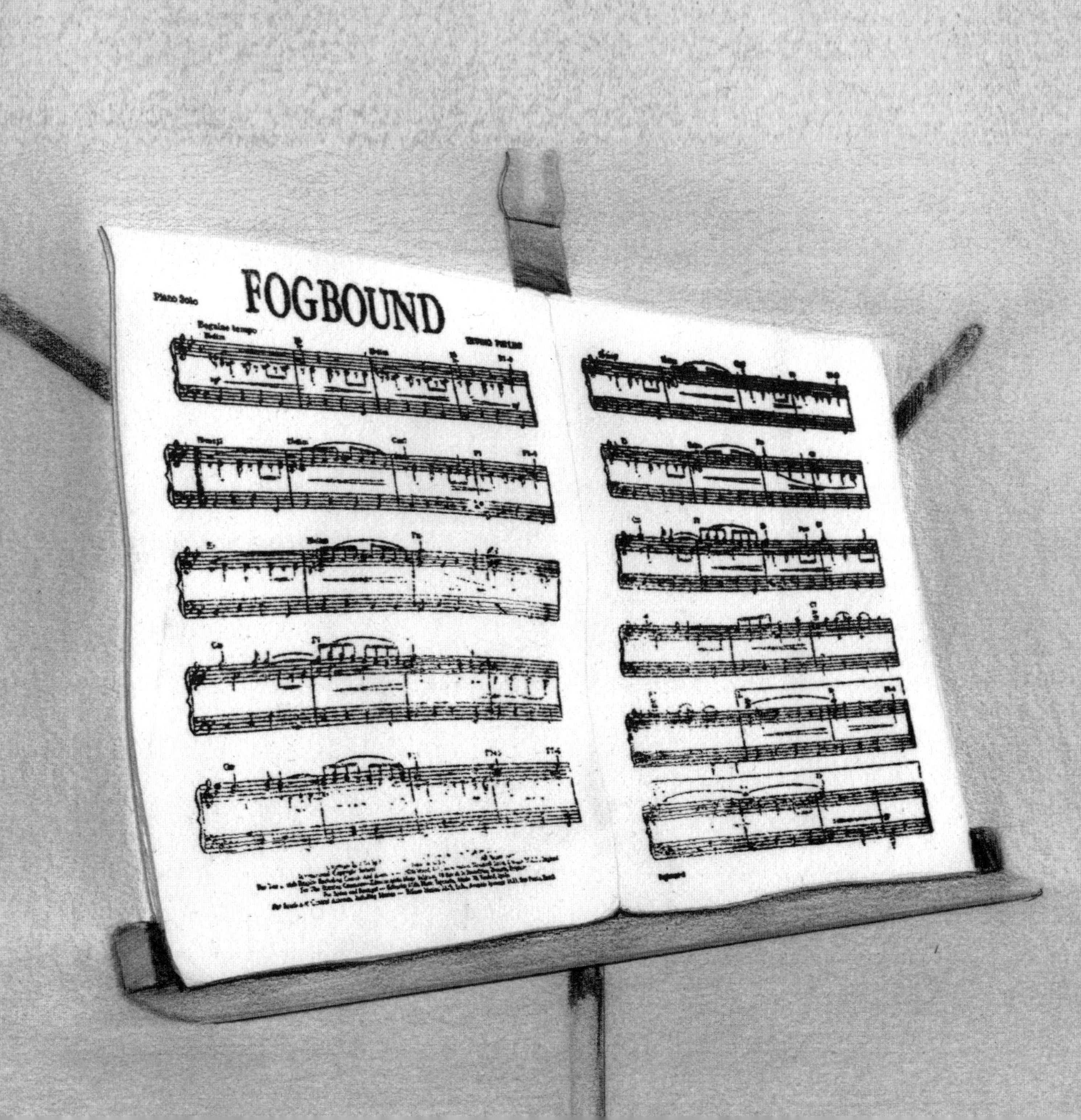

Piano Solo
FOGBOUND
Beguine tempo
FOGBOUND

Standard Song Edition

YOU SMELL SO GOOD

Lyric and Music by

HARRY STONE
TOMMY WOLF

Price 75¢

03014

WOLF-MILLS MUSIC, INC.

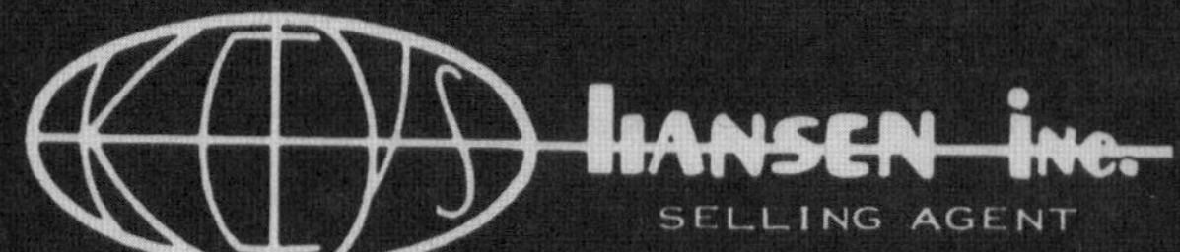

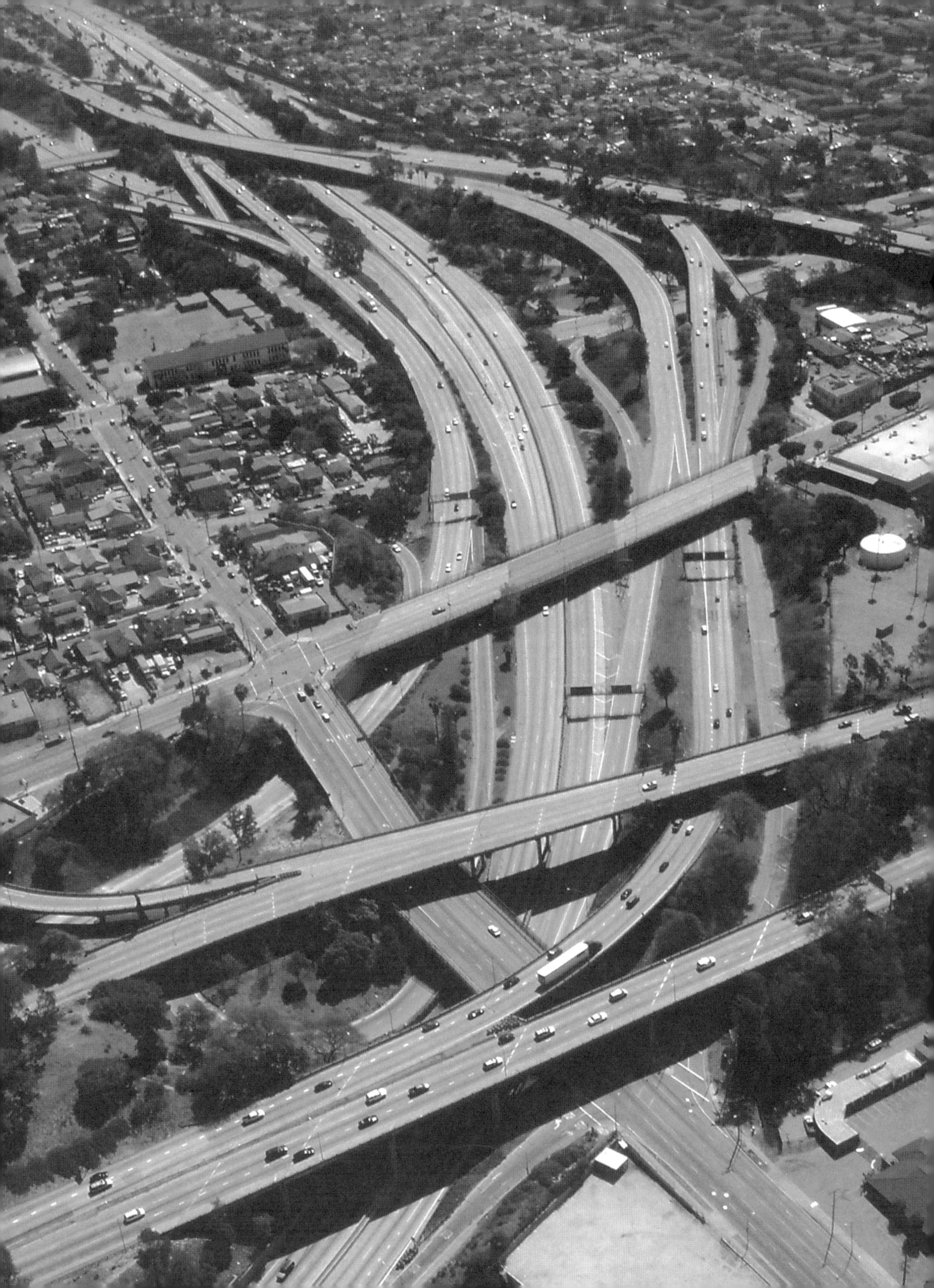

I'LL ALWAYS BE WITH YOU 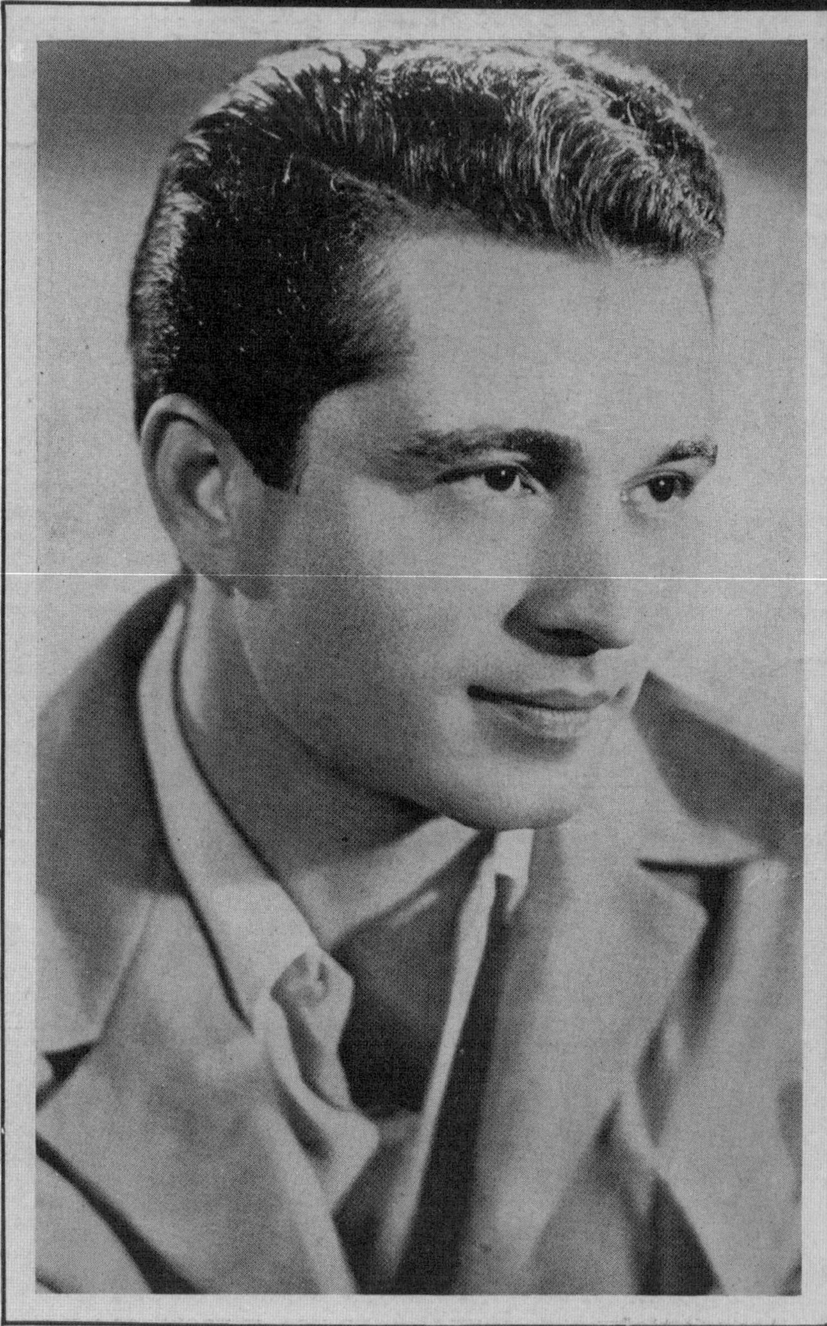
WORDS AND MUSIC
BY
MARJORIE GOETSCHIUS
AND
EDNA OSSER
Featured by
PERRY COMO
MANNING
BROADWAY MUSIC CORPORATION
WILL VON-TILZER PRESIDENT

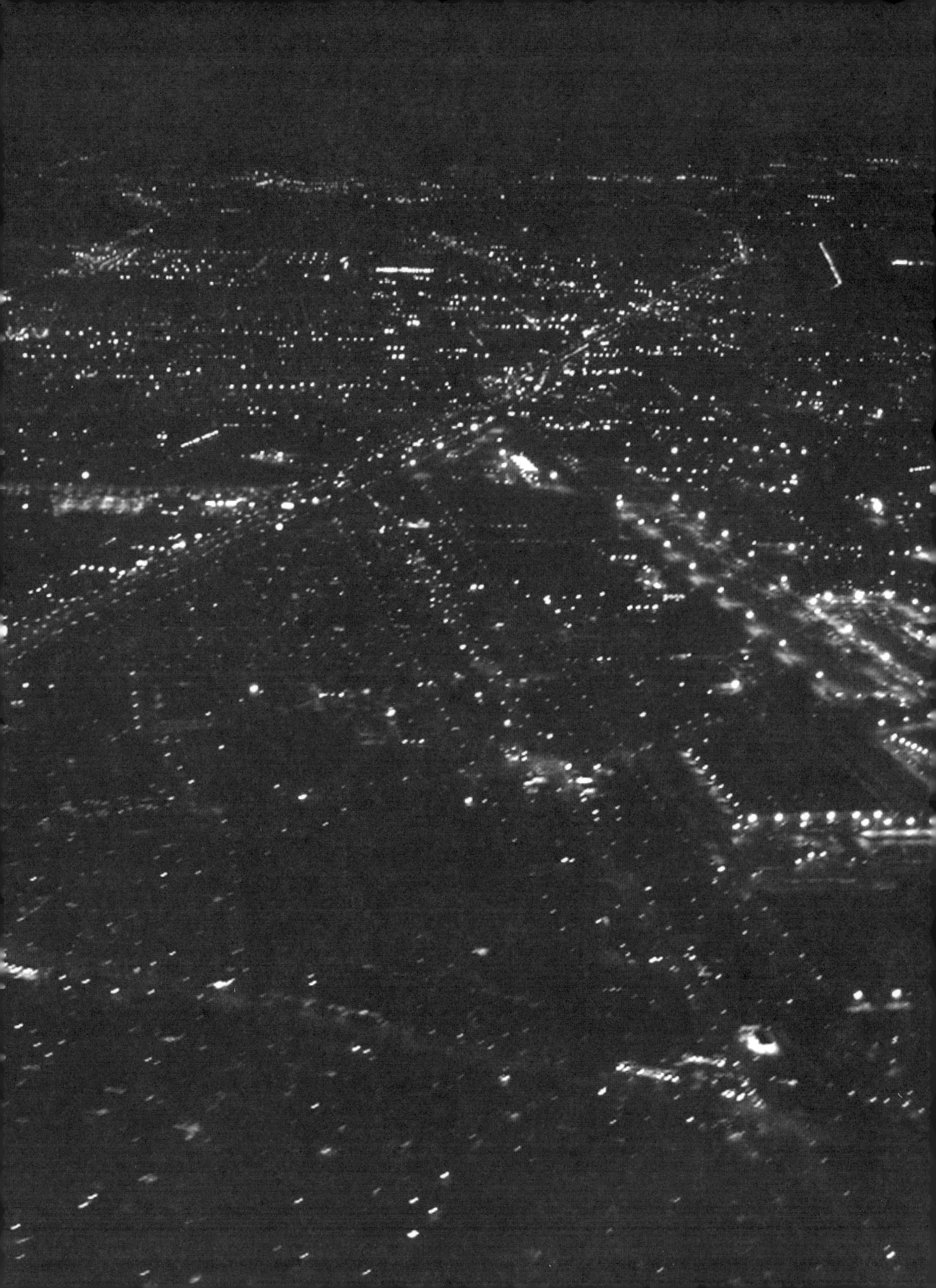

LITTLE BIRD

From the Score to PAULA JACOBI's all Negro Play "The Adamses"

Music and Lyric by

MARK BUCCI

Price Sixty Cents

in U.S.A.

BOTH CONCERT AND SIMPLIFIED VERSIONS INCLUDED

LEEDS MUSIC CORPORATION

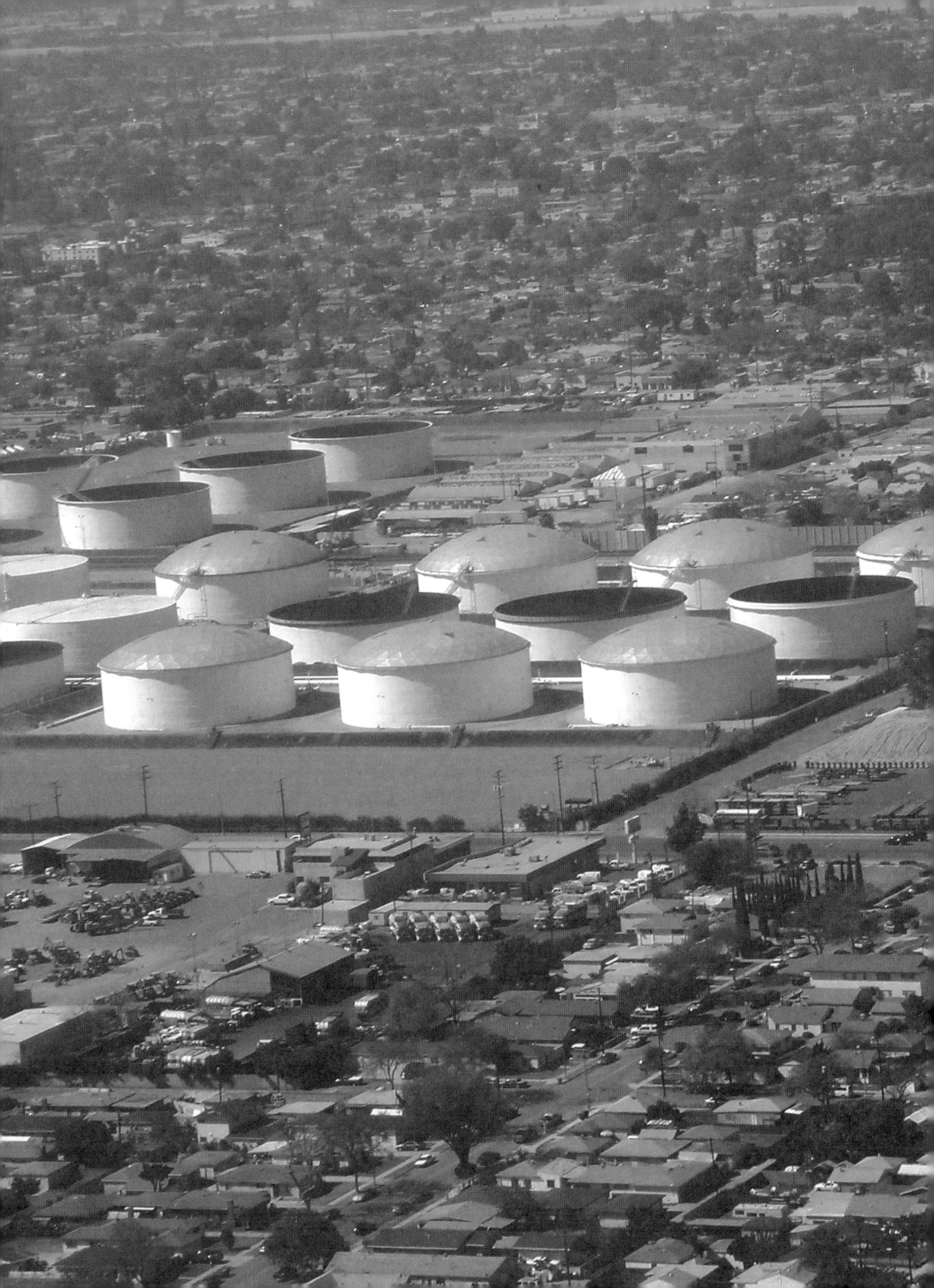

MAKE LOVE TO ME

LYRIC BY
KIM GANNON
A.S.C.A.P.

MUSIC BY
PAUL MANN AND
STEPHAN WEISS
A.S.C.A.P.

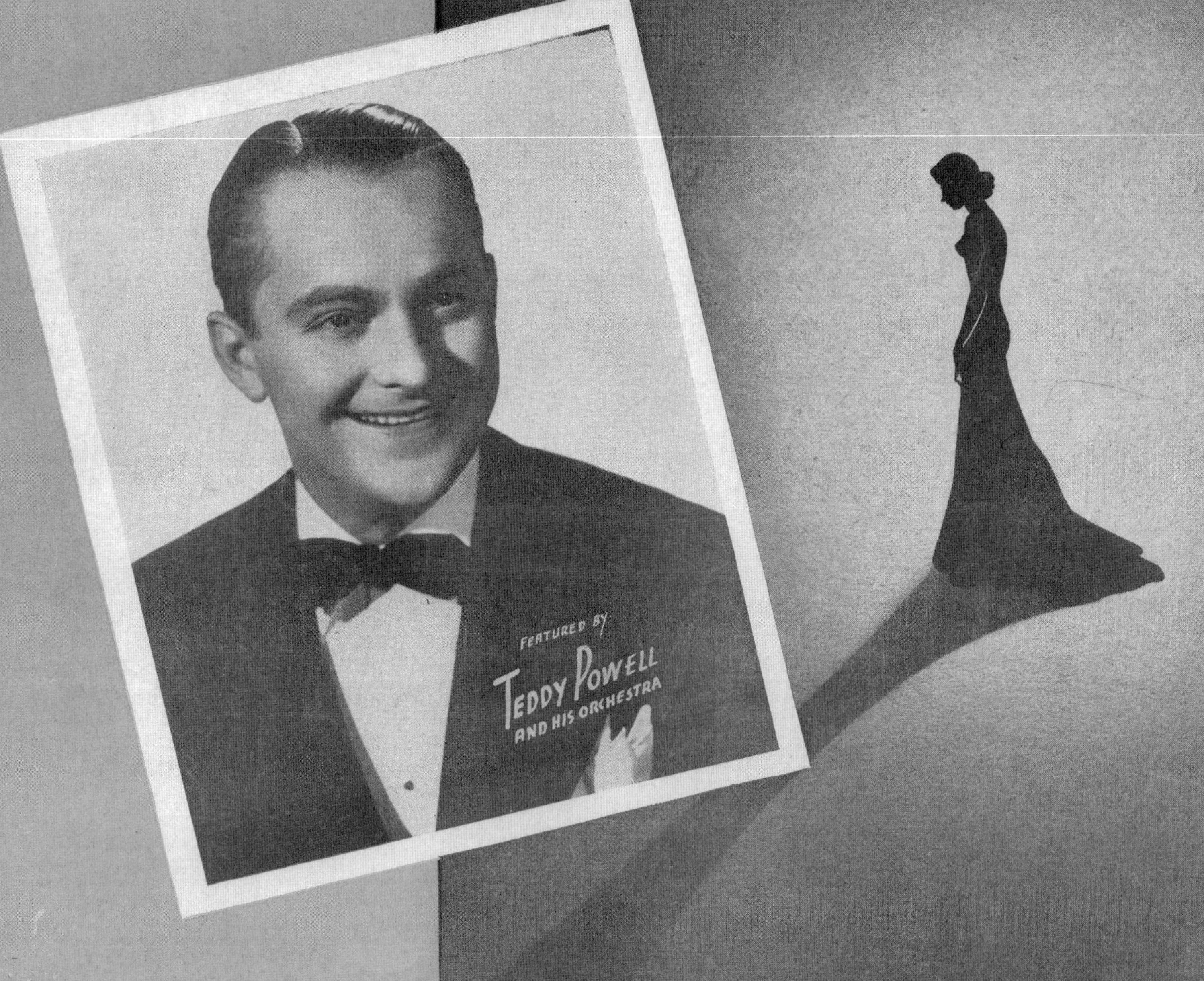

M. WITMARK & SONS
NEW YORK

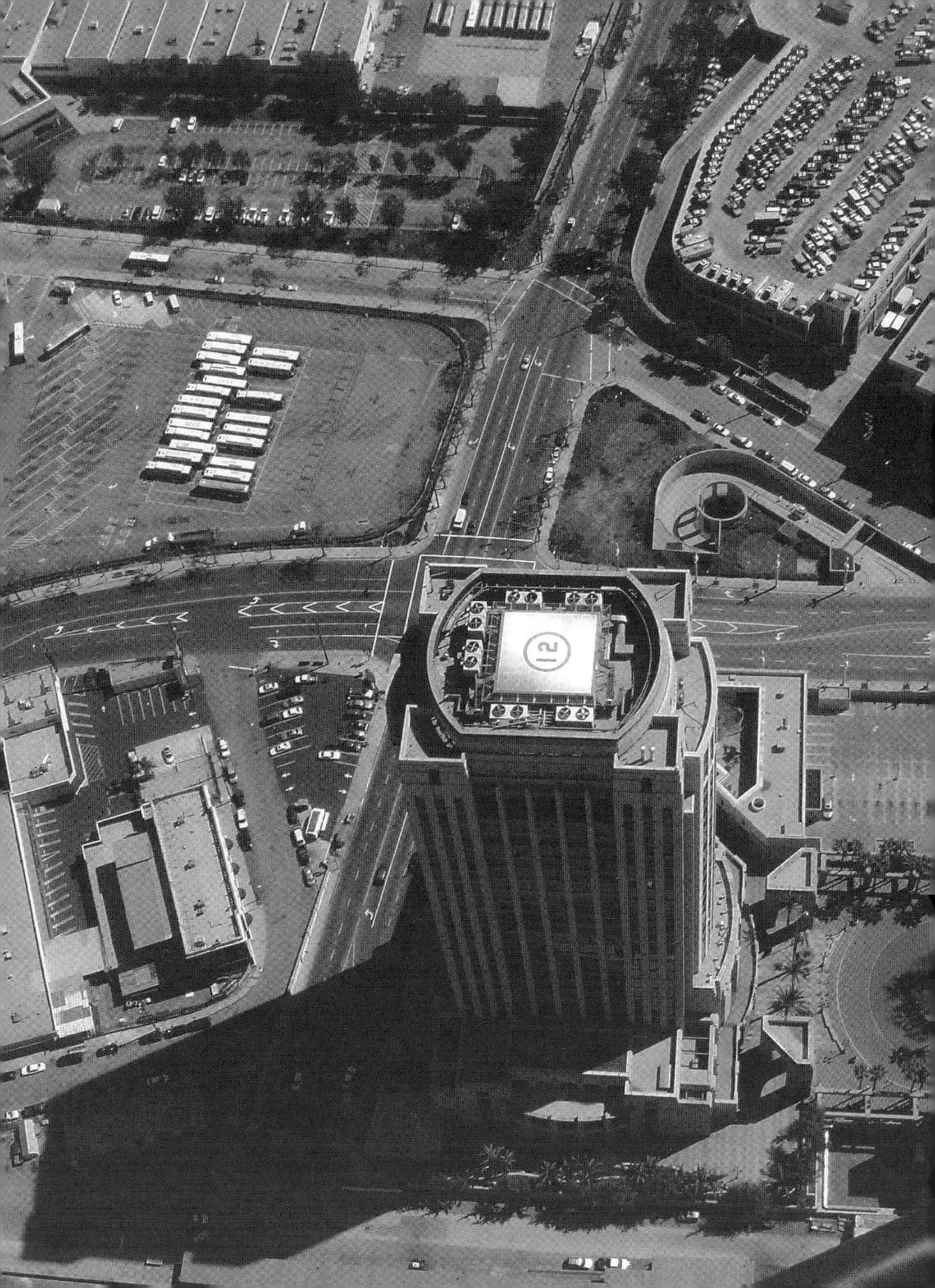

FACE TO FACE

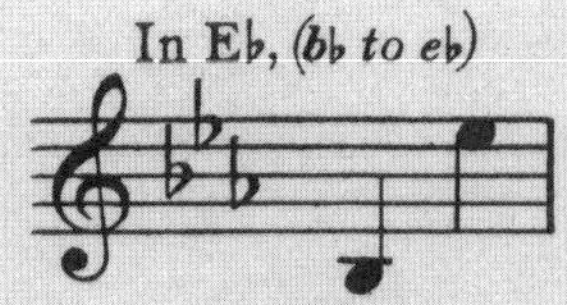

WORDS BY

SAMMY CAHN

MUSIC BY

SAMMY FAIN

Price 60 Cents

IN U.S.A.

M. WITMARK & SONS, NEW YORK

PRINTED IN U.S.A.

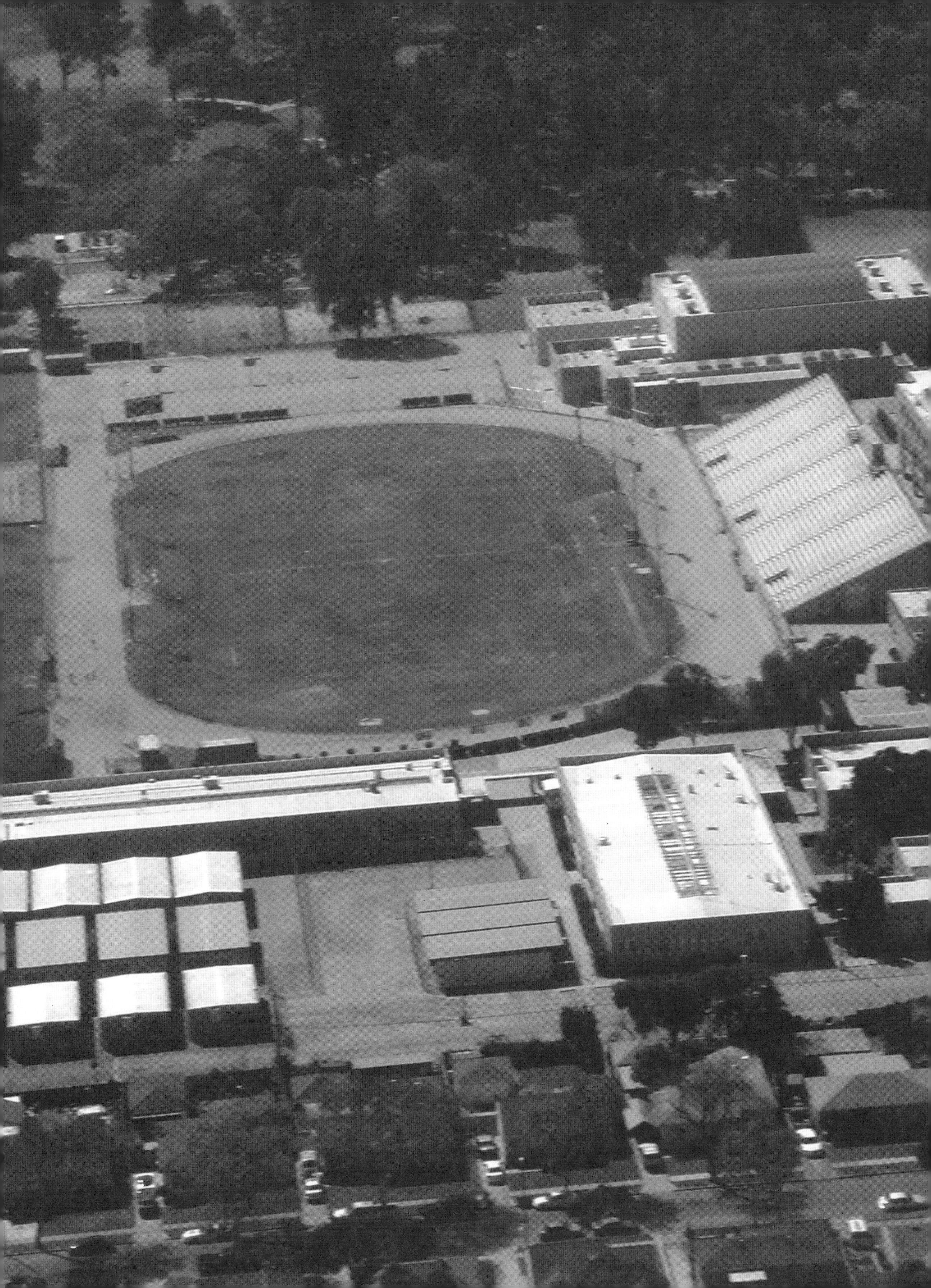

BACK IN YOUR OWN BACK YARD

By AL JOLSON, BILLY ROSE and DAVE DREYER

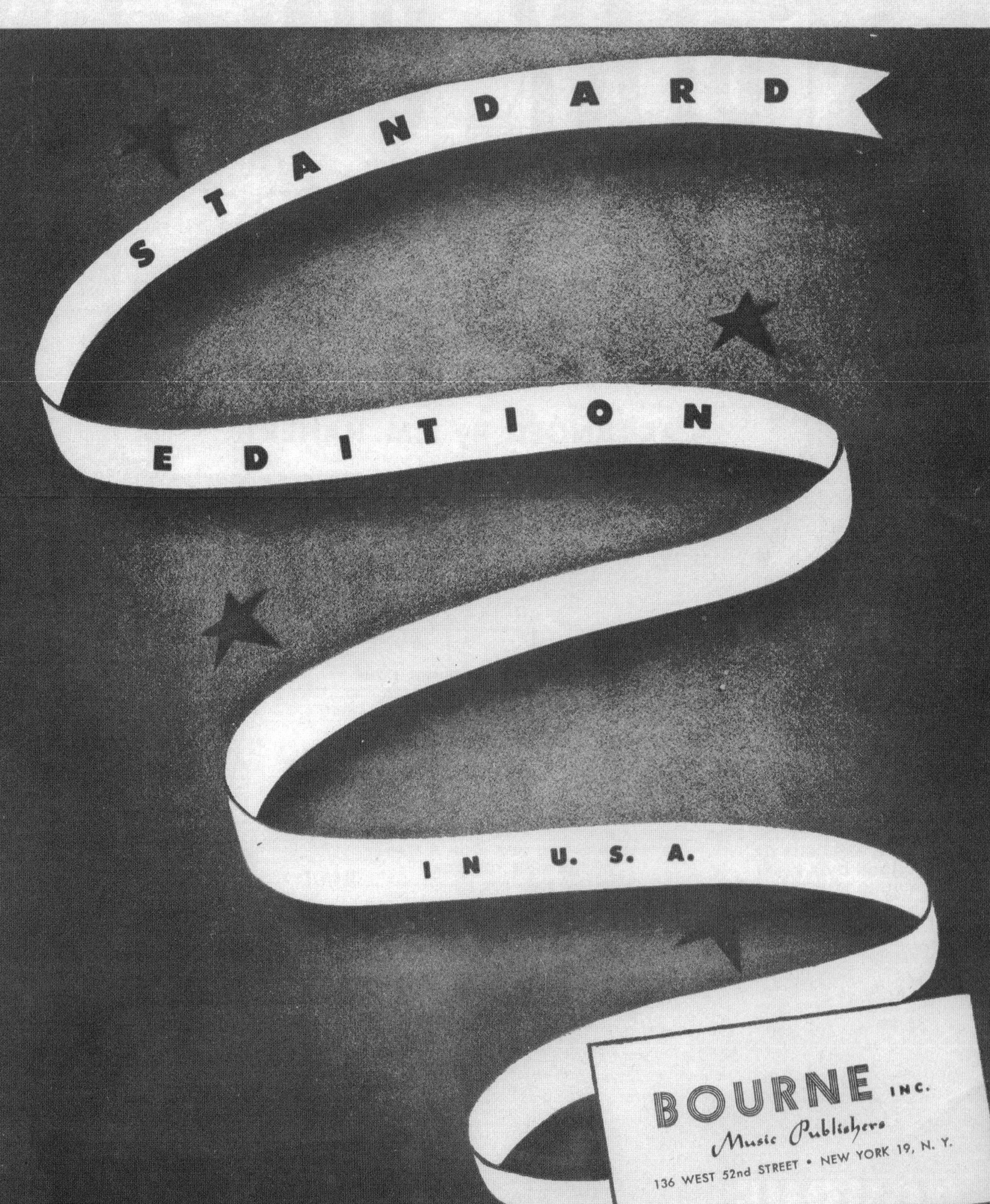

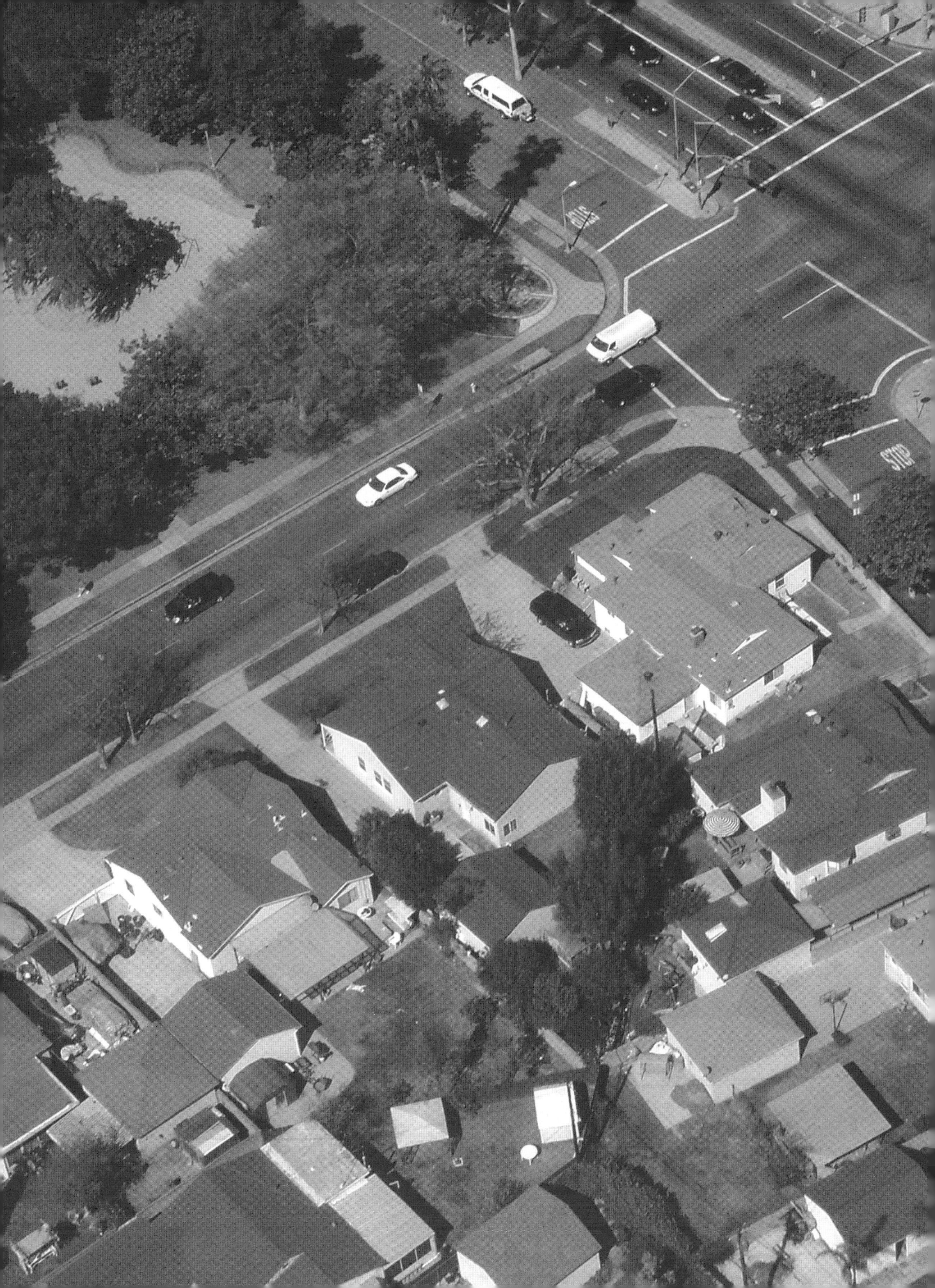

Just For Now

Words by
DORY PREVIN
Music by
ANDRÉ PREVIN

Price 75¢

ANDOR, INC.
Sole Selling Agent: **VALANDO MUSIC CORP.**, 22 West 48th Street, New York 36, N. Y.

Draw Me A Circle

Words and Music by CY YOUNG

Standard Vocal Edition

75c

in U.S.A.

THURSDAY MUSIC CORP.
New York, N.Y.

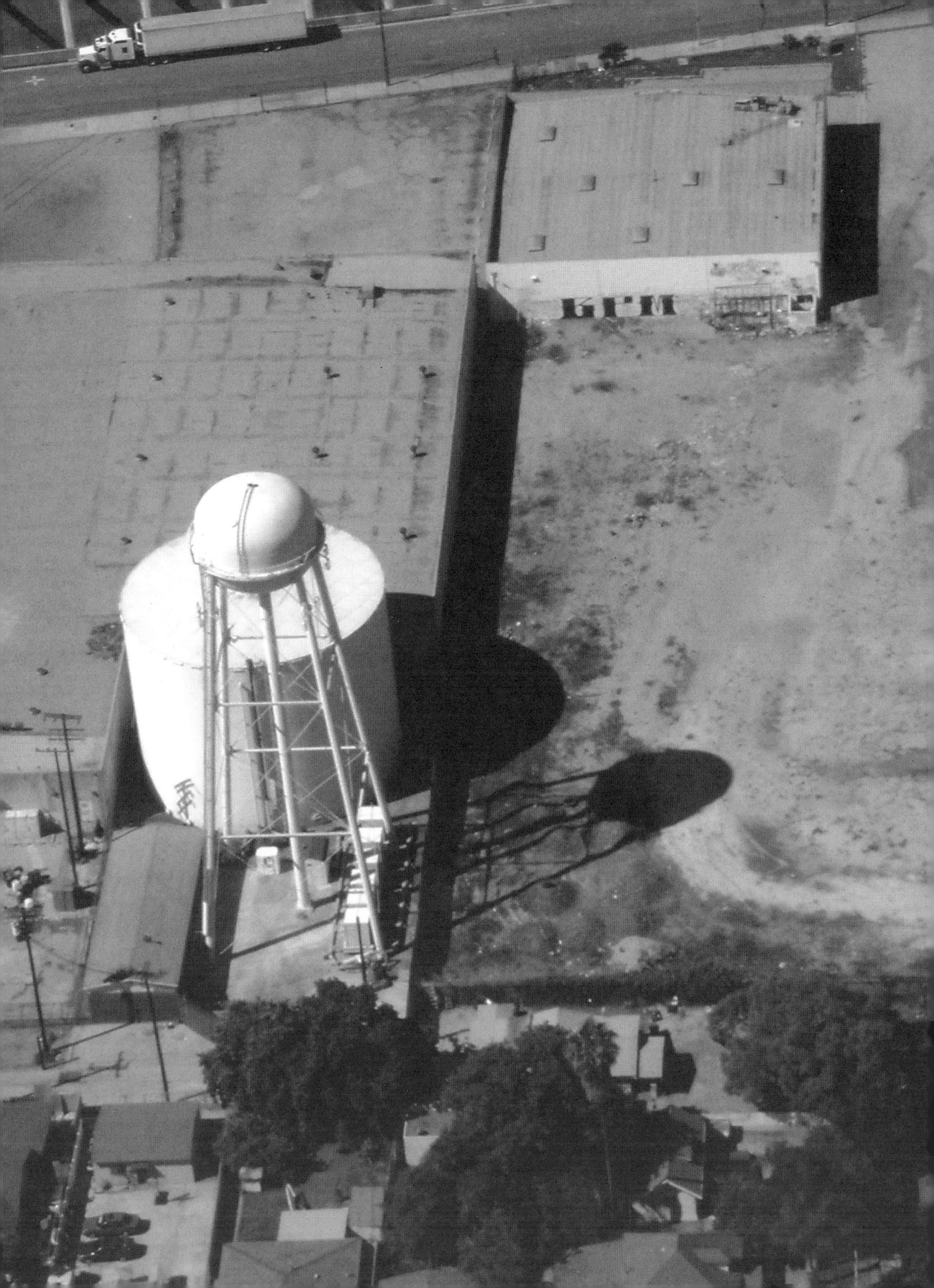

Always In My Heart

Lyric By
Kim Gannon

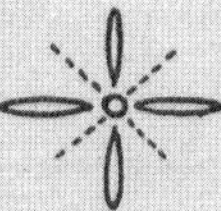

Music By
Ernesto Lecuona

Southern Music Publishing Co., Inc.
1619 Broadway, New York, 19, N.Y.

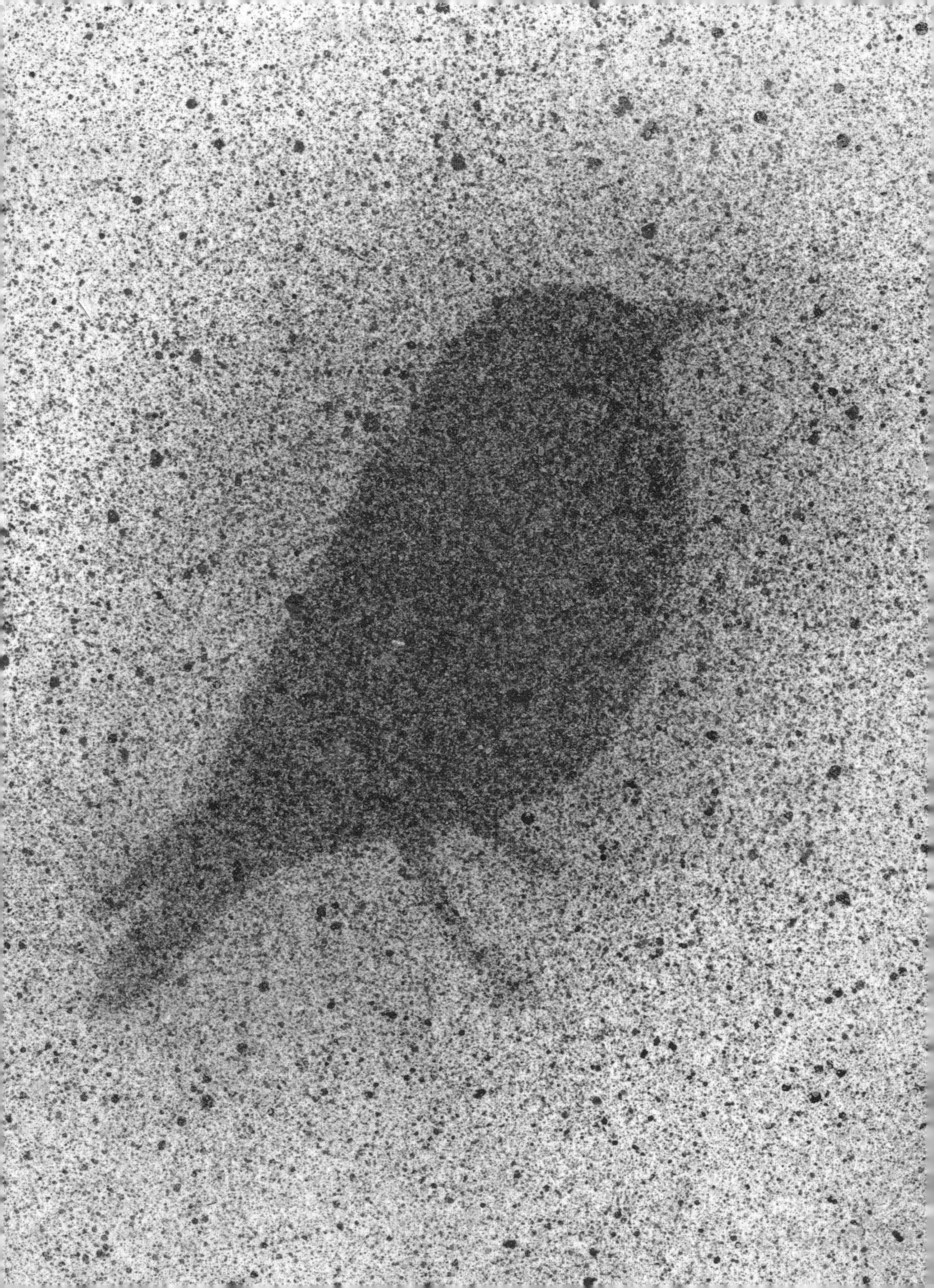

STANDARD EDITION

IT'S A GOOD DAY

Featured in the 20th Century-Fox Production

"WITH A SONG IN MY HEART"

By PEGGY LEE
and DAVE BARBOUR

Price
60c

CRITERION MUSIC CORPORATION

RKO Building • Radio City • New York 20, N. Y.

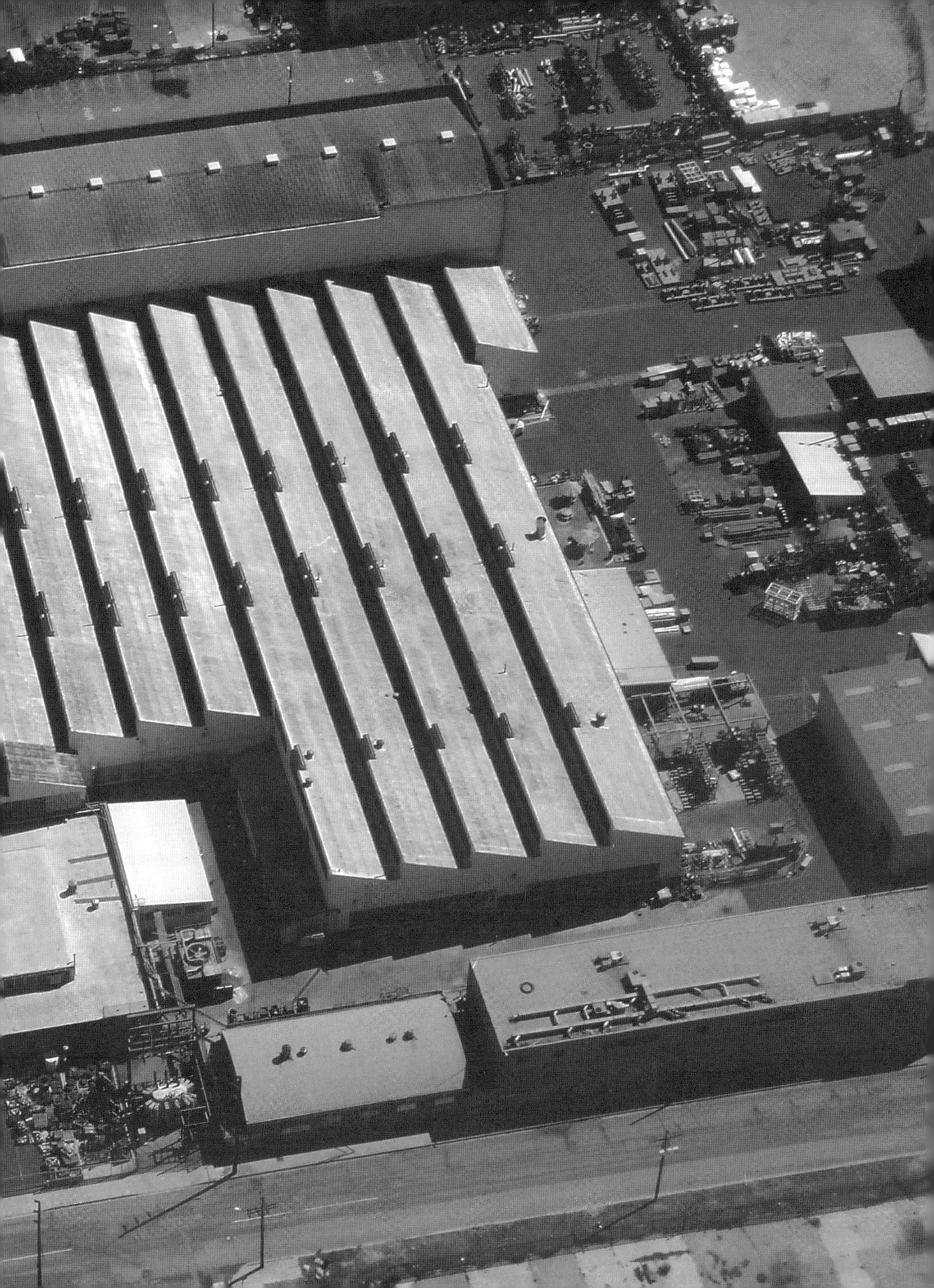

IT'S A BIG WIDE WONDERFUL WORLD

Words and Music by JOHN ROX

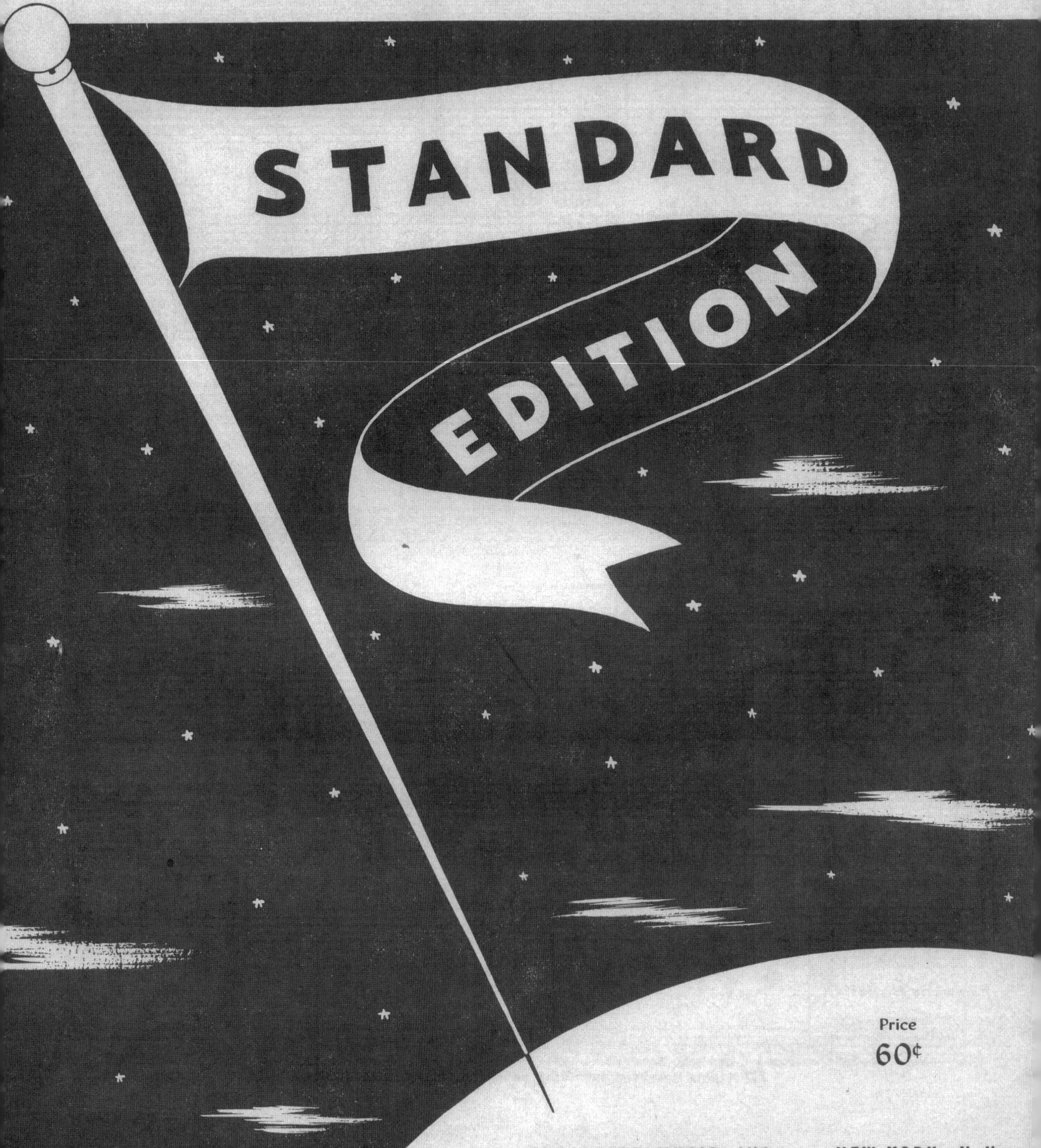

Price
60¢

BROADCAST MUSIC, INC. • NEW YORK, N.Y.

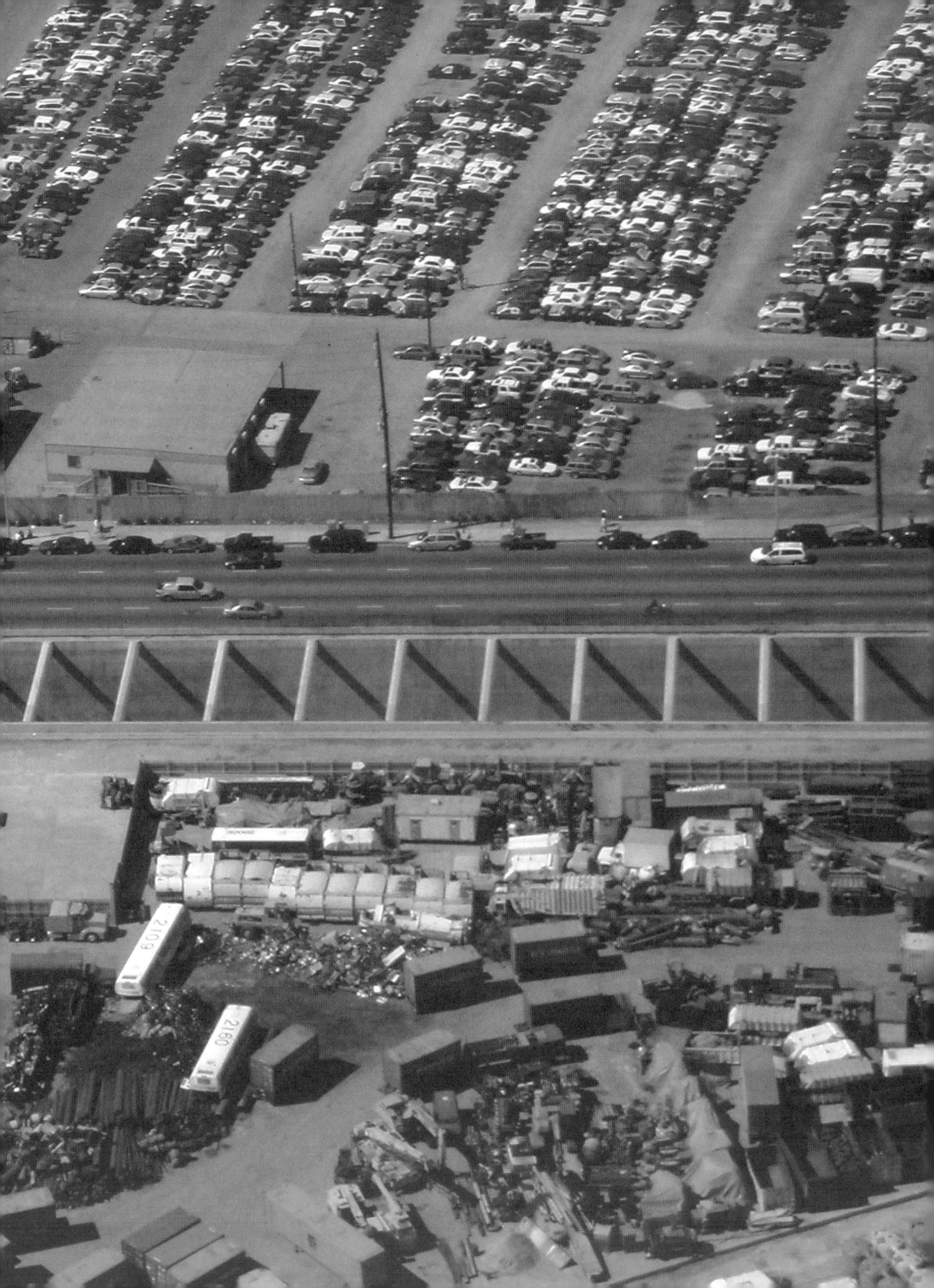

FALLING LEAVES

Piano Solo

COMPOSED AND ARRANGED BY

FRANKIE CARLE

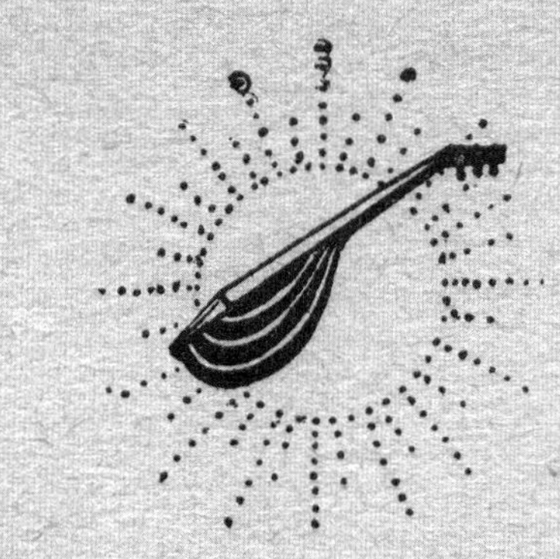

Price

60c

JEWEL MUSIC PUBLISHING CO. INC.,
1674 Broadway, New York, N.Y.

DECEMBER

Words and Music by AL RINKER *and* FLOYD HUDDLESTON

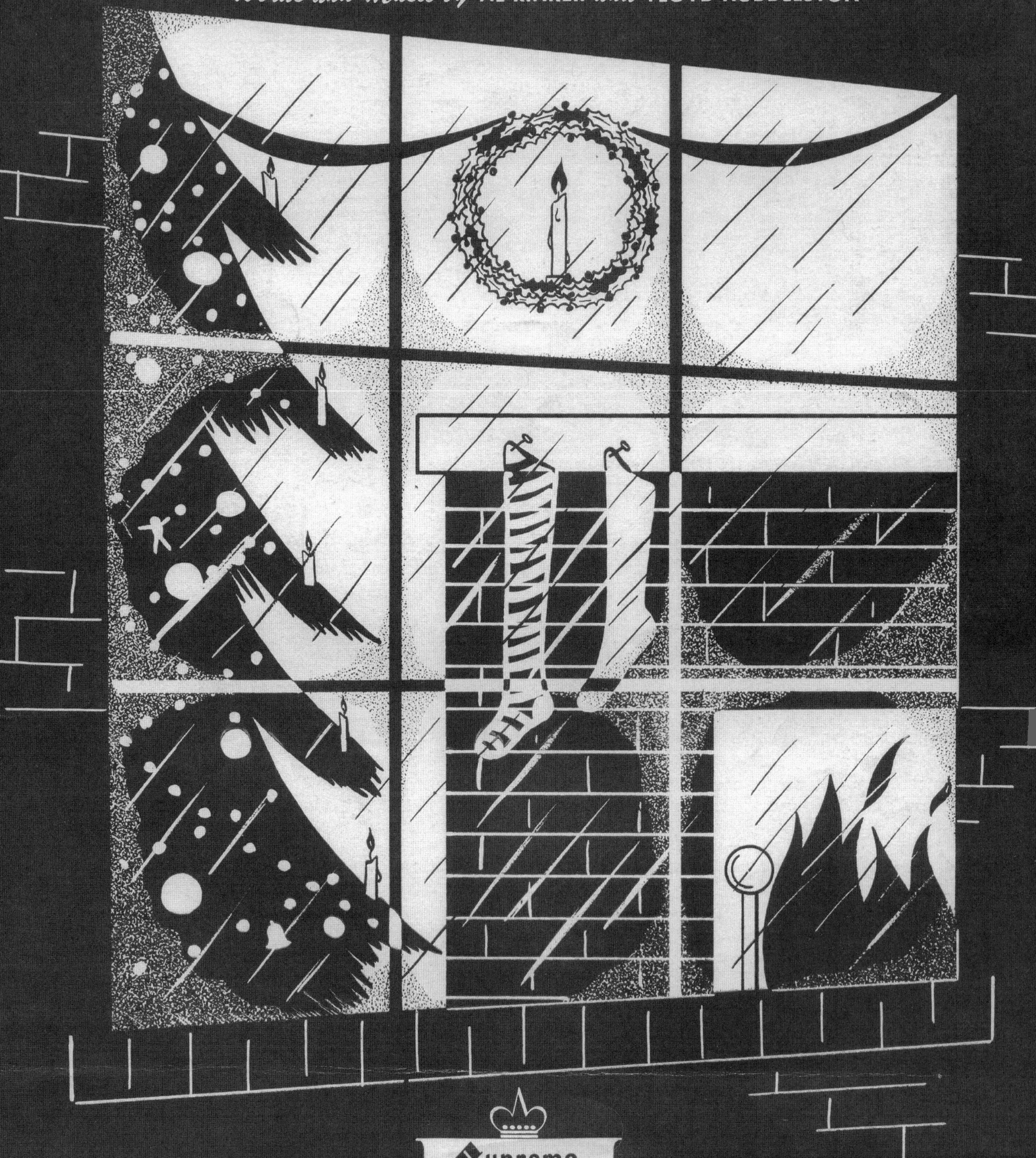

Supreme
MUSIC CORPORATION
1619 BROADWAY • NEW YORK 19, N. Y.

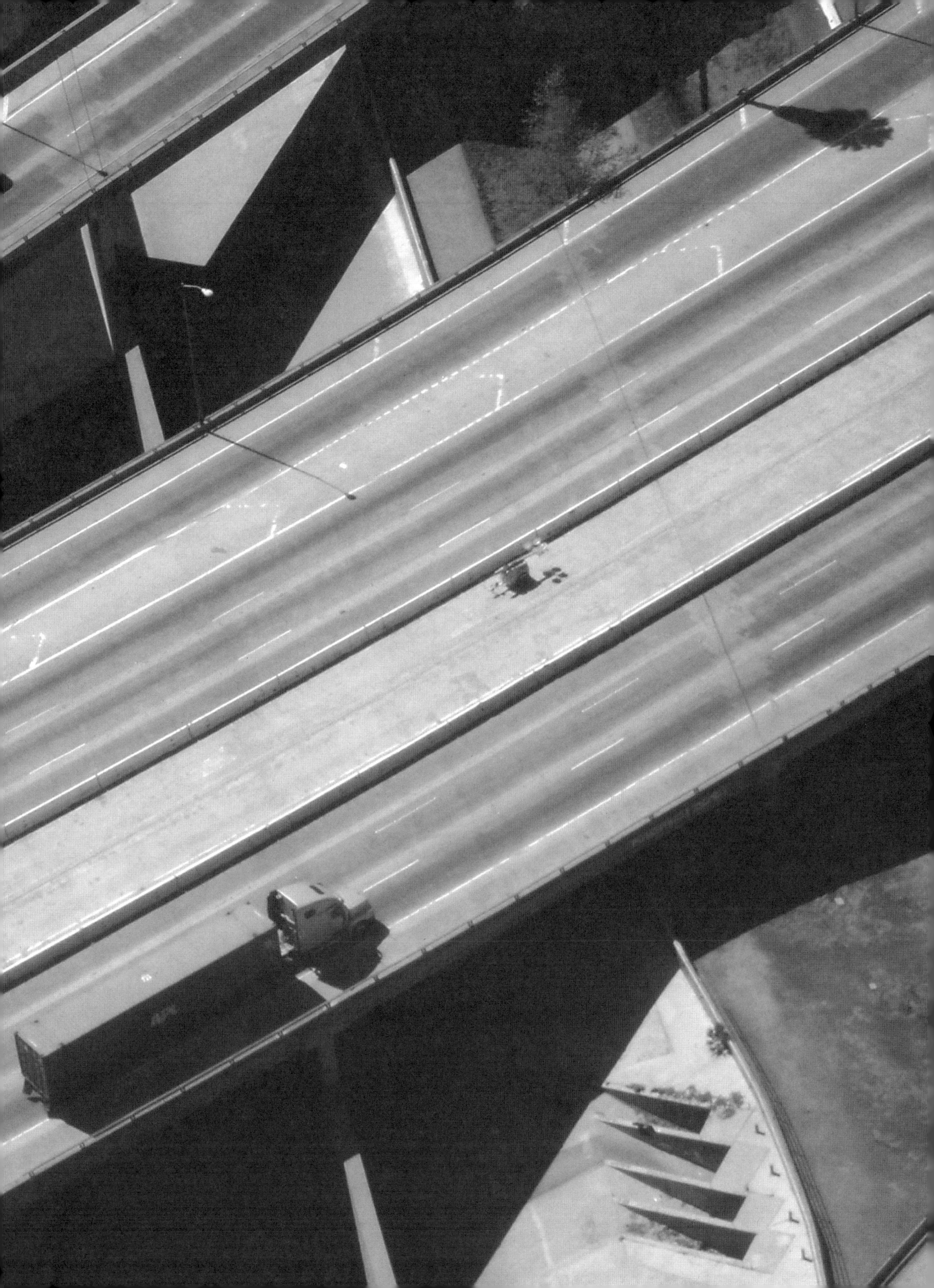

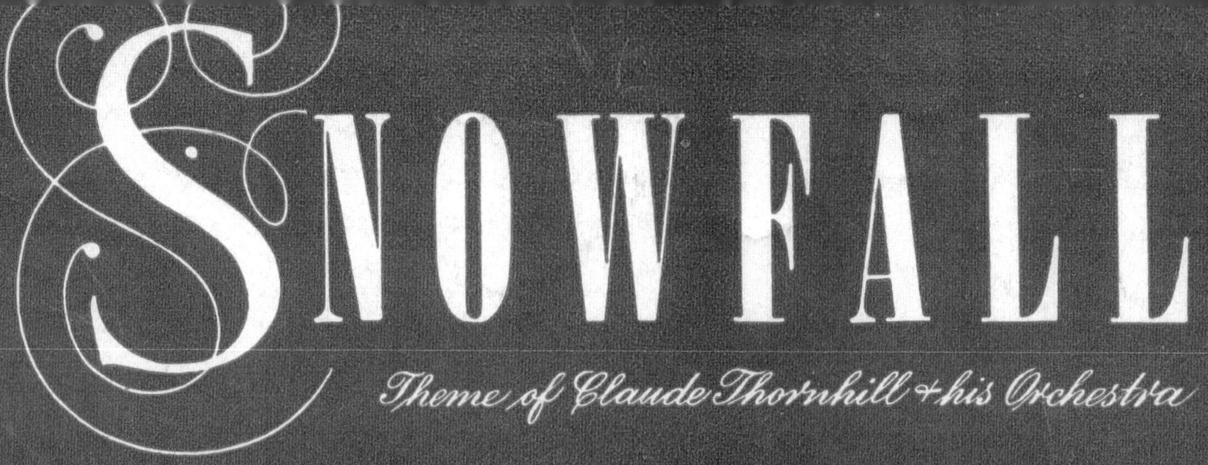

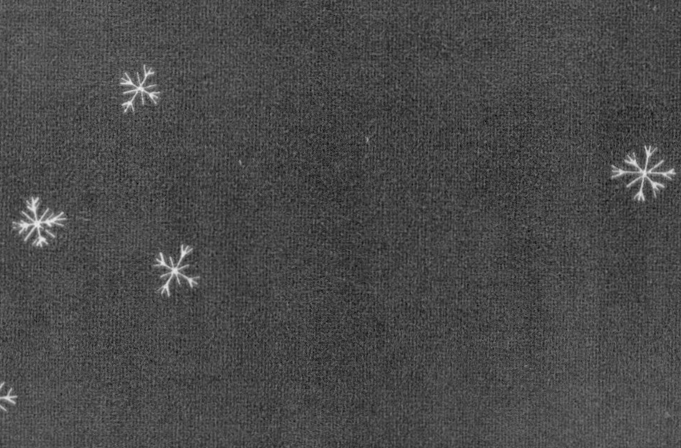

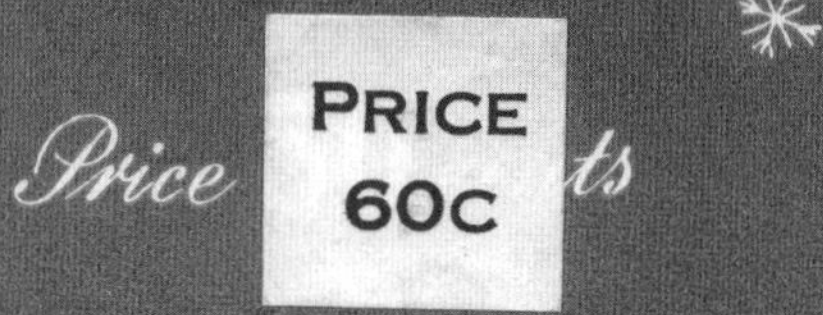

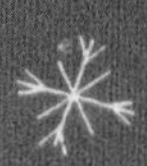

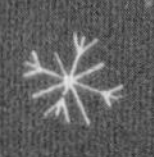

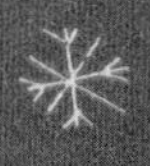

MUTUAL MUSIC SOCIETY, Inc.
1270 SIXTH AVENUE, NEW YORK, N.Y.

THROUGH A LONG AND SLEEPLESS NIGHT

☆

Lyric by
MACK GORDON

Music by
ALFRED NEWMAN

PRICE **60¢** IN U.S.A.

MILLER MUSIC CORPORATION
799 SEVENTH AVENUE • NEW YORK 19, N. Y,

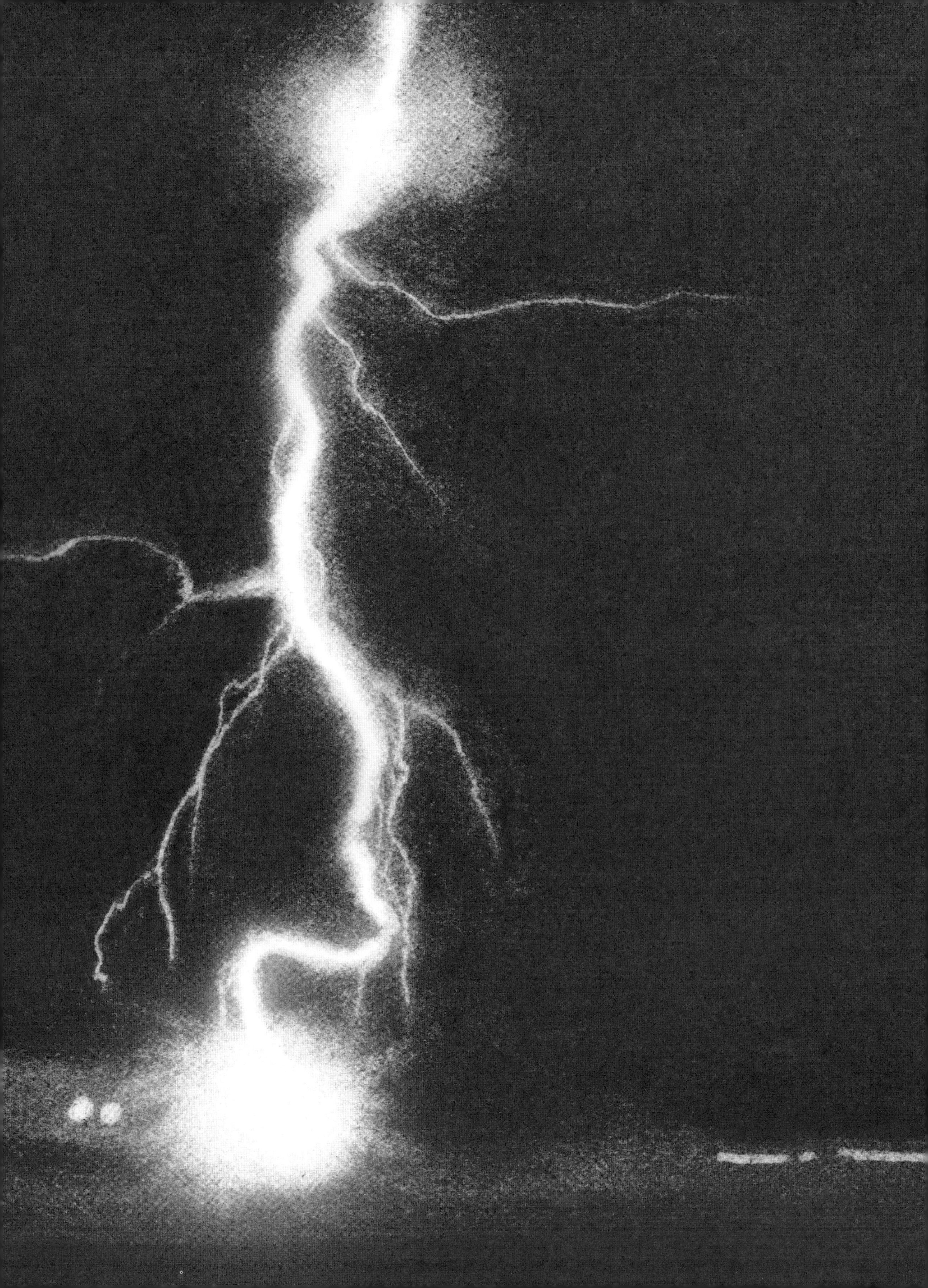

THE STARLIT HOUR

by

PETER DE ROSE

A Modern Composition
for the Piano

PRICE **75¢** IN U.S.A.

ROBBINS MUSIC CORPORATION
799 SEVENTH AVENUE • NEW YORK 19, N. Y.

Moonlight Mood

Lyric by

HAROLD ADAMSON

Music by

PETER DE ROSE

PRICE **60c** IN U.S.A.

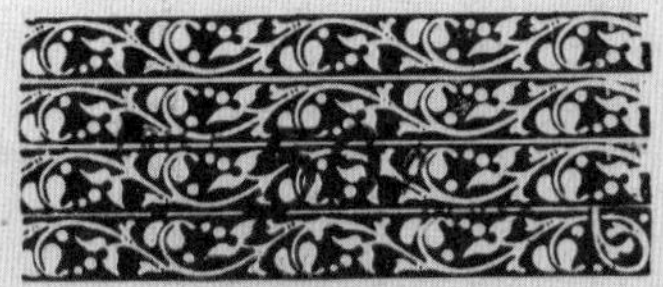

ROBBINS MUSIC CORPORATION
799 SEVENTH AVENUE · NEW YORK

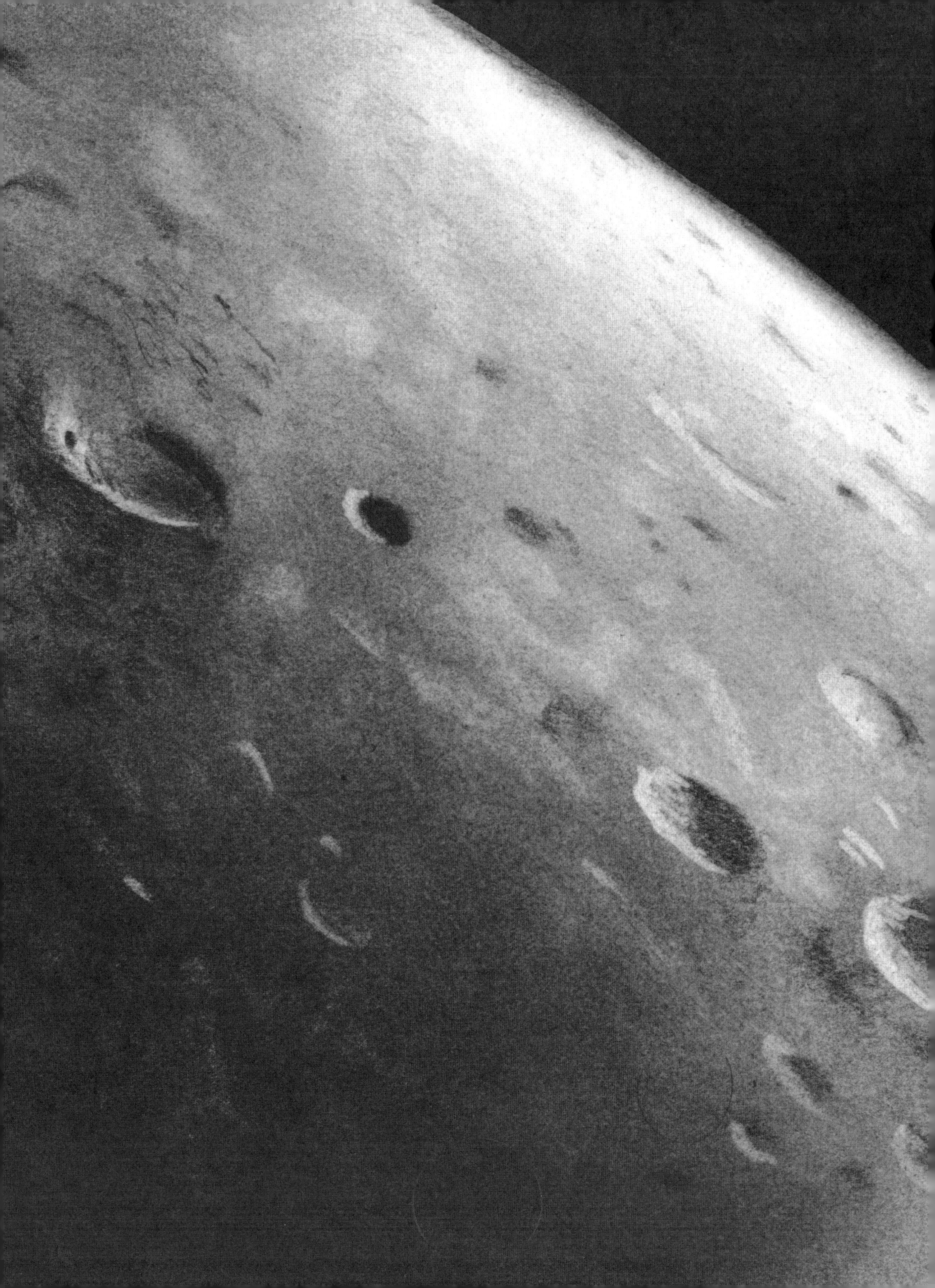

HOW BEAUTIFUL IS NIGHT

PIANO SOLO

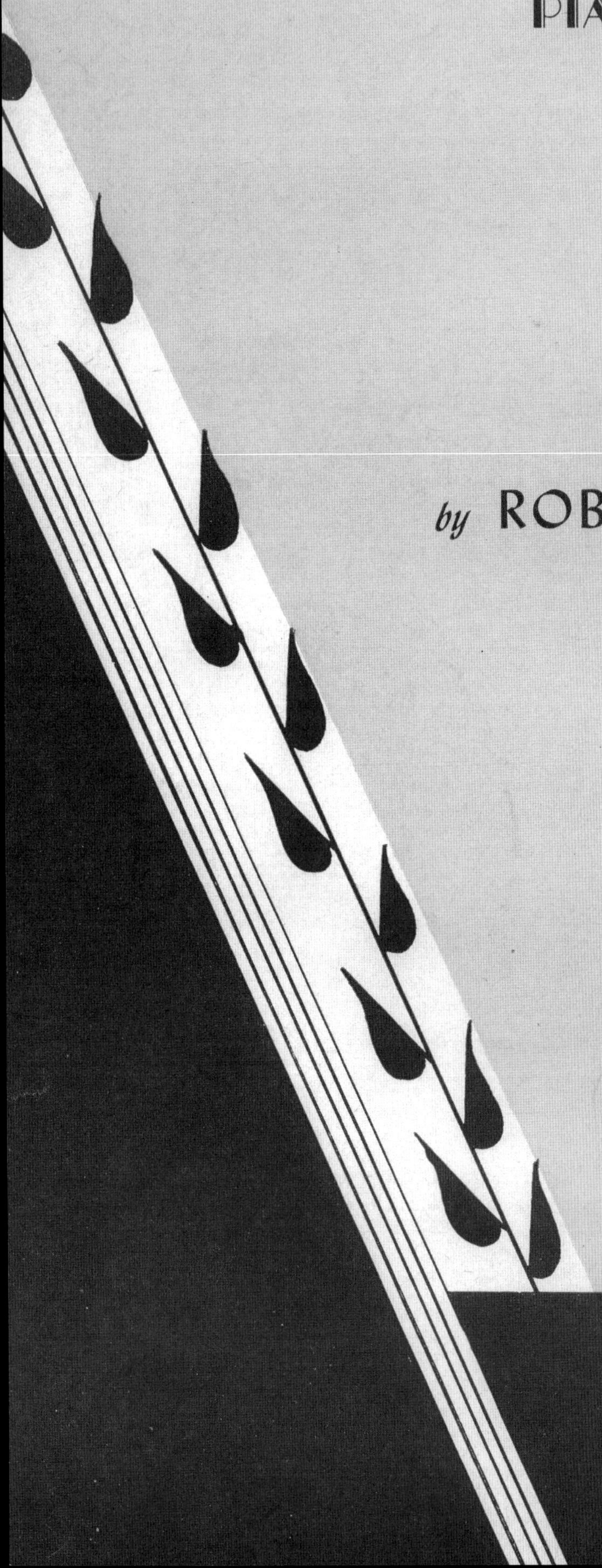

by ROBERT FARNON

PRICE
60¢

CHAPPELL
& CO · INC·
RKO BUILDING
ROCKEFELLER
CENTER · N · Y · C
CHAPPELL
MADE IN U·S·A · & CO · LTD · LONDON

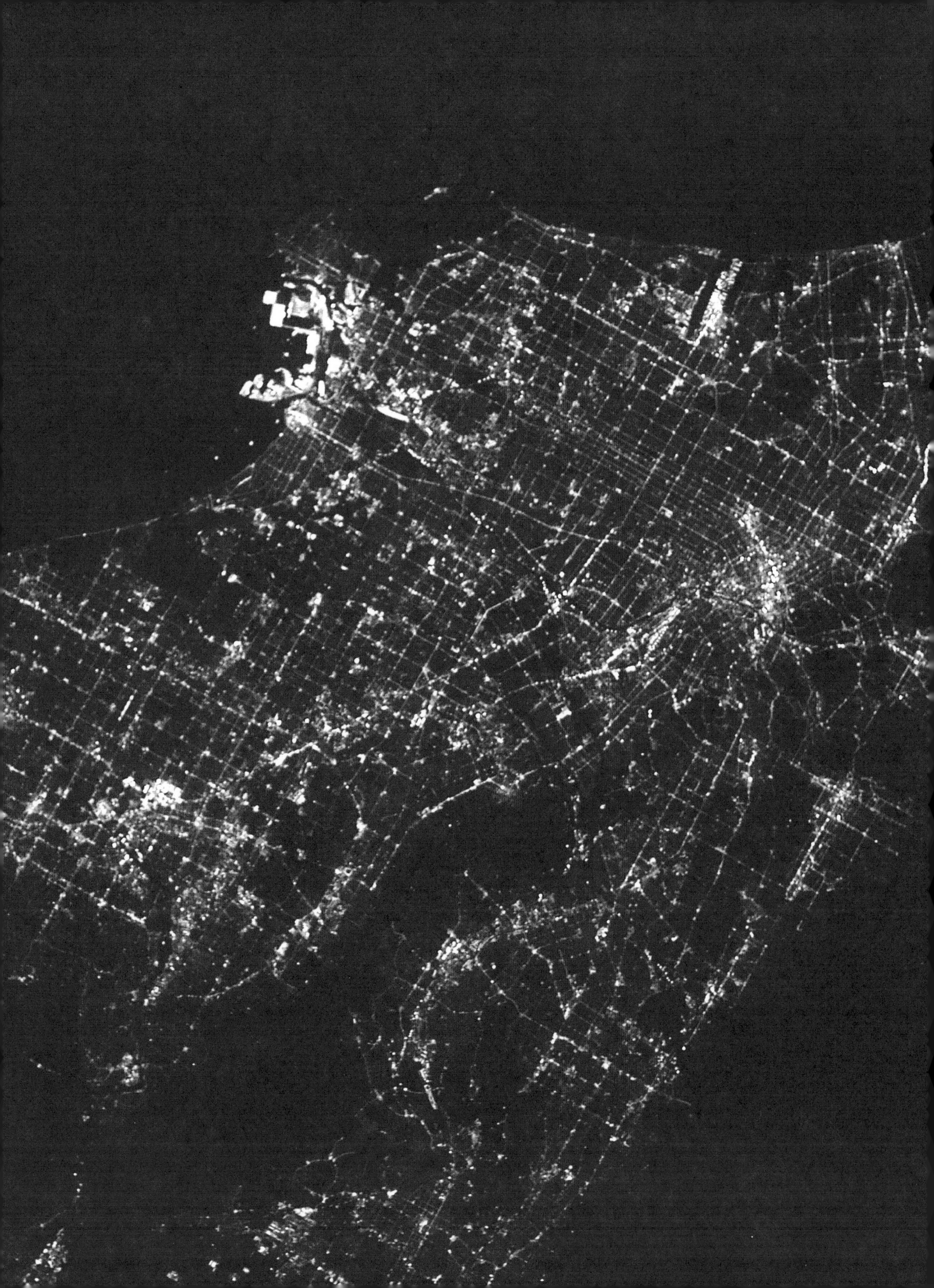

THERE ARE SUCH THINGS

Words and Music by
STANLEY ADAMS
ABEL BAER and
GEO. W. MEYER

PRICE
50¢
IN U. S. A.

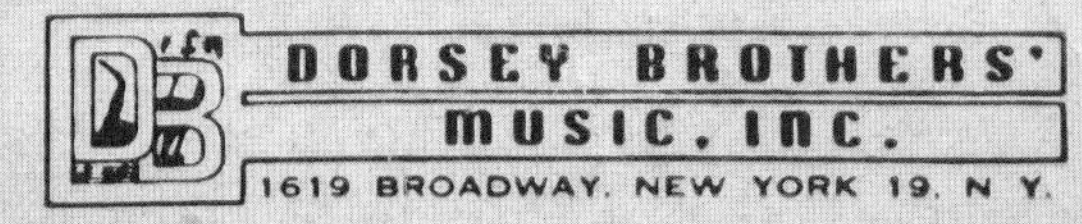

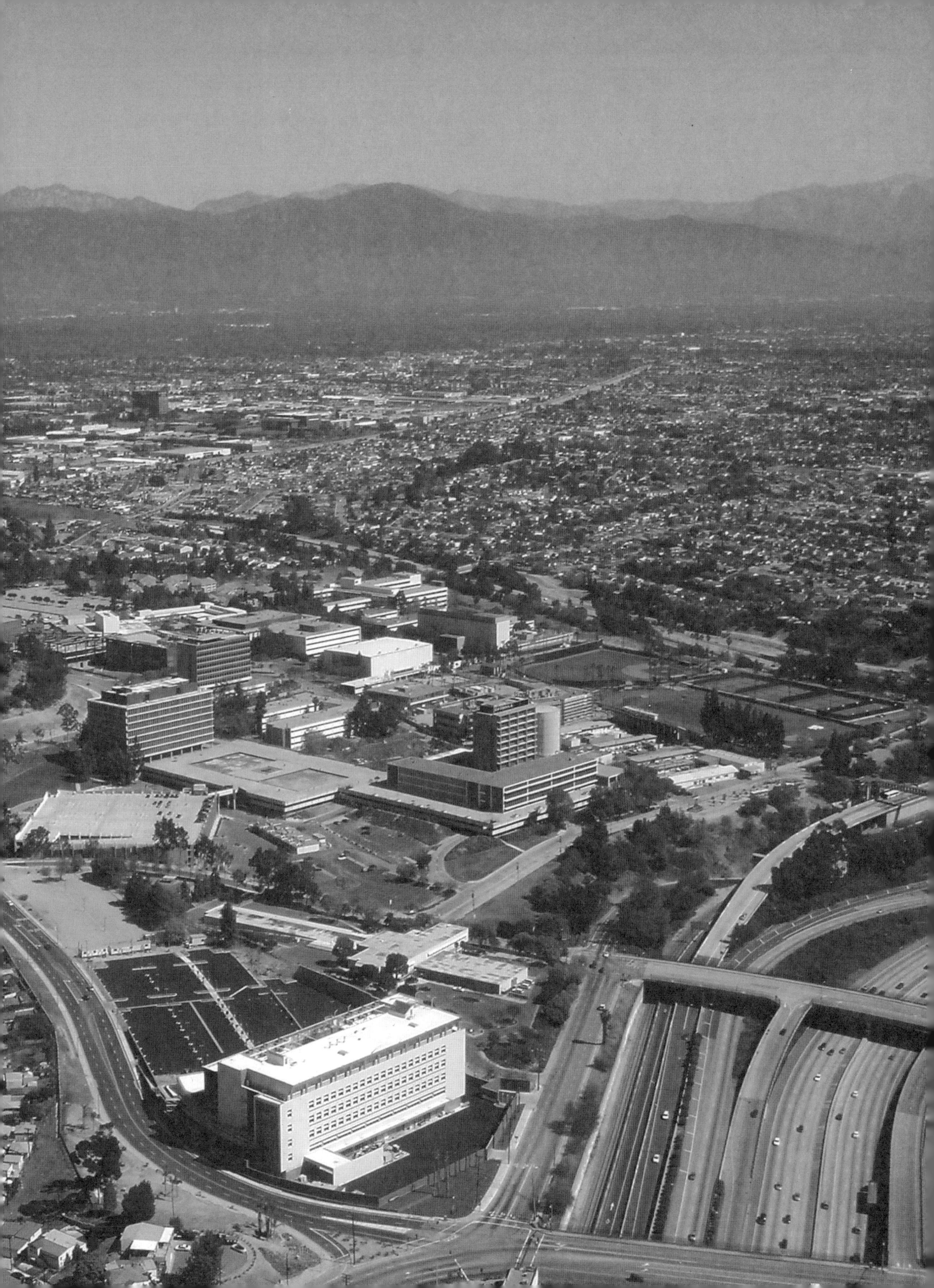

I NEVER KNEW

(I COULD LOVE ANYBODY LIKE I'M LOVING YOU)

by

TOM PITTS, RAY EGAN
and ROY K. MARSH

Revised by
PAUL WHITEMAN

PRICE **60¢** IN U.S.A.

Leo Feist inc.

799 SEVENTH AVENUE • NEW YORK 19, N. Y.

ALL THROUGH THE NIGHT

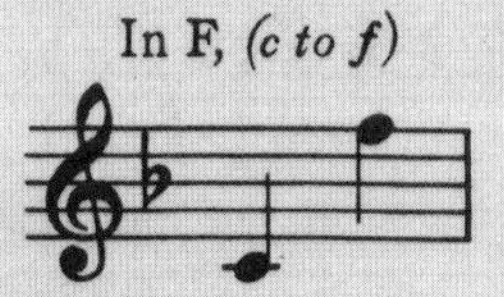

FROM THE MUSICAL COMEDY

"ANYTHING GOES"

WORDS AND MUSIC
BY

COLE PORTER

PUBLISHED IN THE FOLLOWING ARRANGEMENTS

Vocal Solo, F 60
Dance Orchestration (Fox Trot) 1.25

HARMS
INCORPORATED
NEW YORK

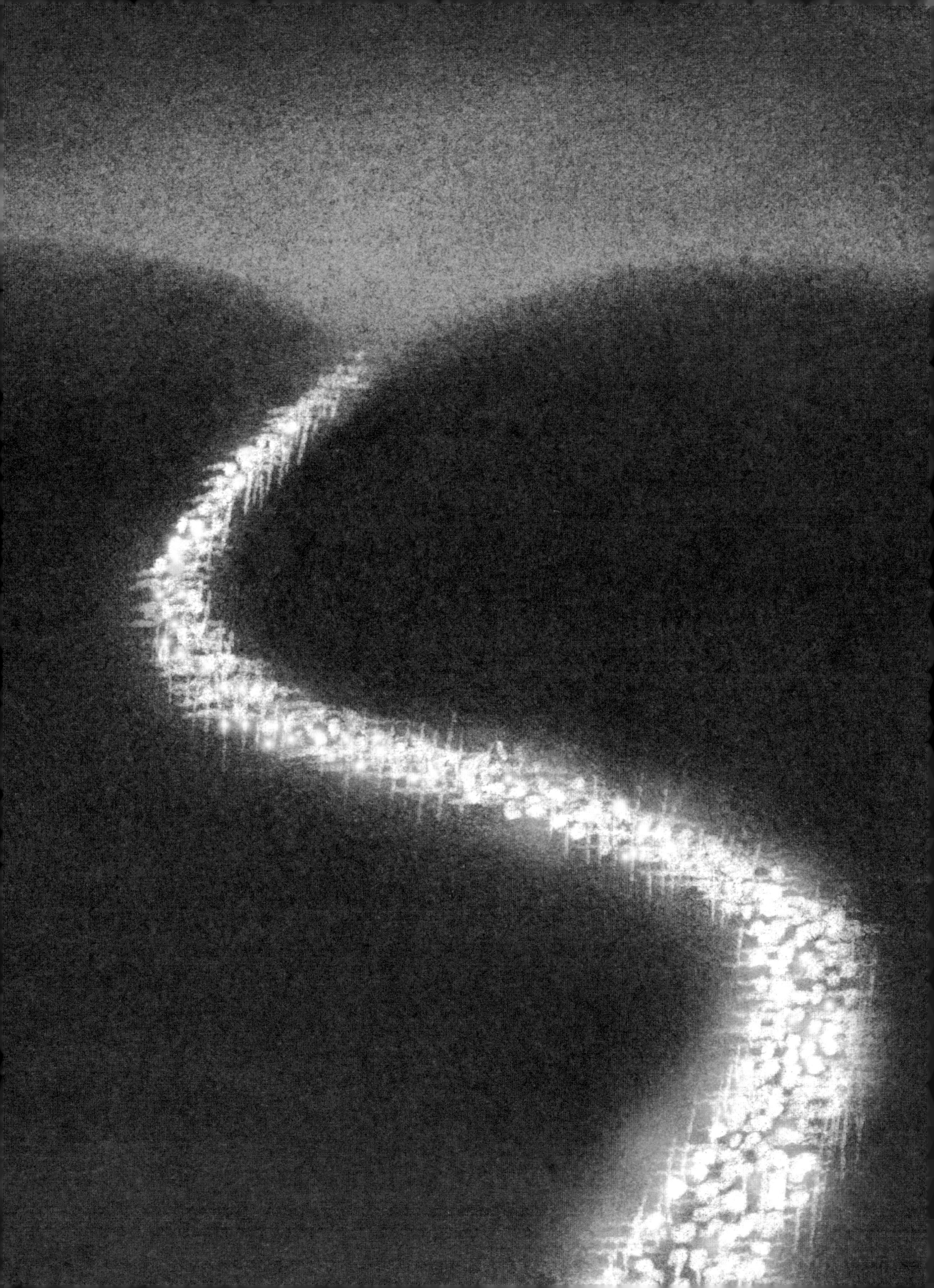

DEEP NIGHT

In C, (c to e)

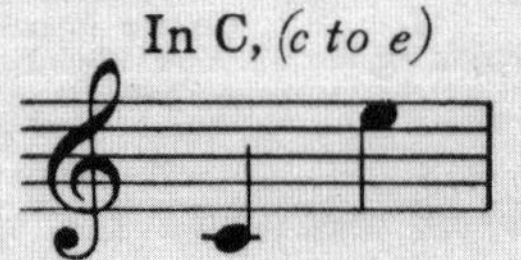

LYRIC BY

RUDY VALLEE

MUSIC BY

CHARLIE HENDERSON

PUBLISHED IN THE FOLLOWING ARRANGEMENTS

Vocal Solo, C 60
4 Part Male (TTBB) 18
Piano Solo (Gotham Classics No. 102) 50
Piano Solo (Concert Paraphrase) 75
Dance Orchestration (Fox Trot) 1.00

WHEN PERFORMING THIS COMPOSITION KINDLY GIVE ALL
PROGRAM CREDITS TO

ADVANCED MUSIC CORPORATION

NEW YORK

DEEP SHITE

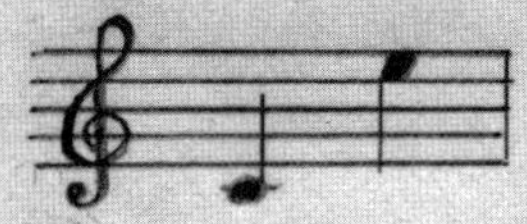

THE BAD AND THE BEAUTIFUL

Words by
DORY LANGDON

Music by
DAVID RAKSIN

PRICE $.75 S.A.

ROBBINS MUSIC CORPORATION
1540 BROADWAY • NEW YORK 36, N. Y.

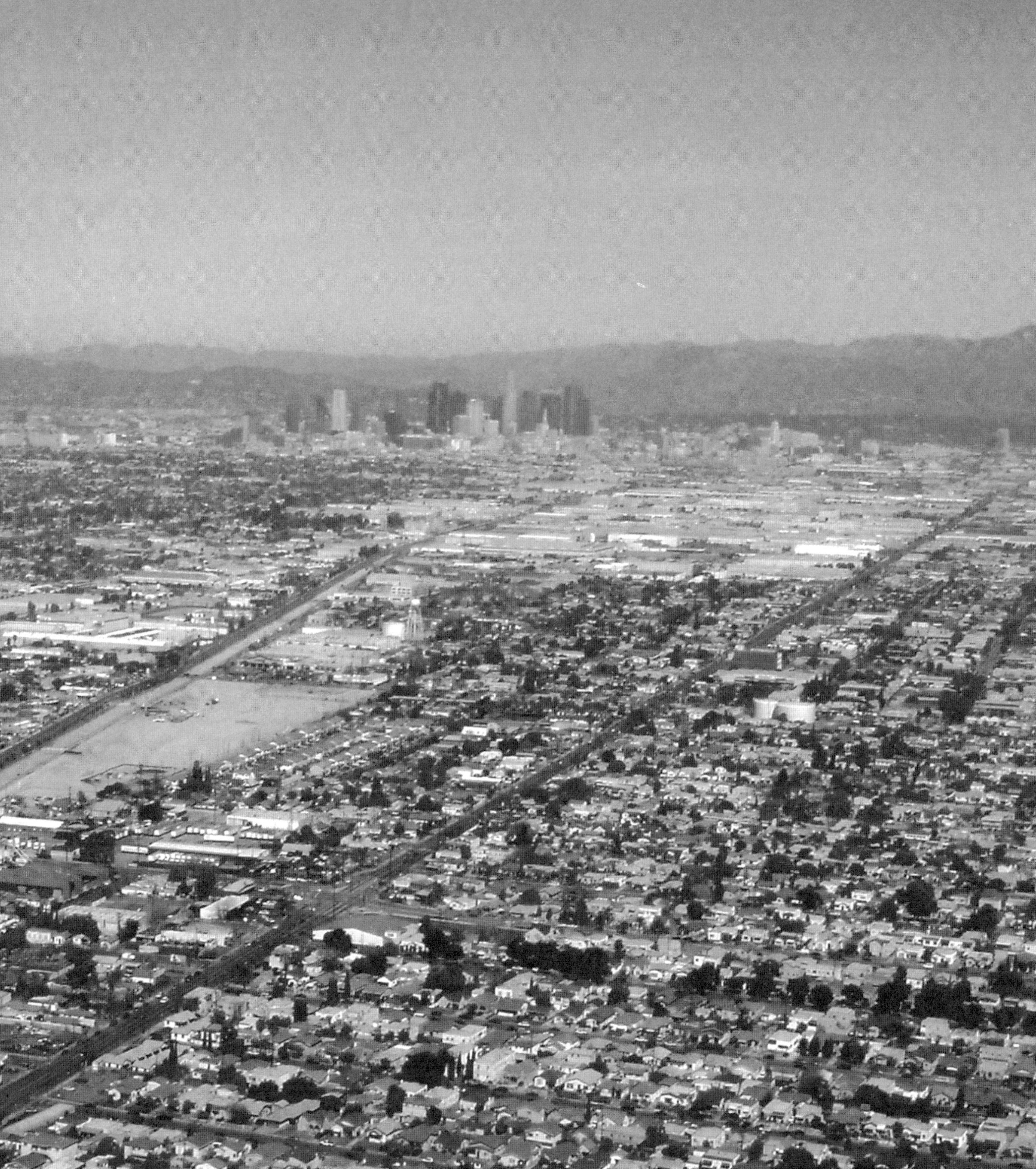

PLEASE BE KIND

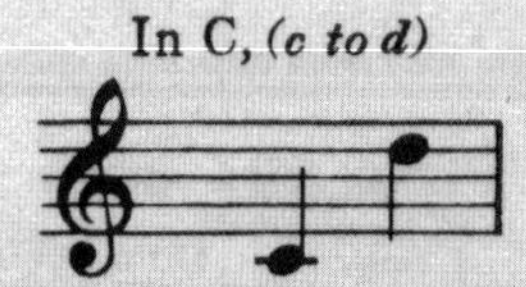

WORDS AND MUSIC BY

SAMMY CAHN
and SAUL CHAPLIN

Price 60 Cents
IN U.S.A.

WHEN PERFORMING THIS COMPOSITION KINDLY GIVE ALL
PROGRAM CREDITS TO

HARMS
INCORPORATED

New York

PRINTED IN U. S. A.

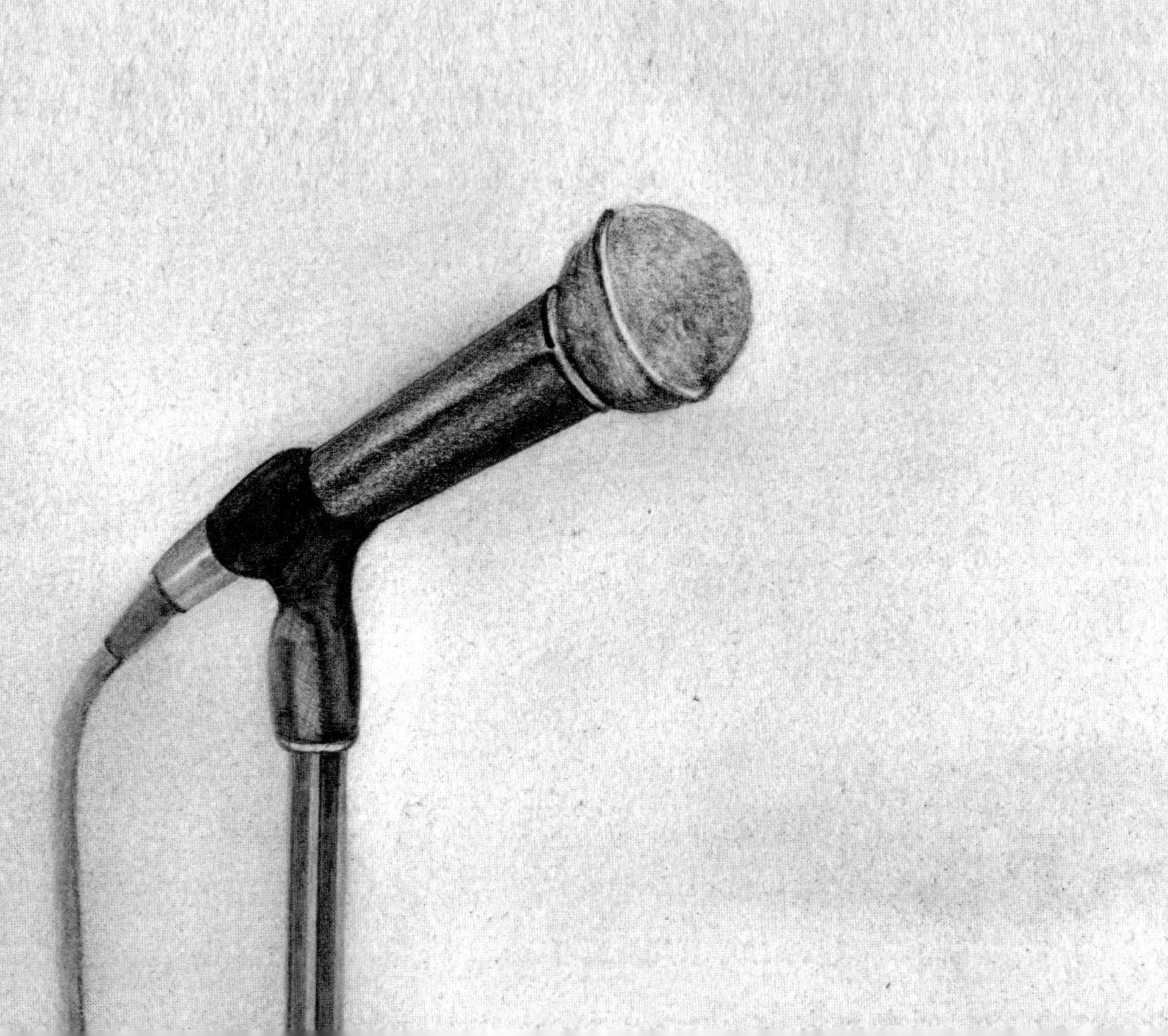

Where, I Wonder

Words by
DORY PREVIN
Music by
ANDRÉ PREVIN

Price 75¢

ANDOR, INC.
Sole Selling Agent: **VALANDO MUSIC CORP.**, 22 West 48th Street, New York 36, N. Y.

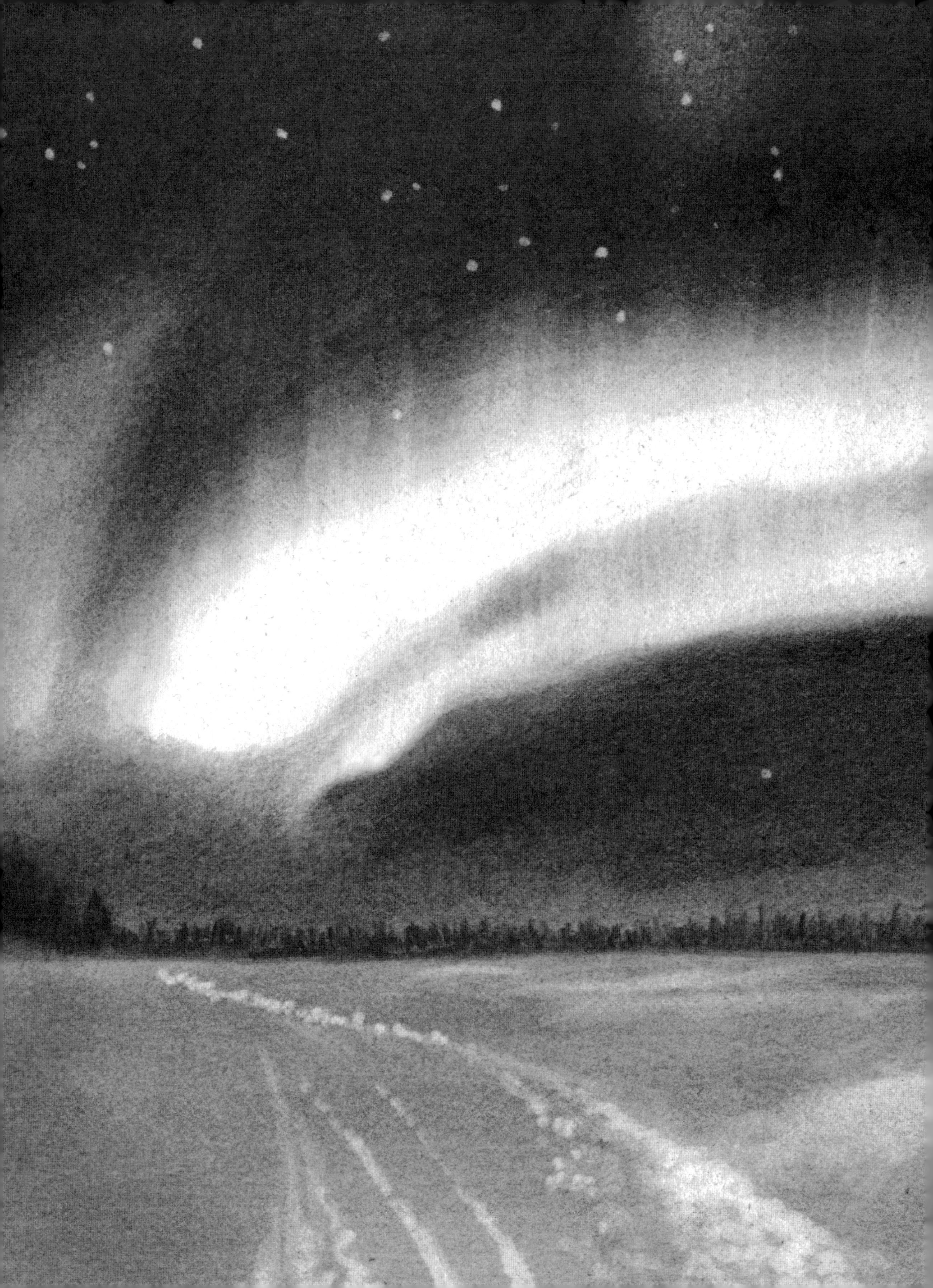

WHERE ARE YOU?

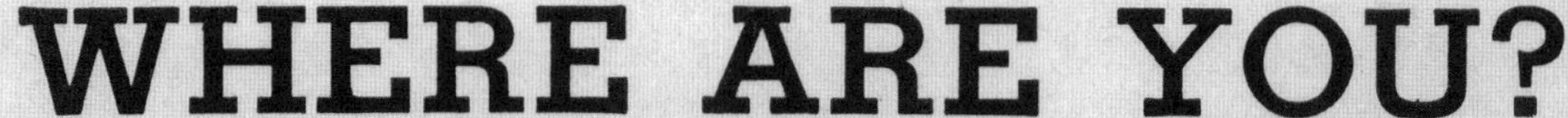

Lyric by

HAROLD ADAMSON

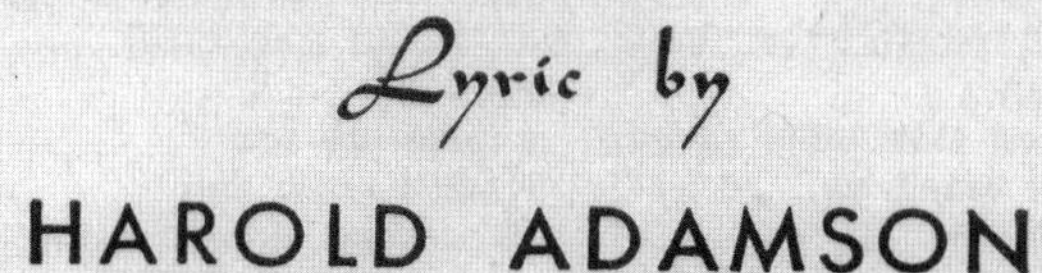

Music by

JIMMY McHUGH

PRICE **60¢** IN U.S.A.

Leo Feist inc.

799 SEVENTH AVENUE • NEW YORK 19, N. Y.

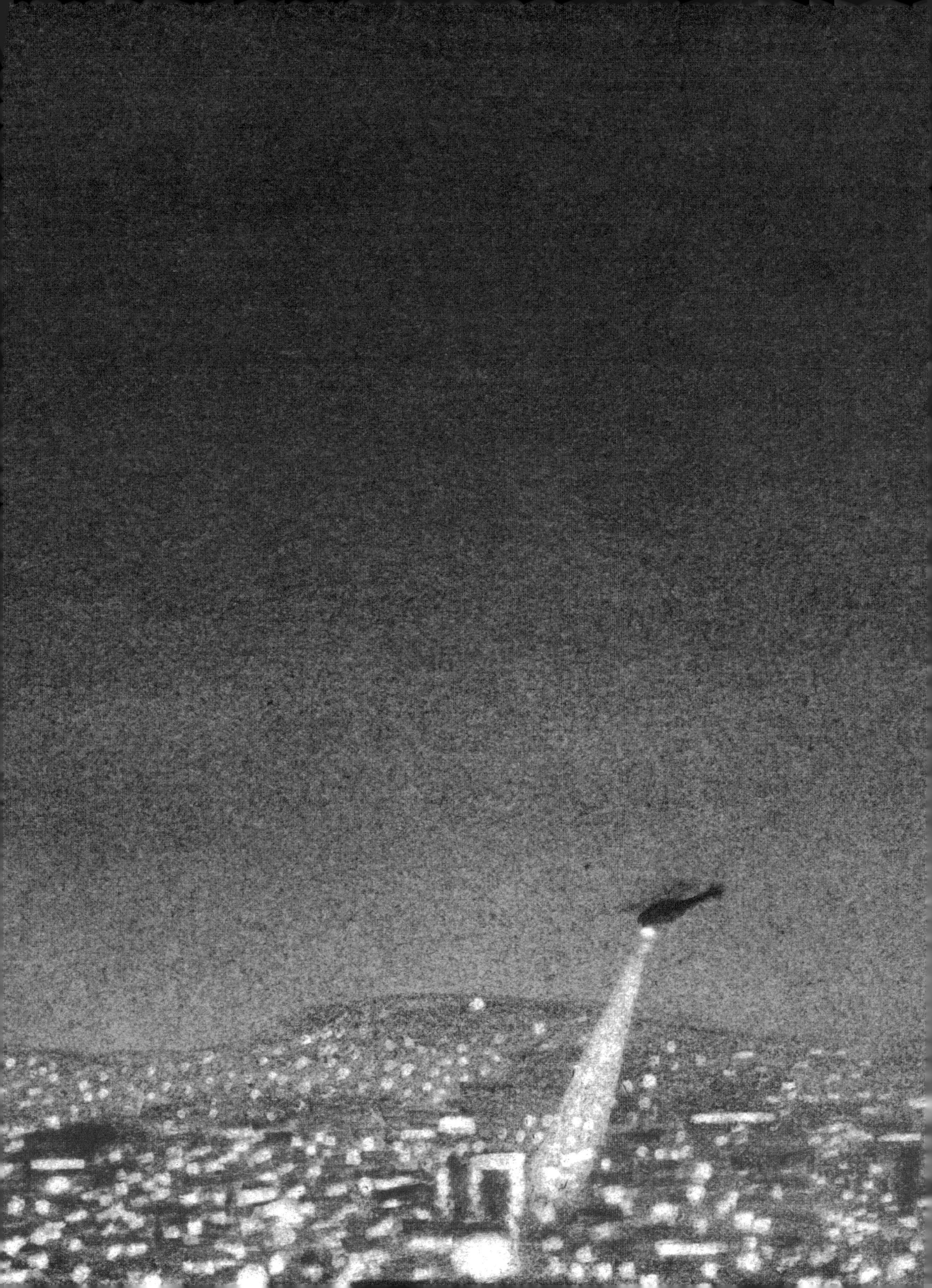

DEEP NIGHT

by
CHARLIE HENDERSON

Paraphrased for Piano by
MAURICE C. WHITNEY

Price **75c** net
in USA

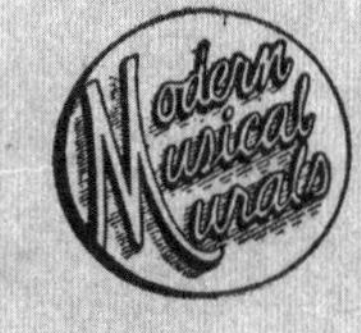

ADVANCED MUSIC CORPORATION

RCA BUILDING, NEW YORK, N. Y.

Printed in U.S.A.

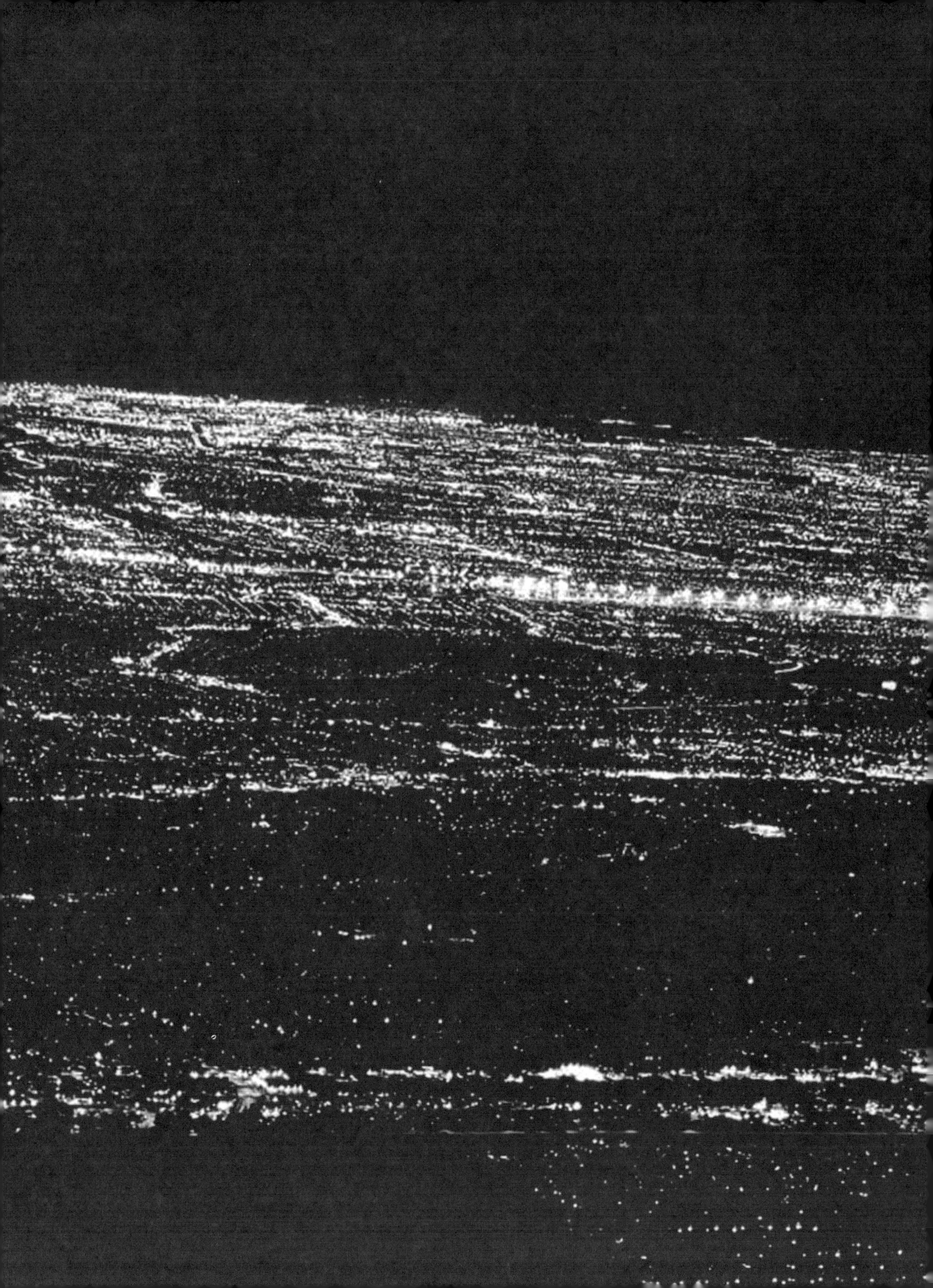

WHERE ARE YOU NOW

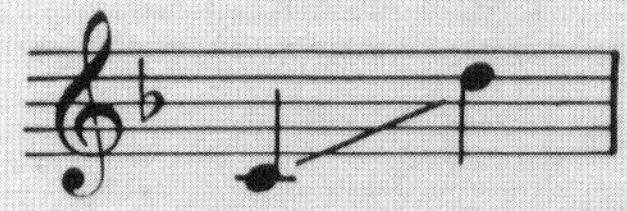

Words and Music by
TONY HATCH
JACKIE TRENT

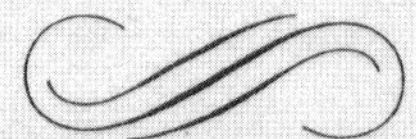

Price
Seventy Five cents
in U.S.A.

DUCHESS MUSIC CORPORATION
A SUBSIDIARY OF
MUSIC CORPORATION OF AMERICA

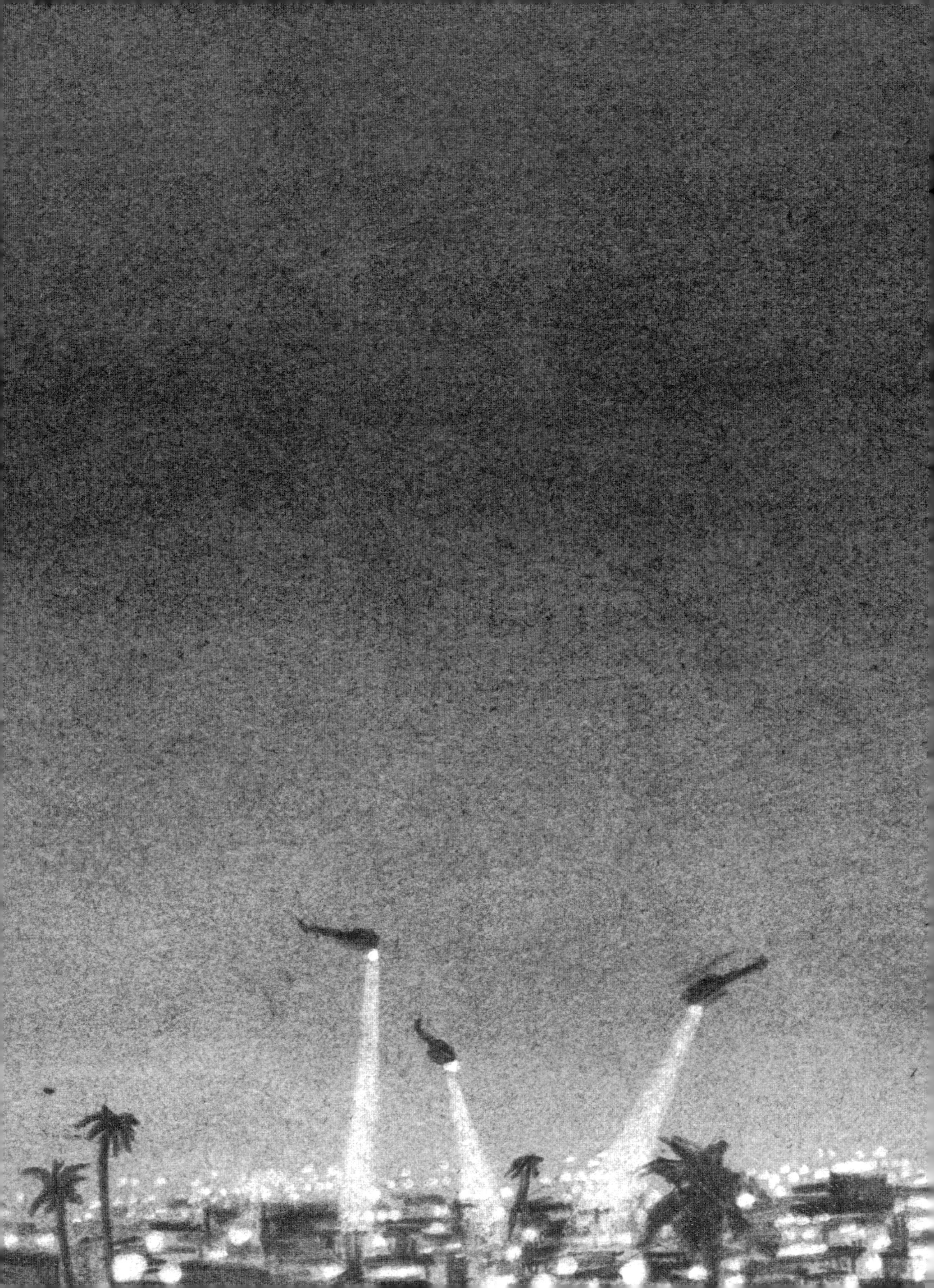

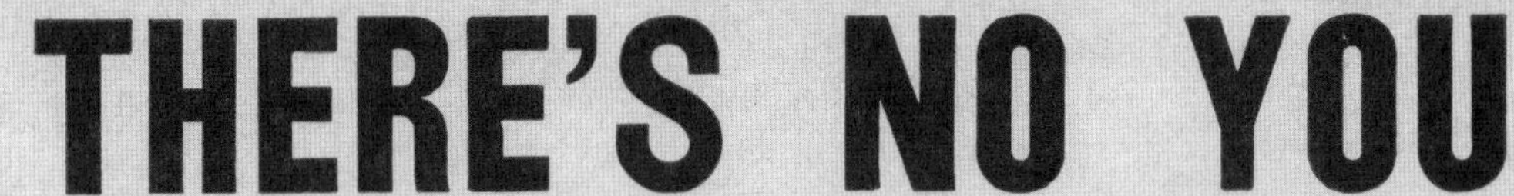

THERE'S NO YOU

Lyric by
TOM ADAIR

Music by
HAL HOPPER

Price **60¢**
IN U.S.A.

1619 BROADWAY **BARTON** NEW YORK CITY
MUSIC CORPORATION

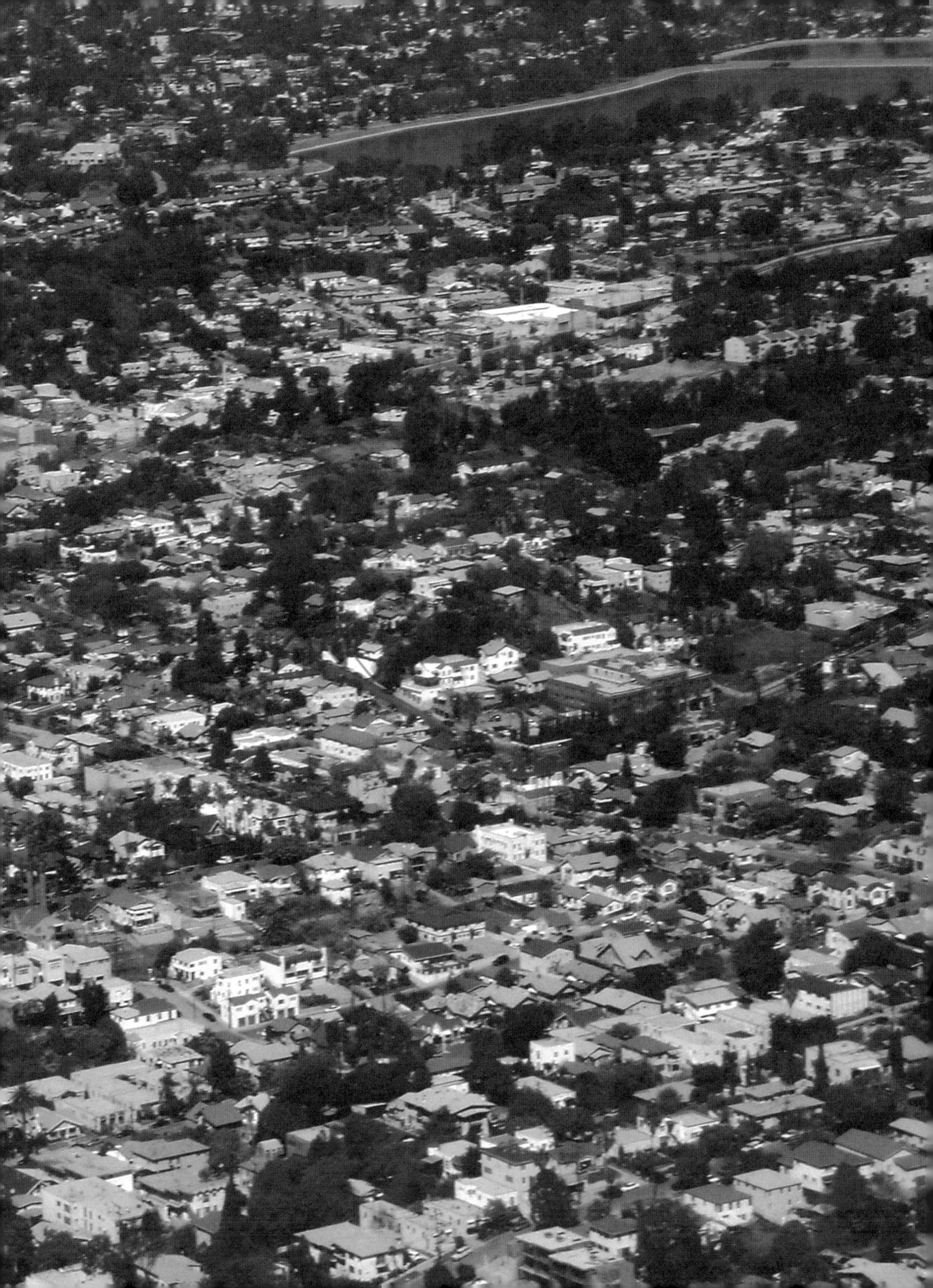

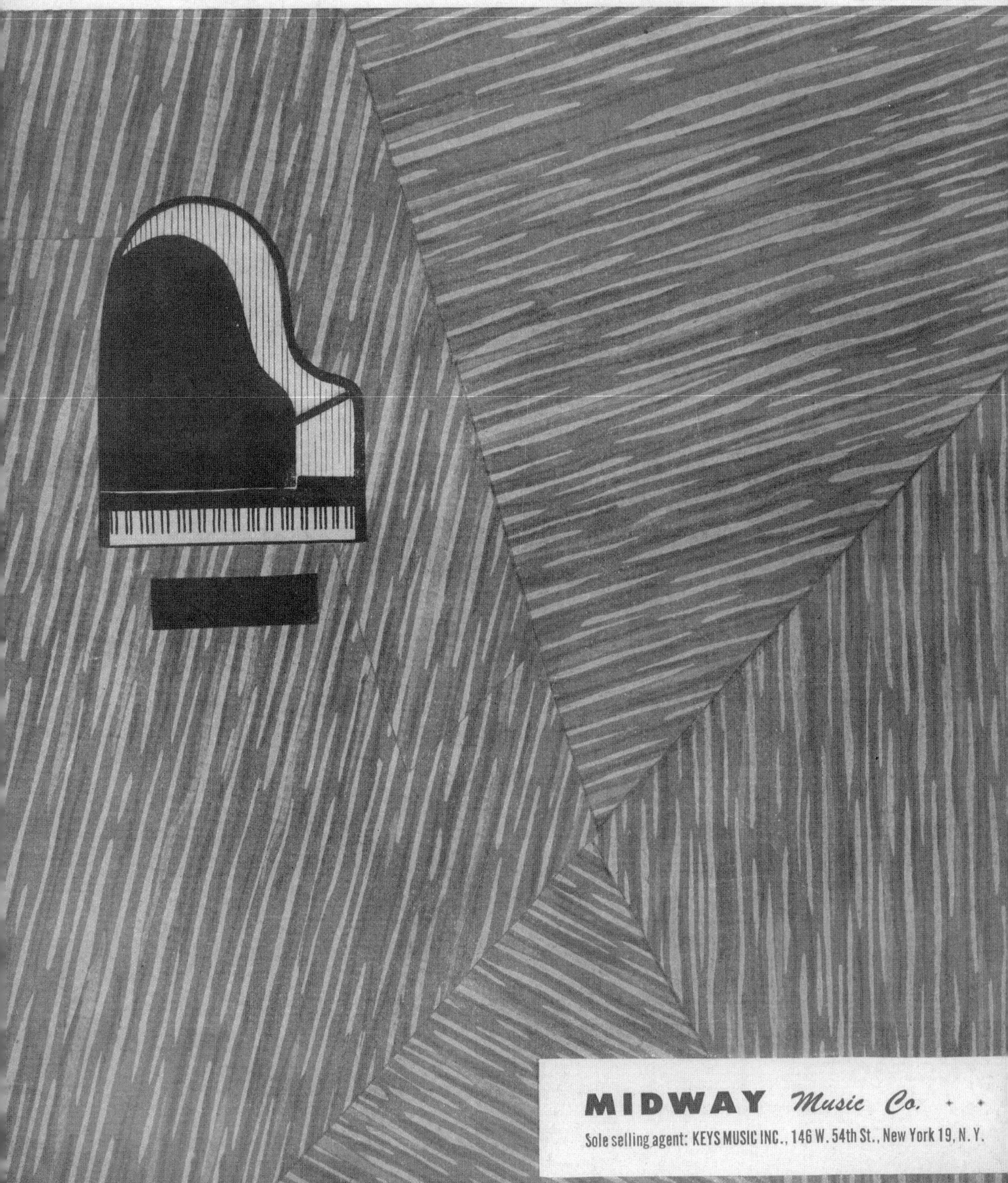

EASY COME, EASY GO LOVER
Words and Music by CHUCK UPHAM and HARVEY COOPER
AS RECORDED BY SARAH VAUGHN FOR DECCA RECORDS
PRICE 60¢ IN U
MIDWAY Music Co.
Sole selling agent: KEYS MUSIC INC., 146 W. 54th St., New York 19, N. Y.

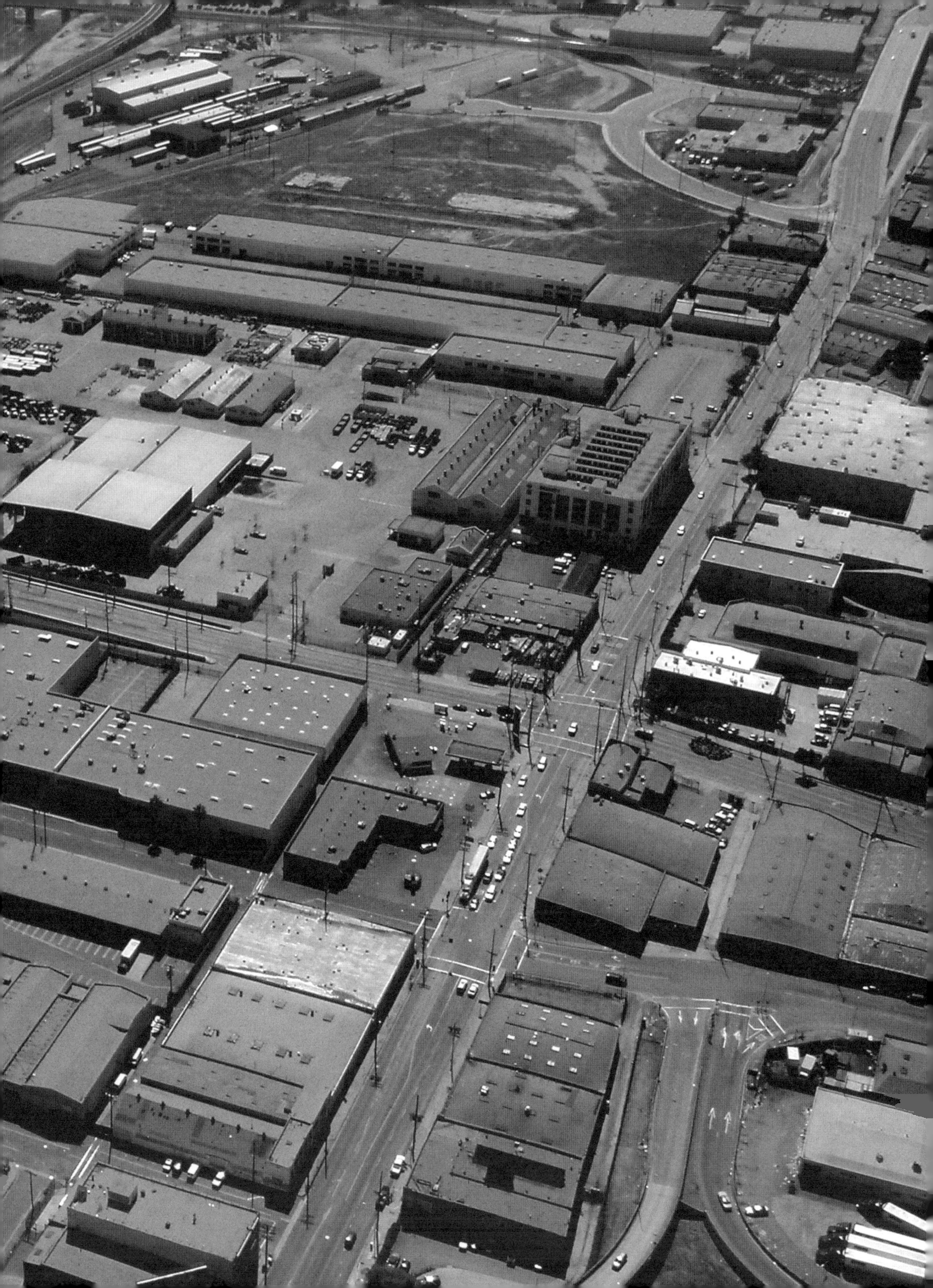

IF I SHOULD LOSE YOU

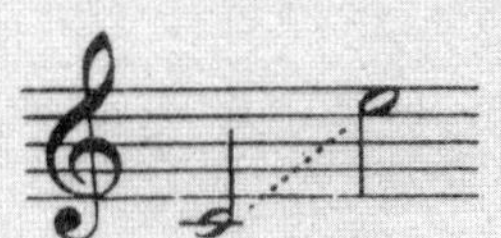

Words and Music by
LEO ROBIN
and
RALPH RAINGER

Published for the following Arrangements

Song 60
Dance Orch.—Fox Trot 1.25

Famous Music Corporation
1619 BROADWAY · NEW YORK, N.Y.

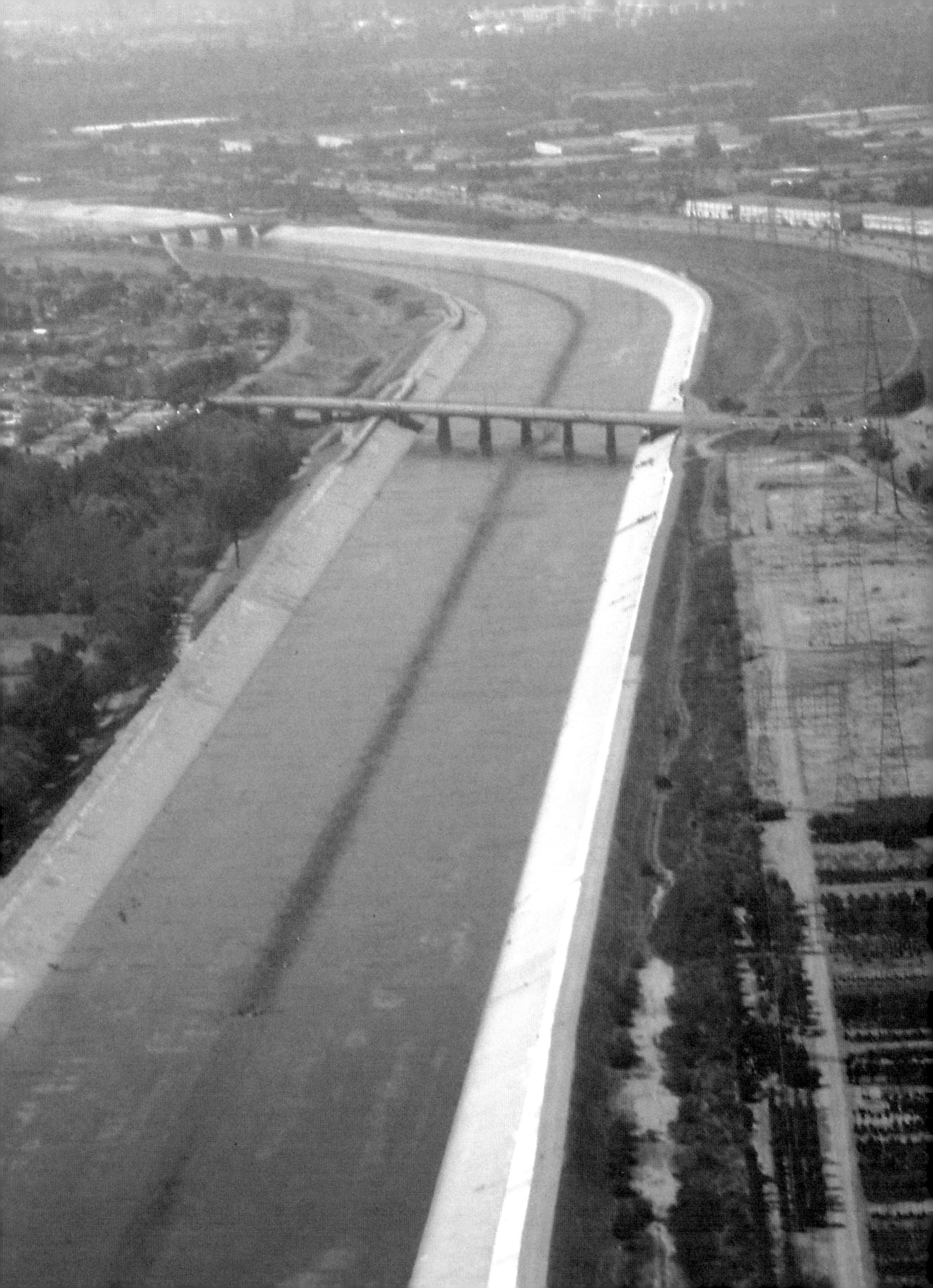

THAT'S THE
BEGINNING OF THE END

MUSIC & LYRIC BY
JOAN WHITNEY
ALEX KRAMER

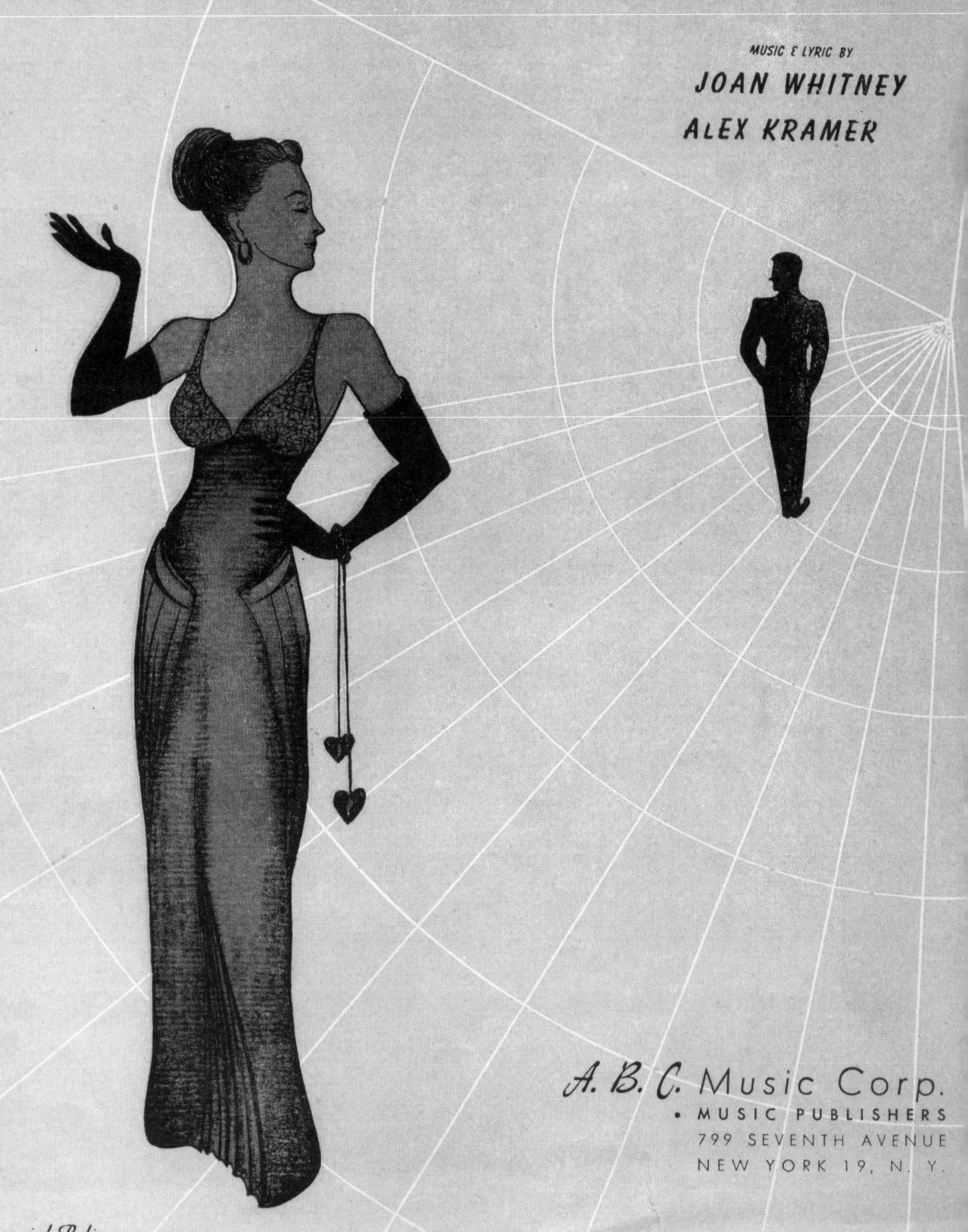

A. B. C. Music Corp.
• MUSIC PUBLISHERS
799 SEVENTH AVENUE
NEW YORK 19, N. Y.

a. joel Robinson

PIANO SOLO EDITION

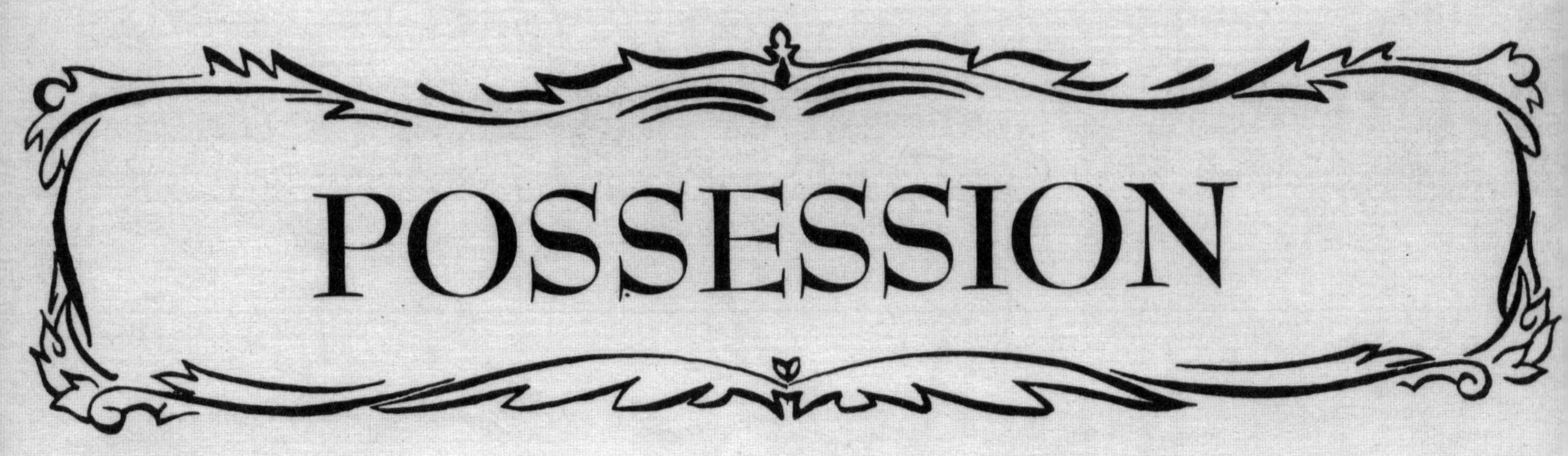

POSSESSION

(Perfume Set To Music Series)

By

HARRY REVEL

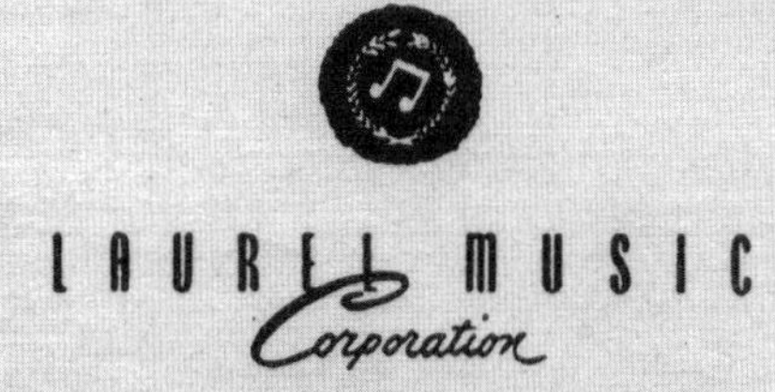

LAUREL MUSIC
Corporation

1619 BROADWAY, NEW YORK

Price 60¢

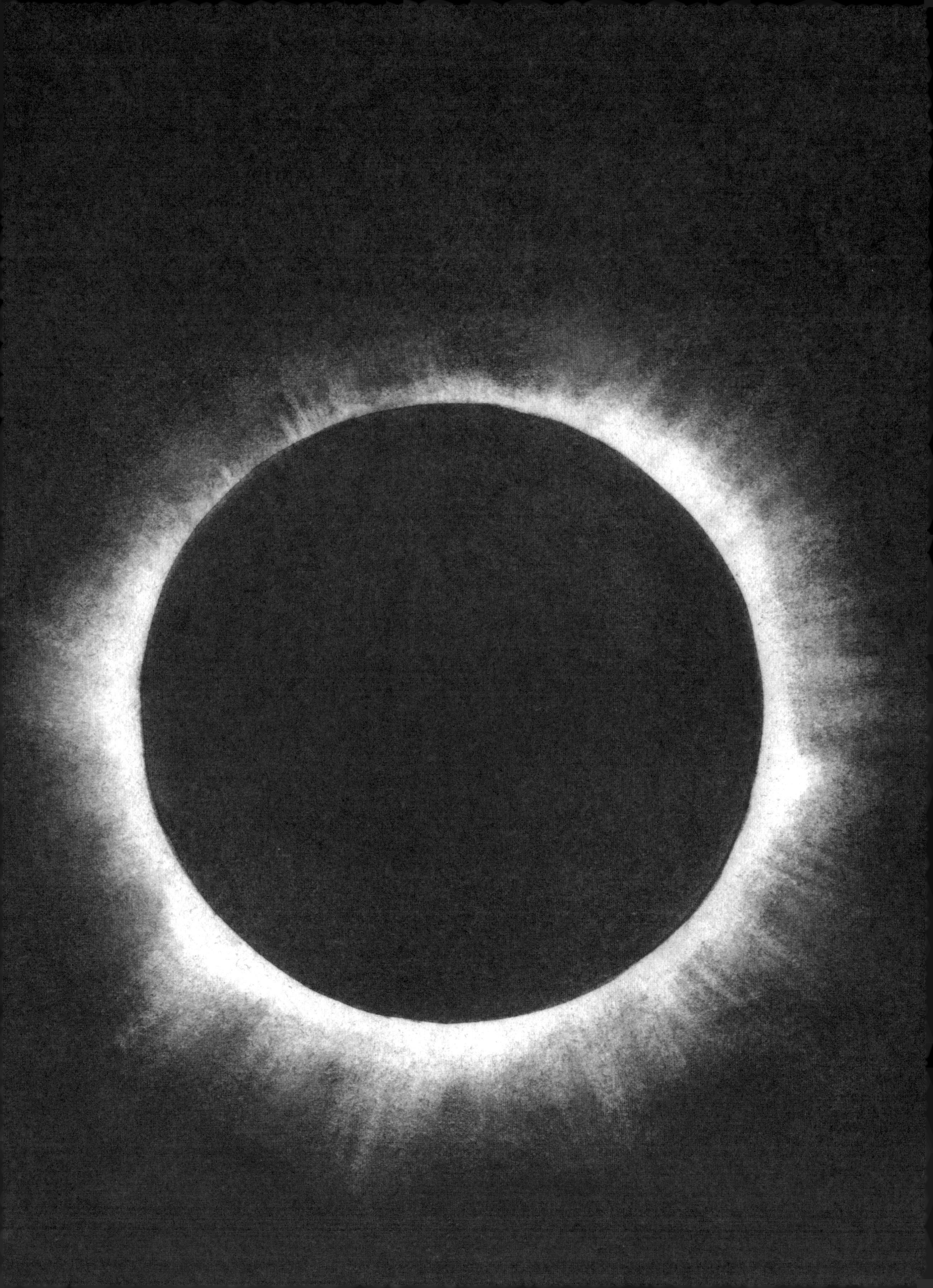

EVERYTHING HAPPENS TO ME

Lyric by **TOM ADAIR**

Music by **MATT DENNIS**

PRICE
60¢
IN U.S.A.

EMBASSY MUSIC CORPORATION
1619 Broadway • New York, N. Y.

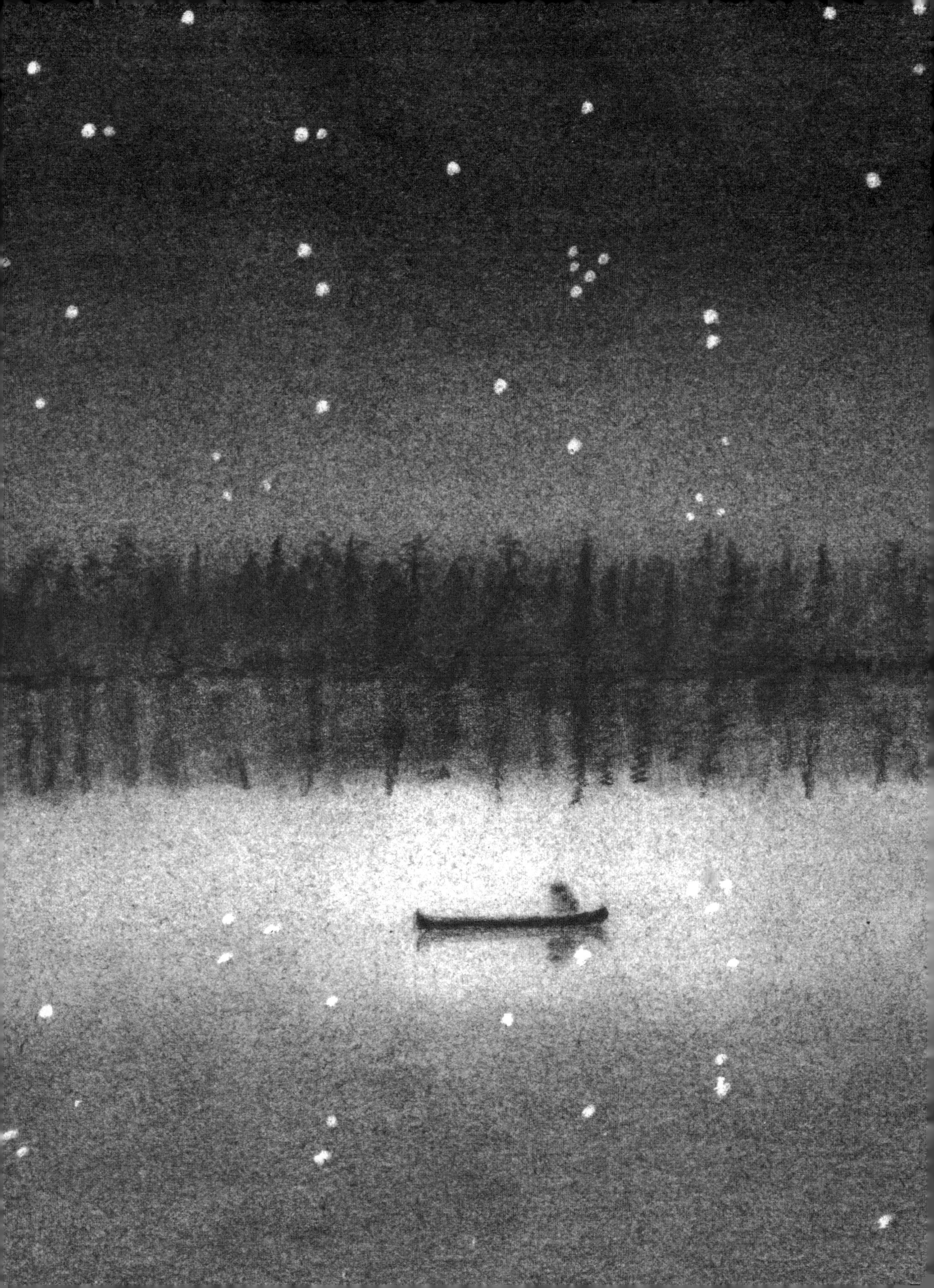

DEEP IN A DREAM

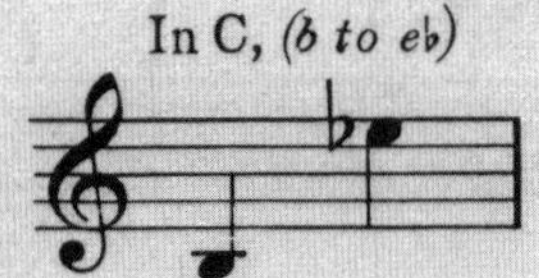

WORDS BY

EDDIE DE LANGE

MUSIC BY

JIMMY VAN HEUSEN

PUBLISHED IN THE FOLLOWING ARRANGEMENTS

Vocal Solo, C 60
Vocal Orchestration, 2 Keys C–G *each* 1.25
Dance Orchestration (Fox Trot) 1.25

WHEN PERFORMING THIS COMPOSITION KINDLY GIVE ALL
PROGRAM CREDITS TO

H A R M S
I N C O R P O R A T E D
New York

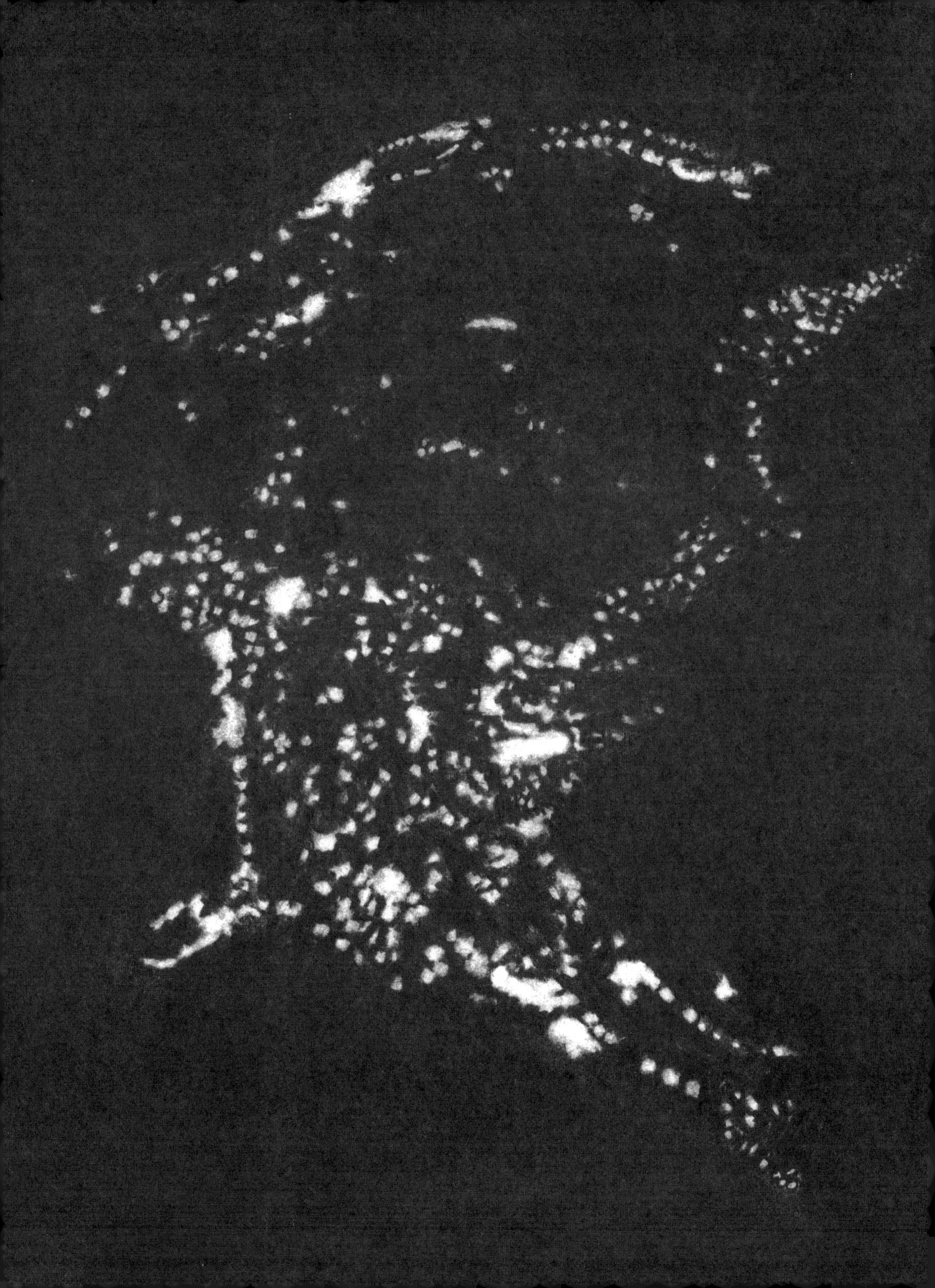

Land of Dreams

WORDS BY

NORMAN GIMBEL

MUSIC BY

EDDIE HEYWOOD

PRICE
.60
IN U.S.A.

MERIDIAN MUSIC CORPORATION   35 WEST 51st STREET   •   NEW YORK 19, N. Y.

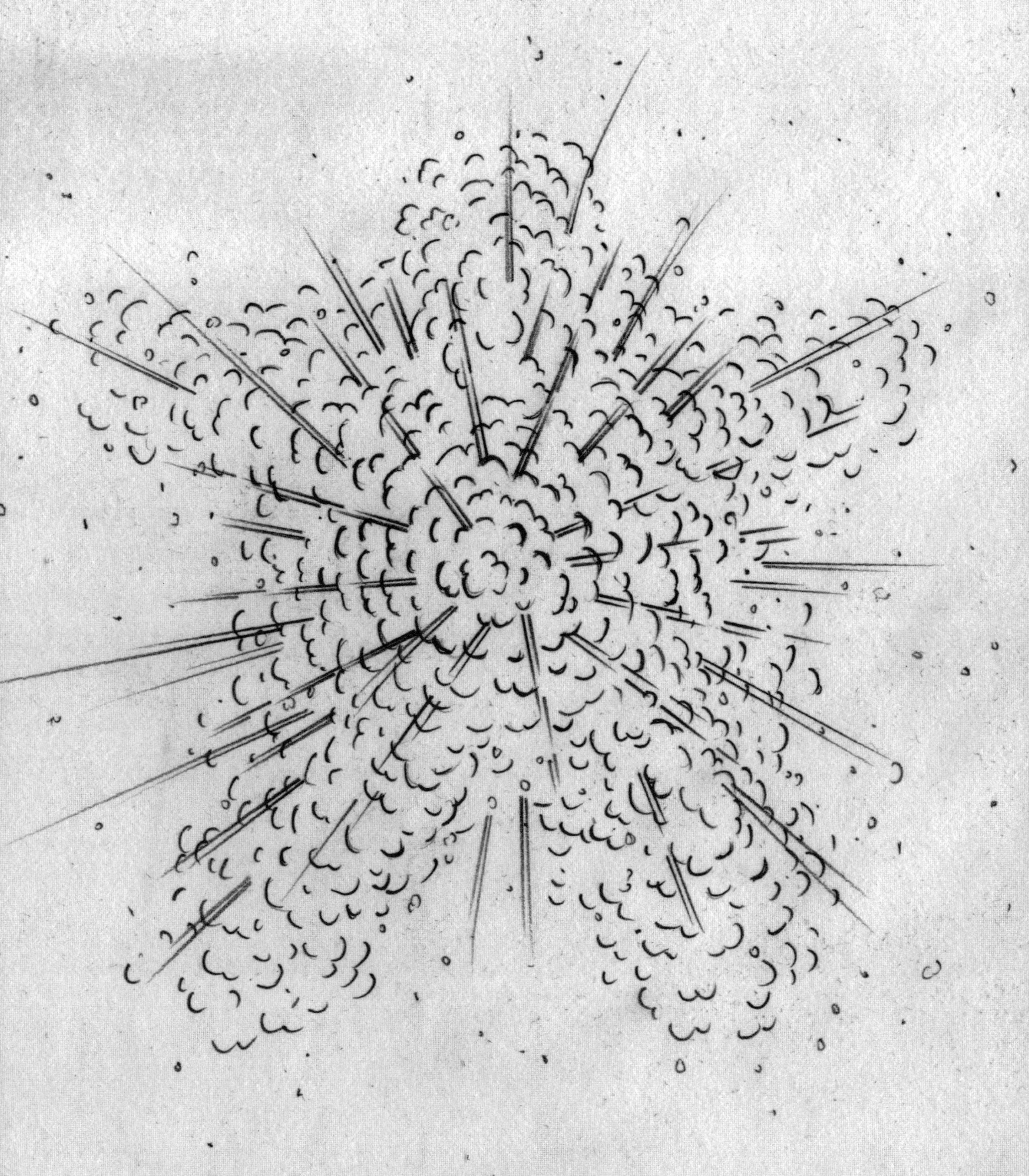

FAR AWAY PLACES

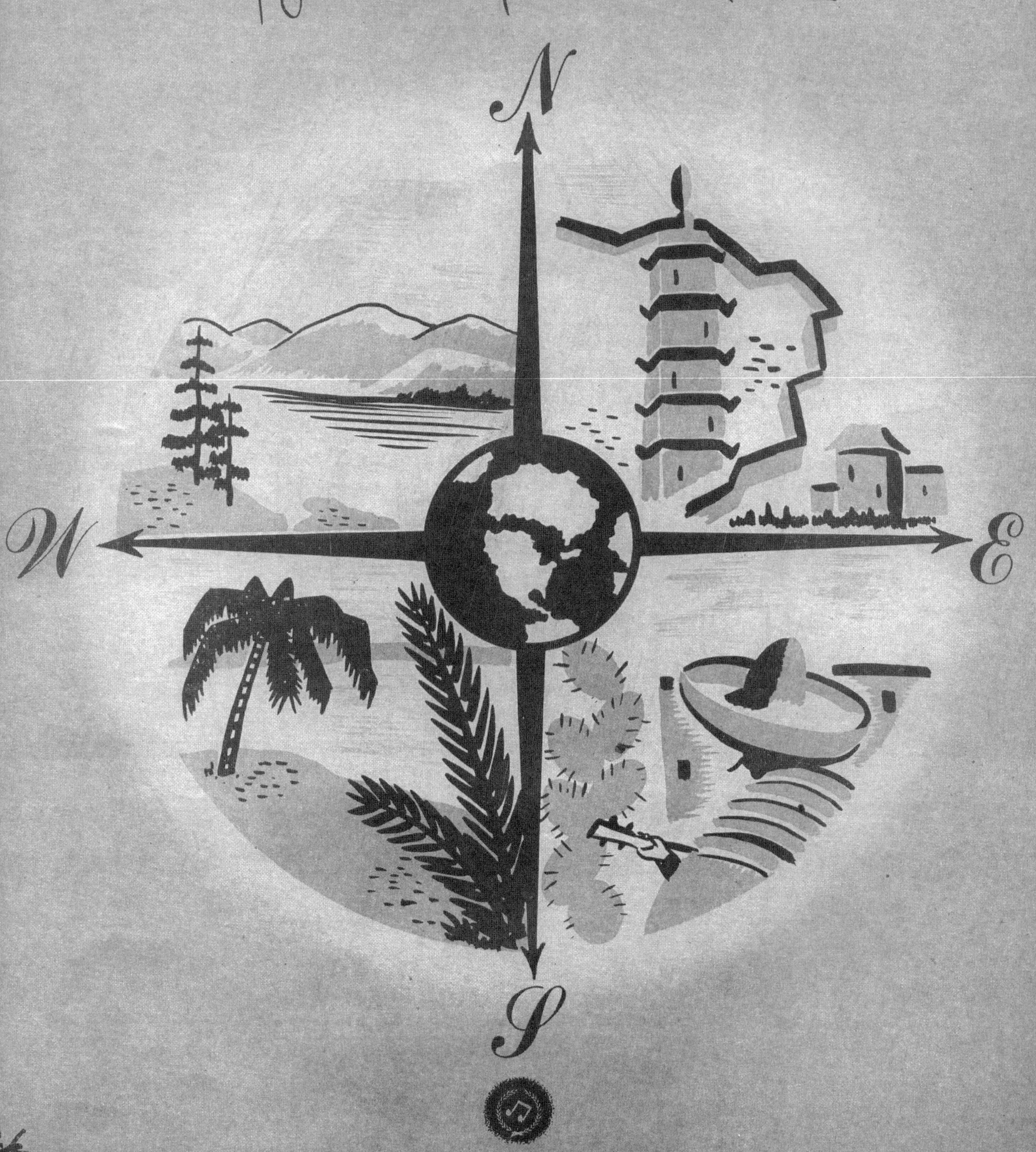

LAUREL MUSIC CO.
1619 BROADWAY, NEW YORK

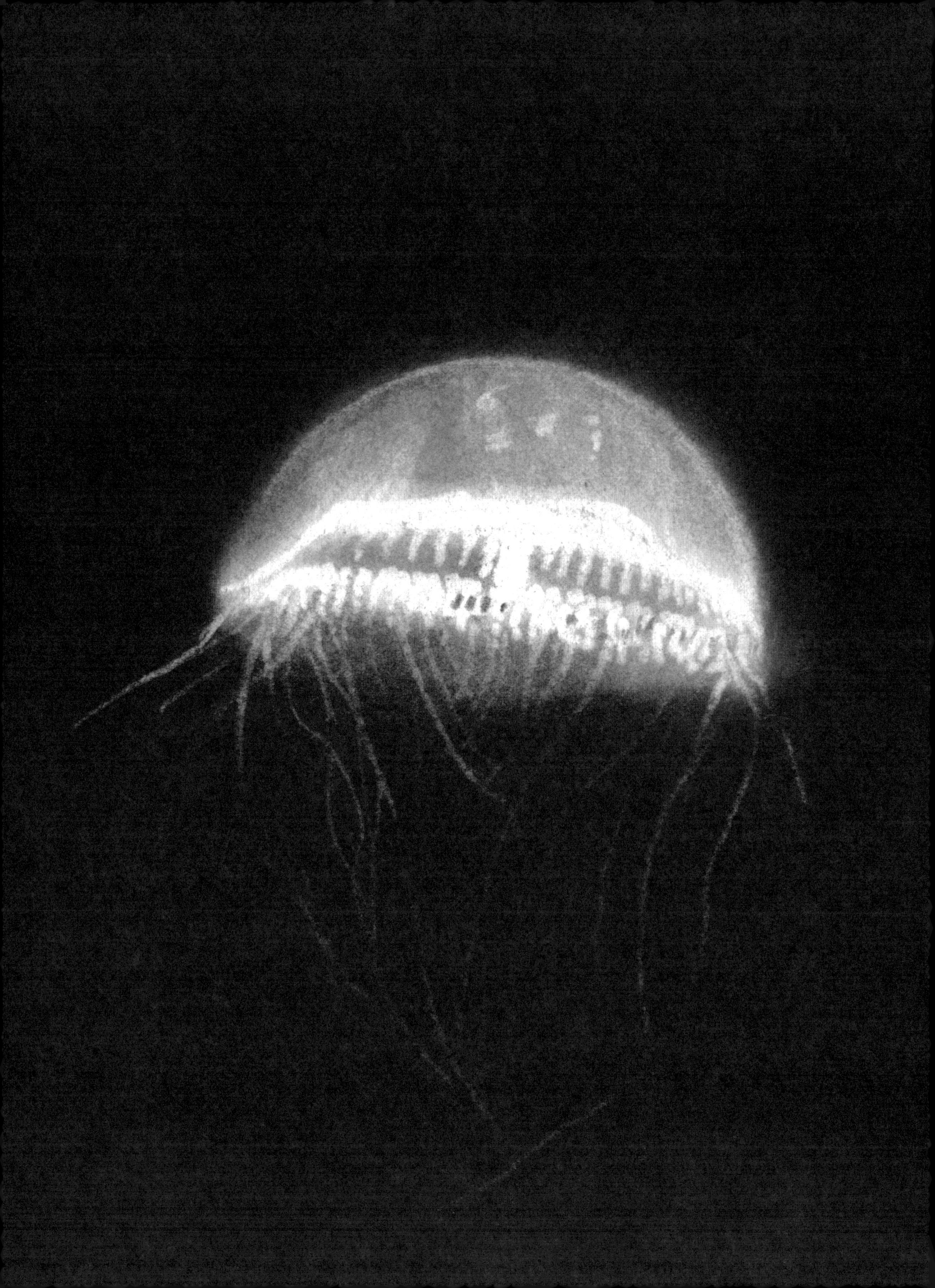

ALMOST PARADISE

By NORMAN PETTY
PIANO SOLO

PRICE
50¢
(In U.S.A.)

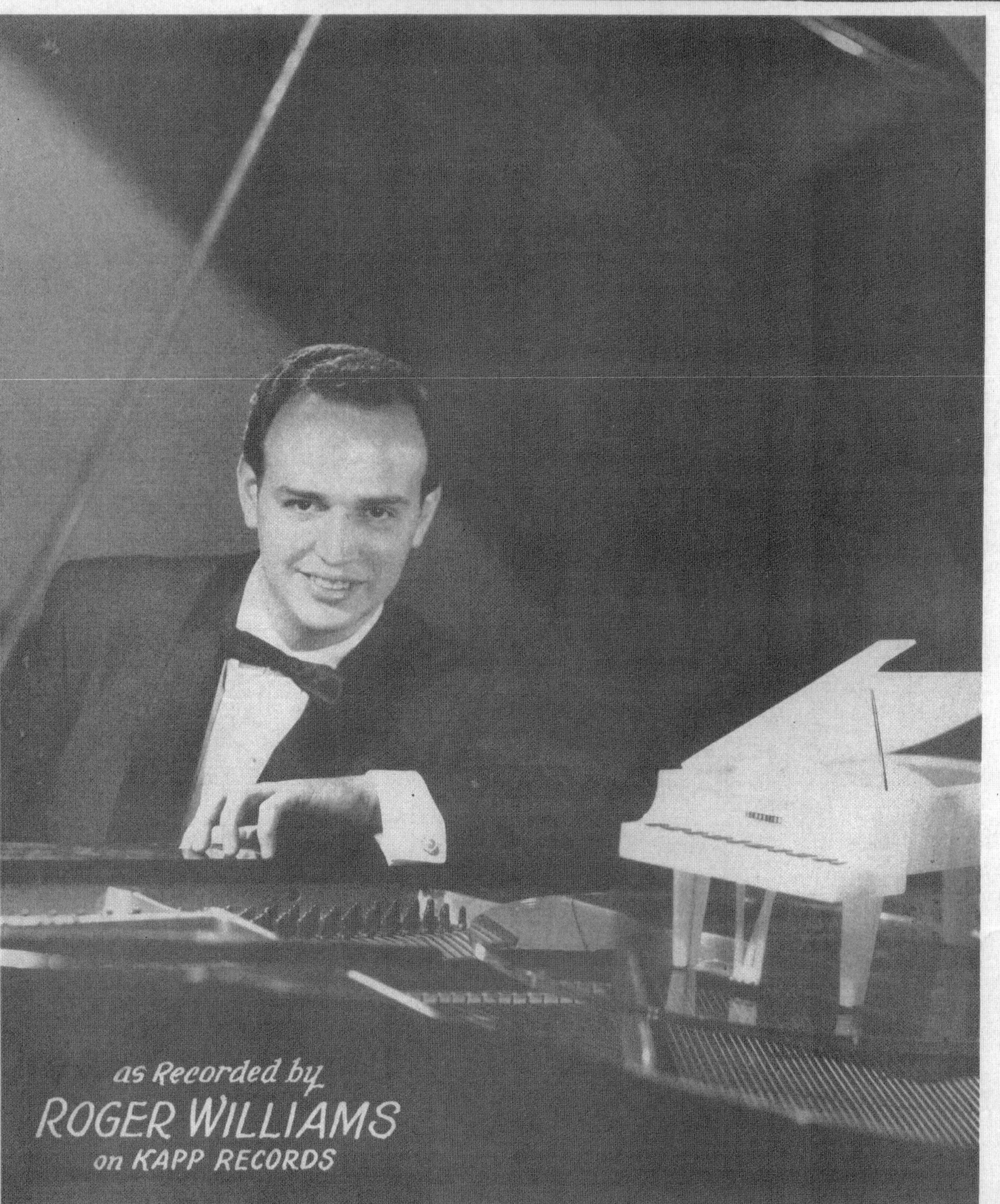

SOLE SELLING AGENT
SOUTHERN MUSIC PUB. CO., INC.

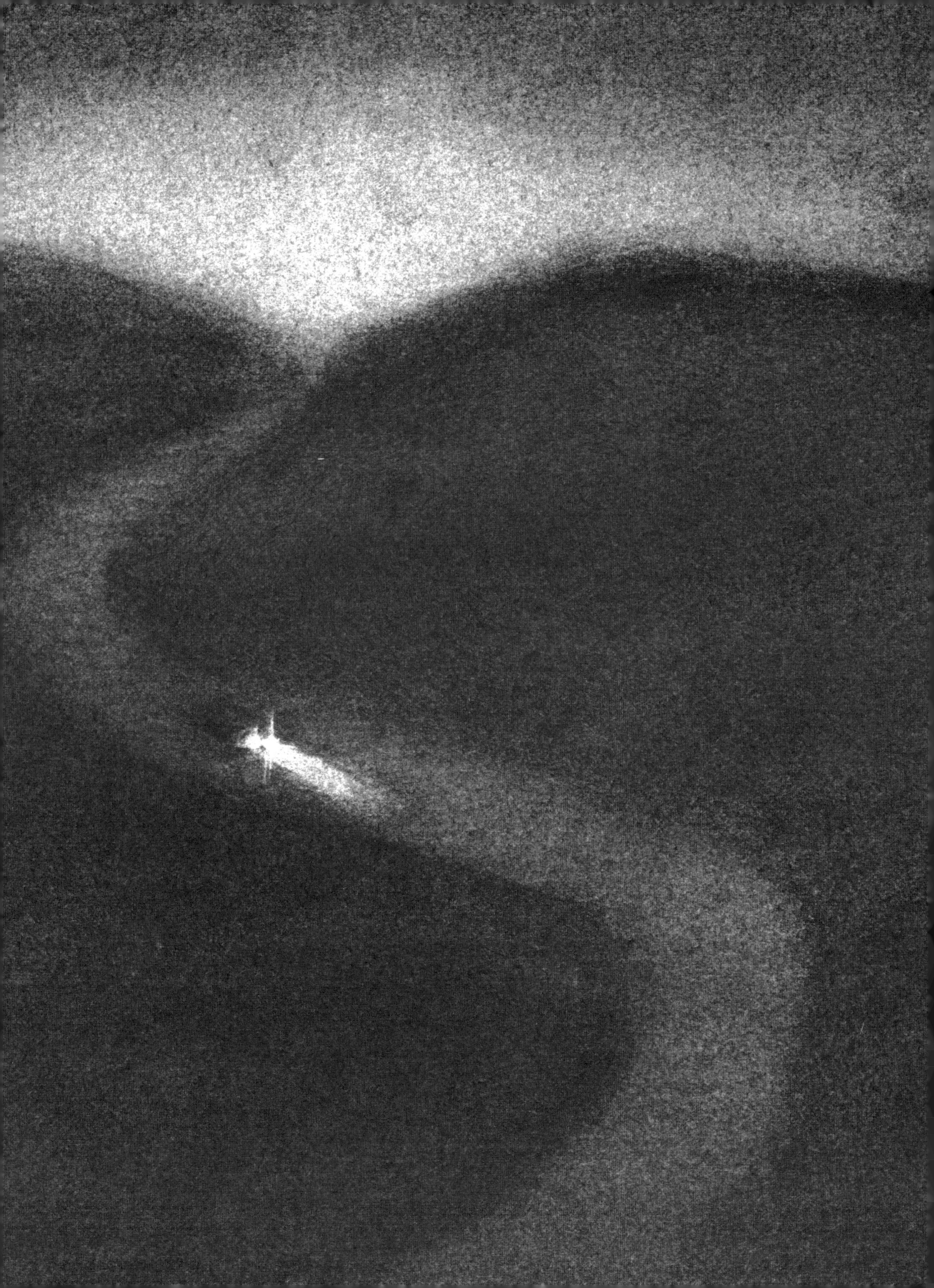

WHERE FLAMINGOS FLY

By HAROLD COURLANDER
EL THEA
JOHN BENSON BROOKS

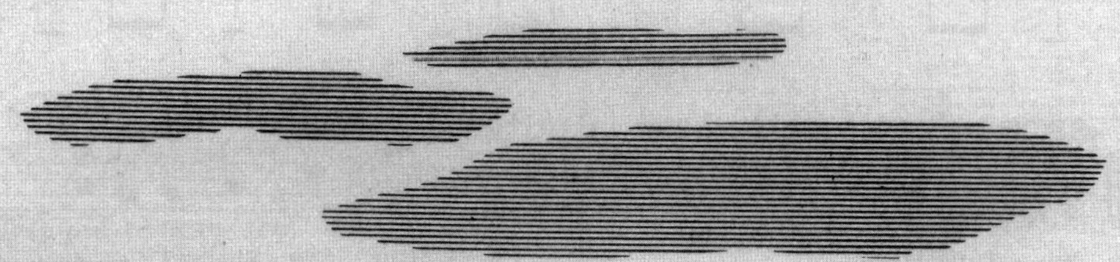

Recorded By

PEGGY LEE

on BRUNSWICK Records

PRICE 75¢

ROOSEVELT MUSIC CO., INC.

Sole Selling Agents:

KEYS-HANSEN, INC.

119 W. 57th St., New York 19, N. Y.

02288

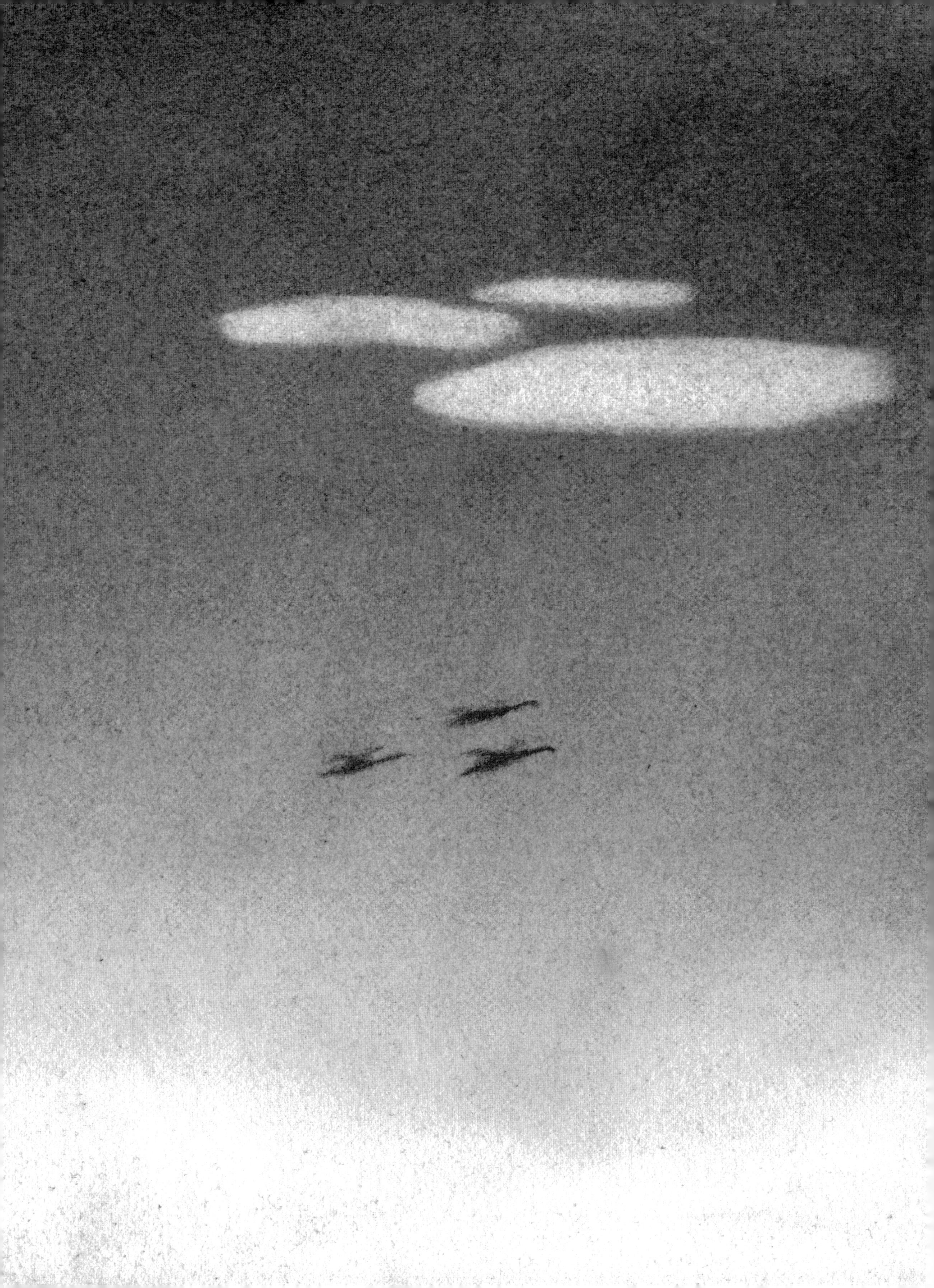

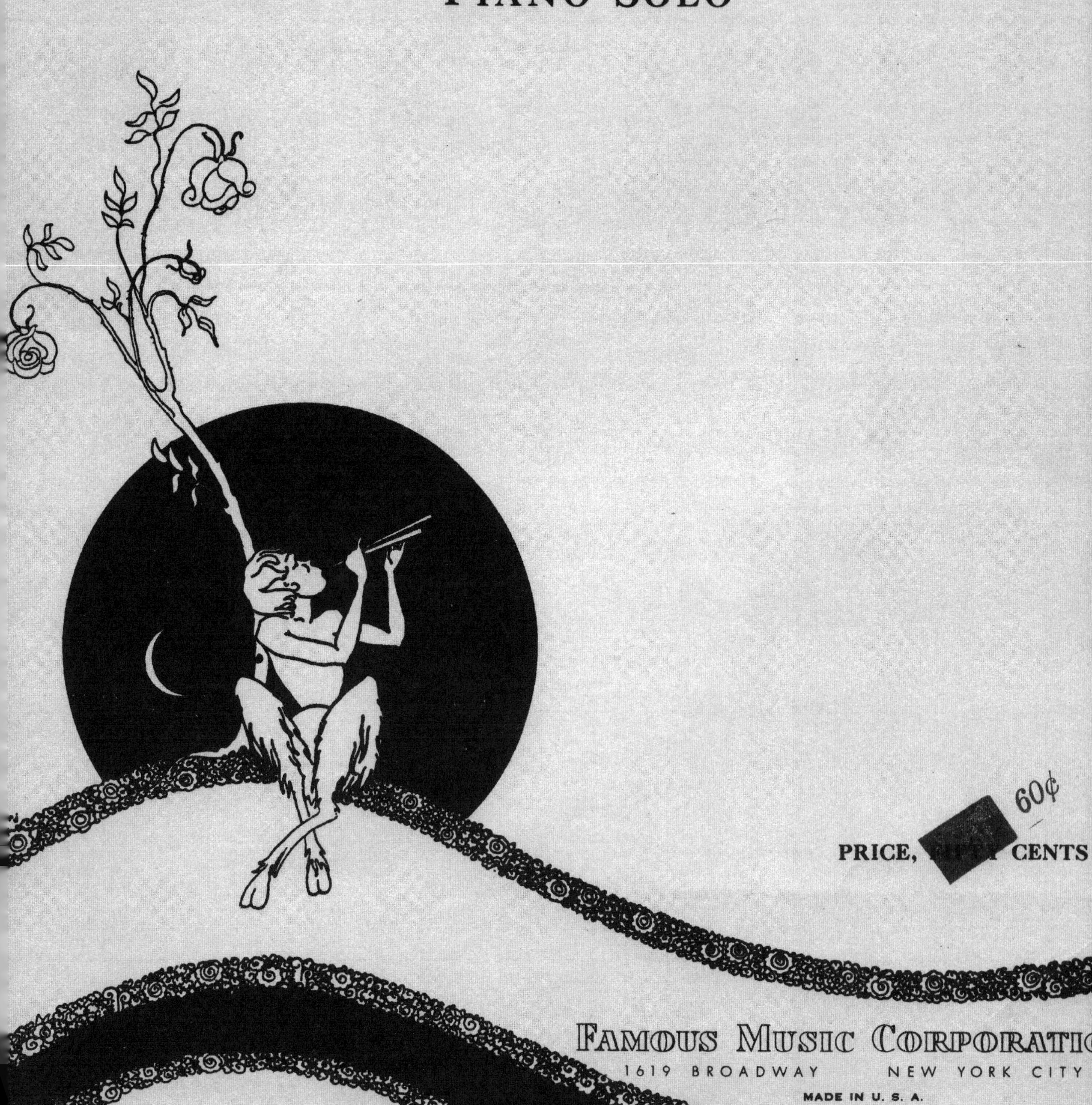

HOAGY CARMICHAEL'S
BLUE ORCHIDS
PIANO SOLO
60¢
PRICE, FIFTY CENTS
FAMOUS MUSIC CORPORATION
1619 BROADWAY   NEW YORK CITY
MADE IN U.S.A.

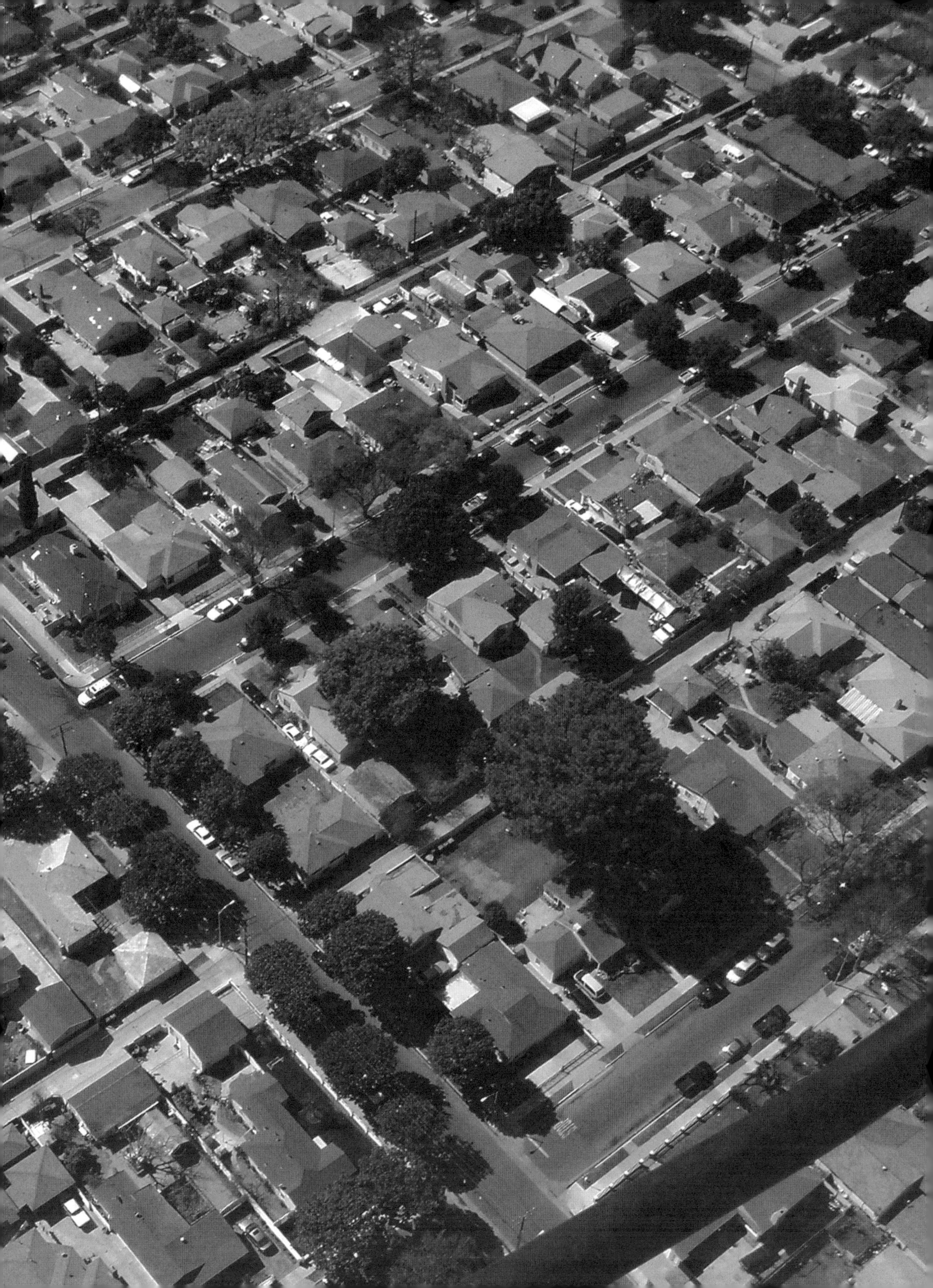

Compared To You

Lyric by
PAUL HERRICK, A.S.C.A.P.

Music by
MATT DENNIS, A.S.C.A.P.

Price 60 cents

DORSEY BROTHERS MUSIC, INC.
33 West 60th Street
New York, N. Y. 10023

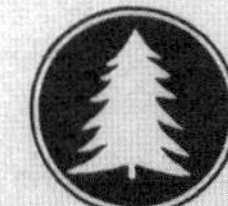

EVERGREEN MUSIC CORPORATION

340 North Camden Drive, Beverly Hills, California
NEW YORK: 240 West 55th Street, New York 19.

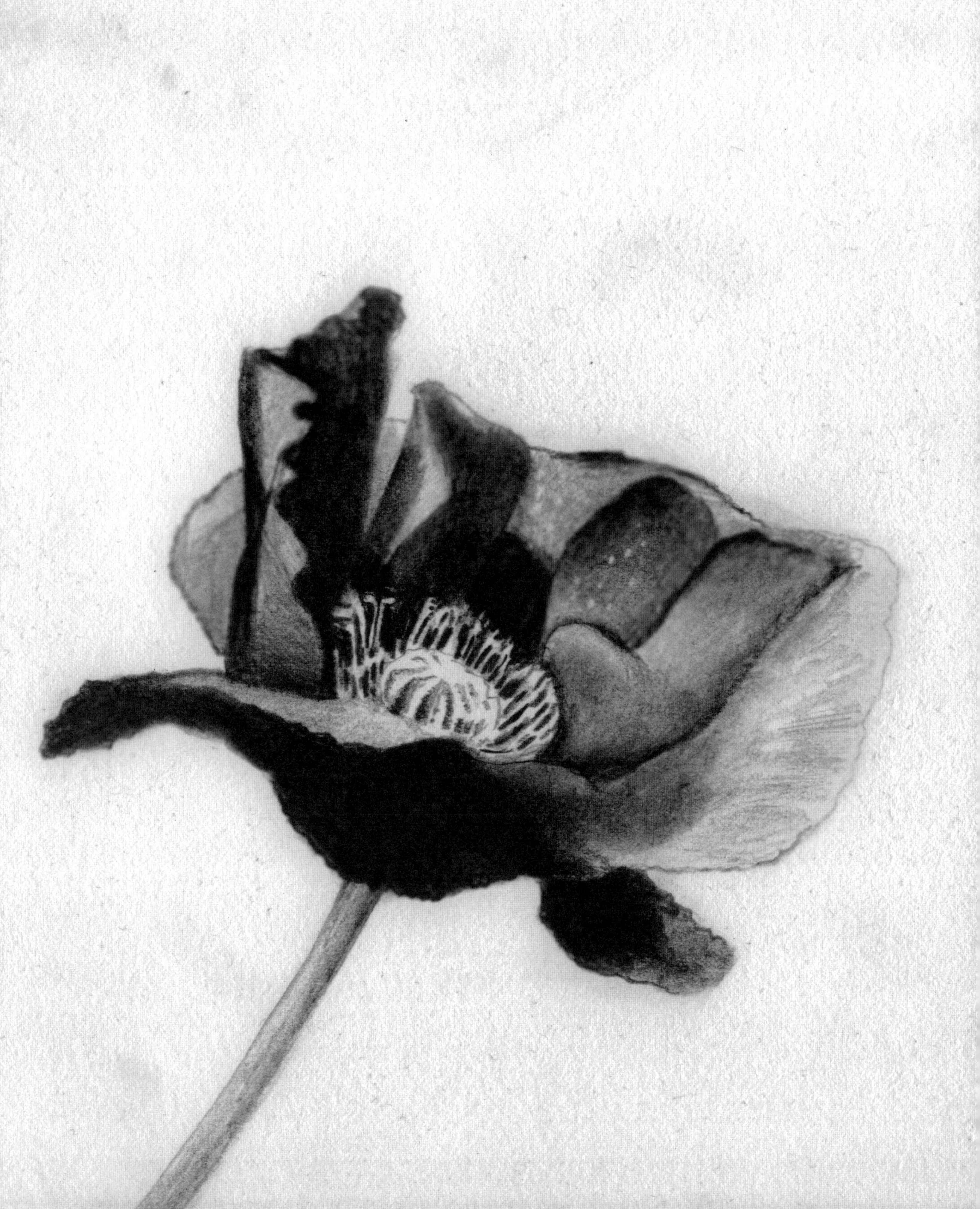

IMAGINATION

Words by JOHNNY BURKE

Music by JIMMY VAN HEUSEN

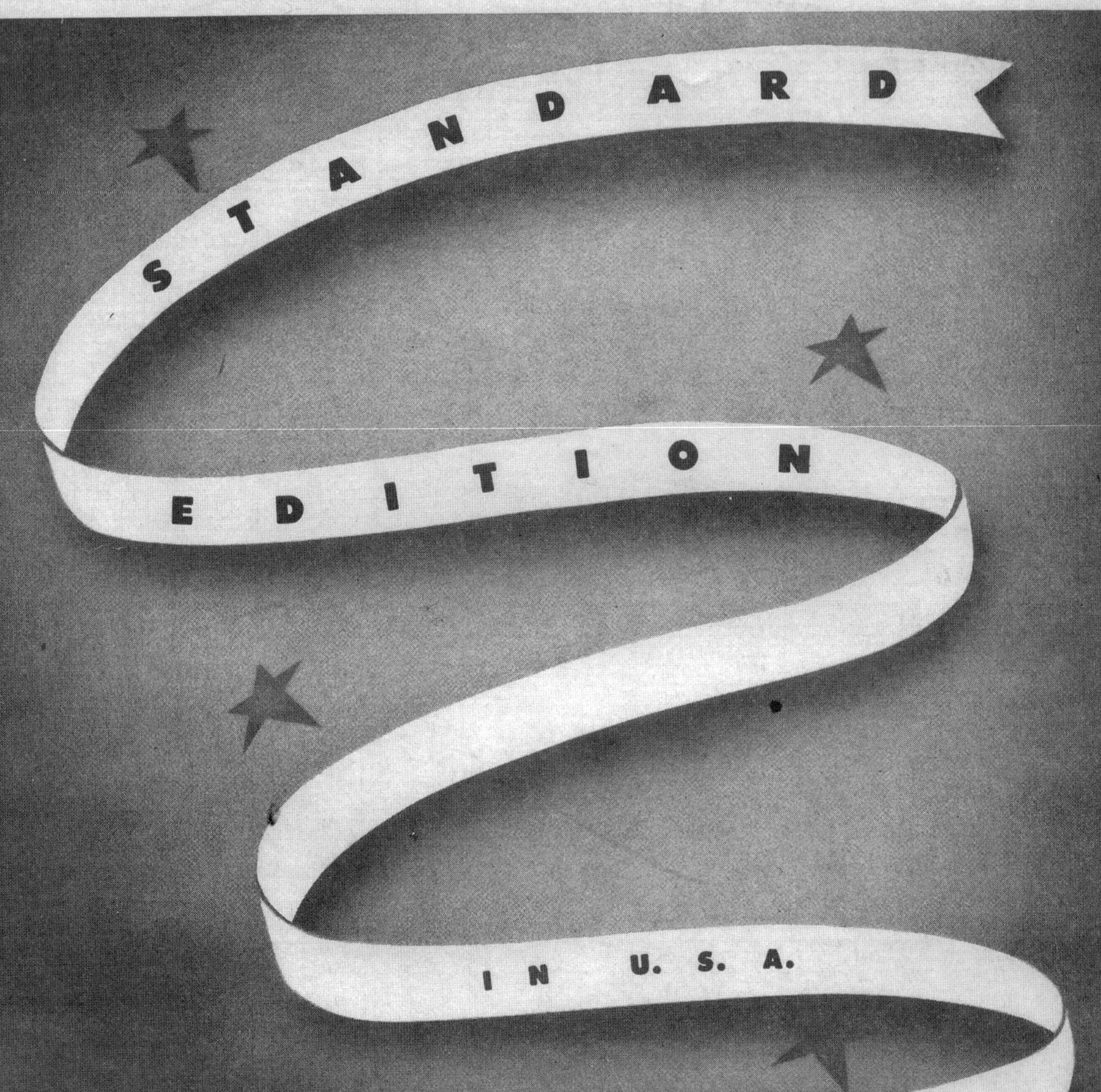

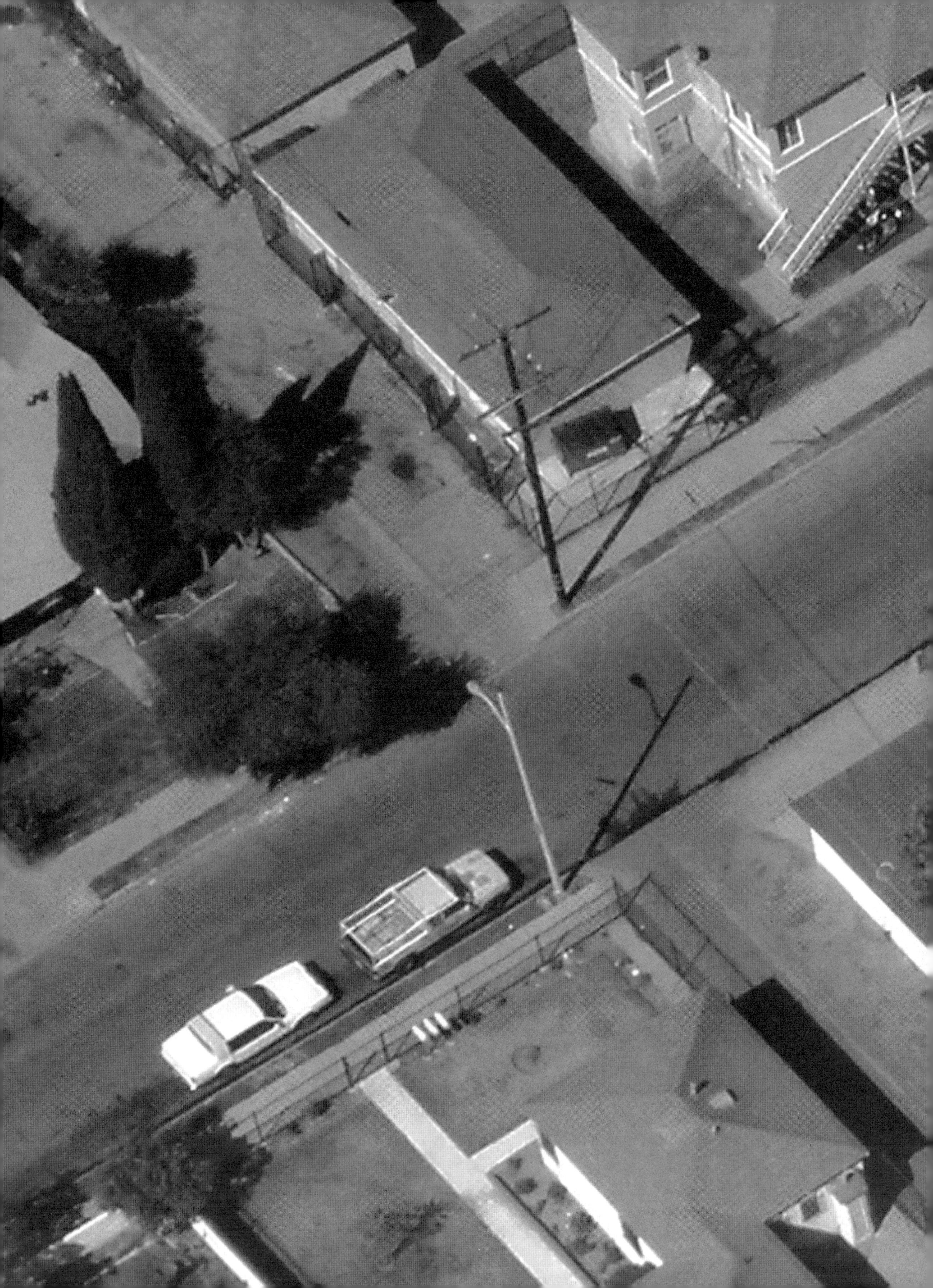

EV'RYWHERE

Words by LARRY KAHN

Music by TOLCHARD EVANS

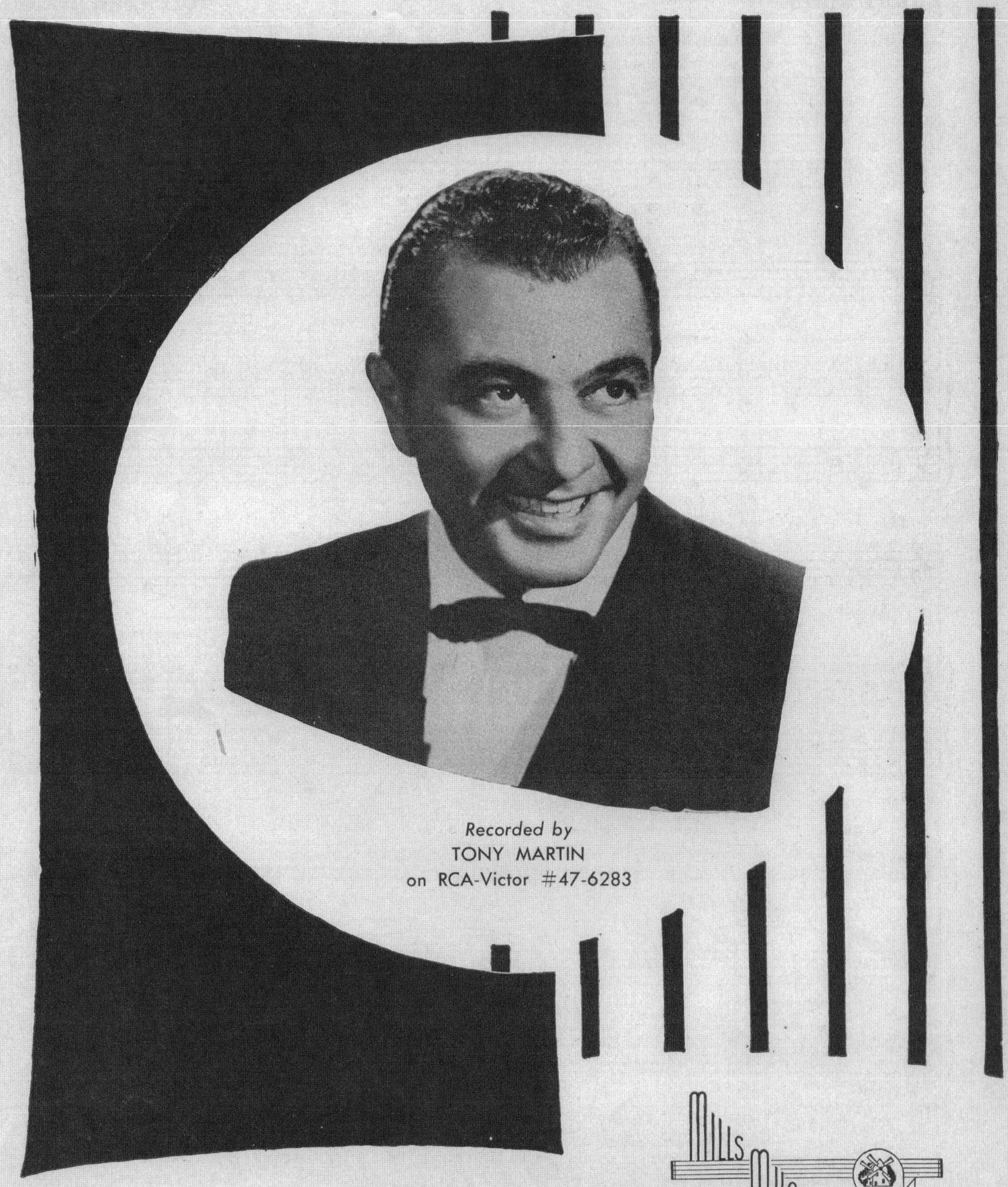

Mills MUSIC, Inc

1619 BROADWAY, NEW YORK, N. Y.

By Arrangement With
SYDNEY BRON MUSIC CO., LTD., LONDON

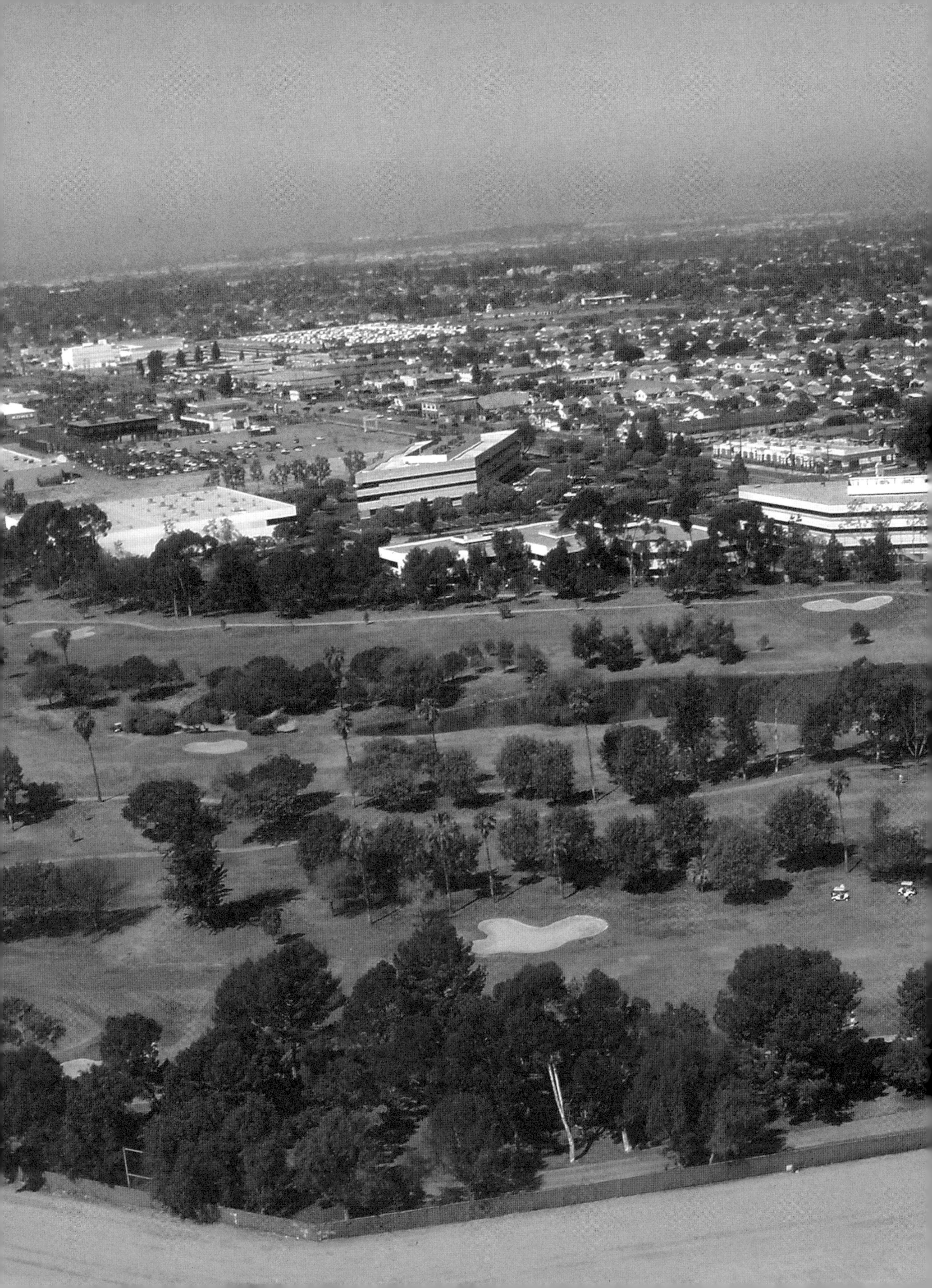

ALL OF ME

By SEYMOUR SIMONS and GERALD MARKS

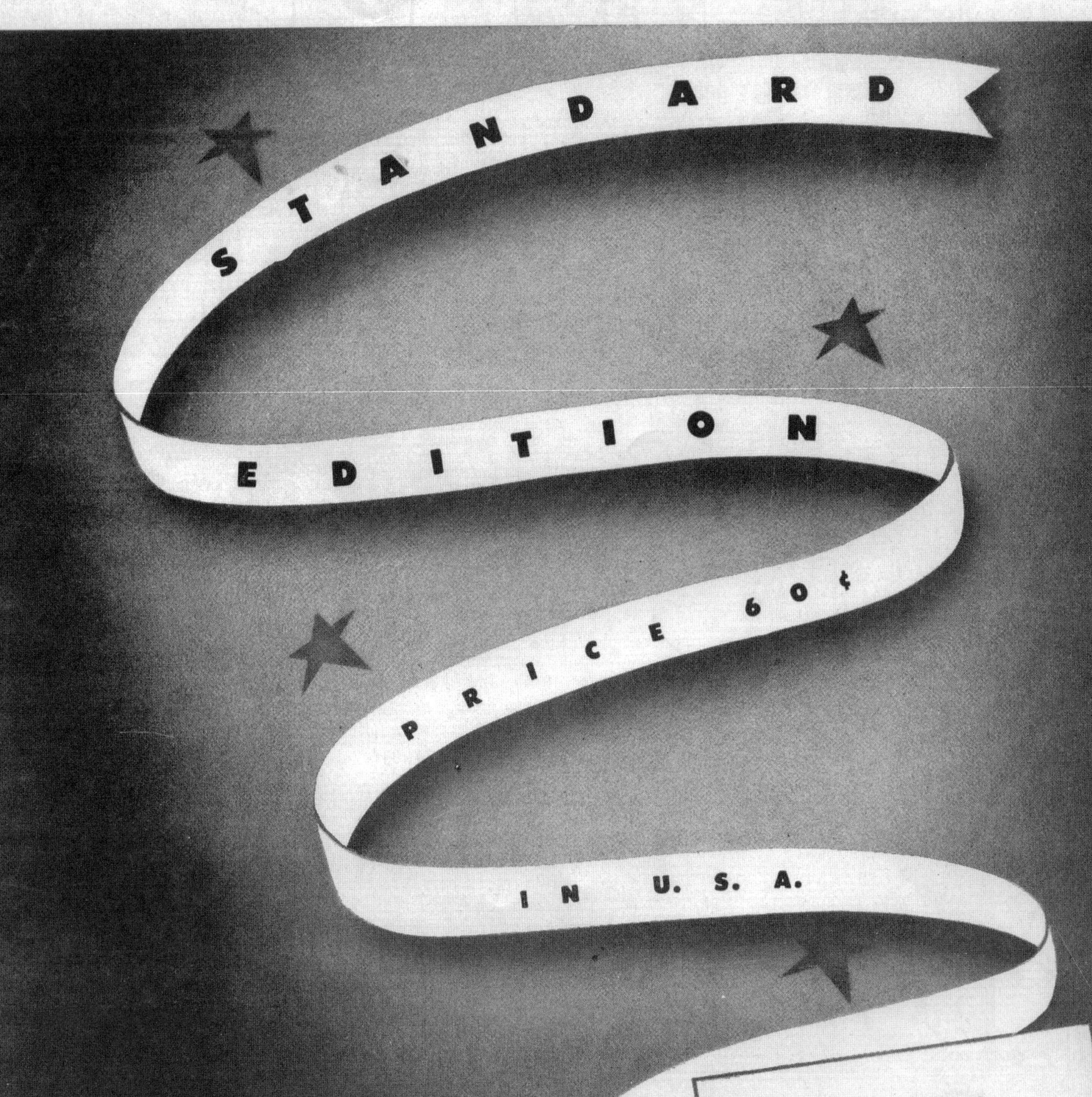

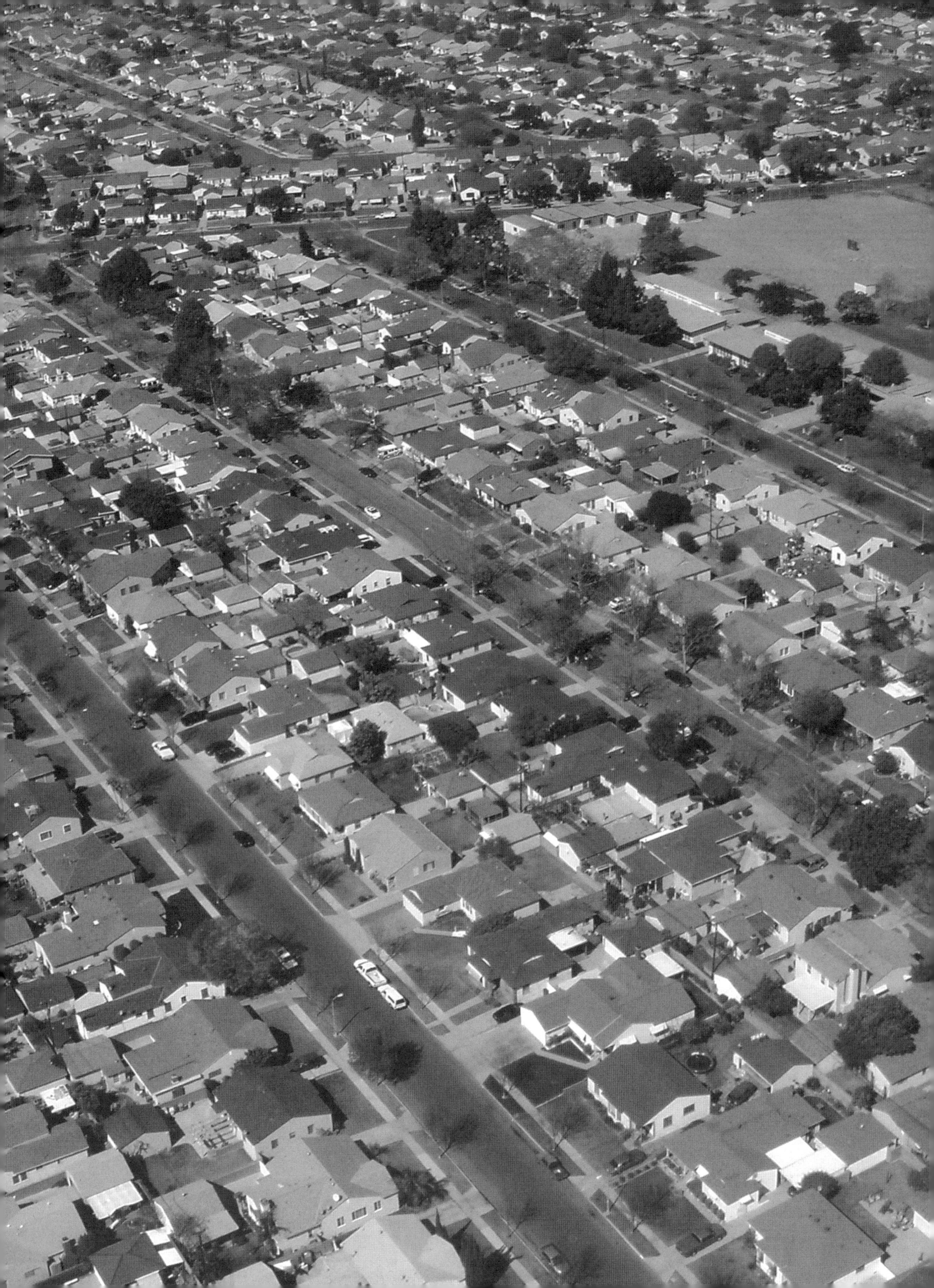

FOGBOUND

PIANO SOLO
by
IRVING FIELDS

1619 BROADWAY, NEW YORK 19, N. Y.

PRICE
75¢

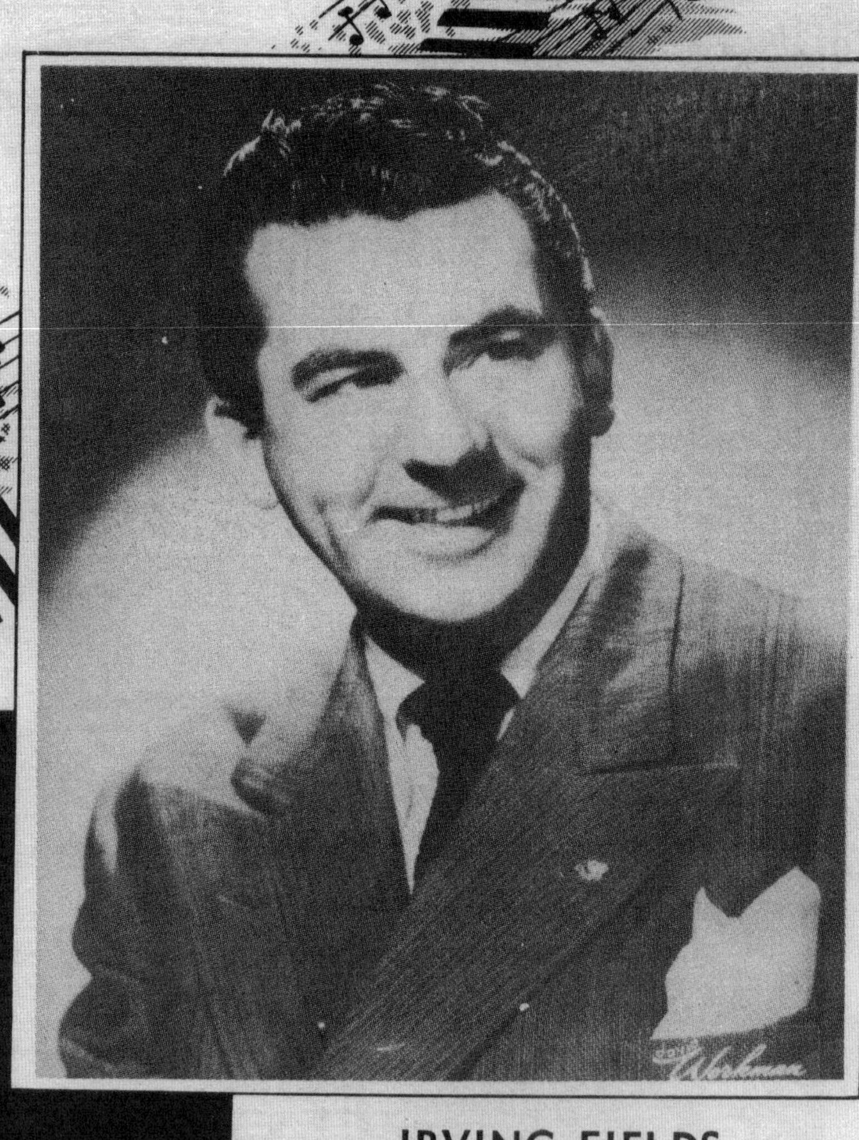

IRVING FIELDS

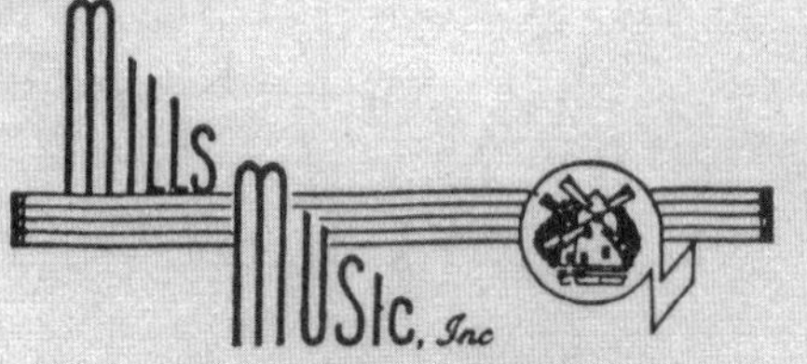

1619 BROADWAY, NEW YORK 19, N. Y.

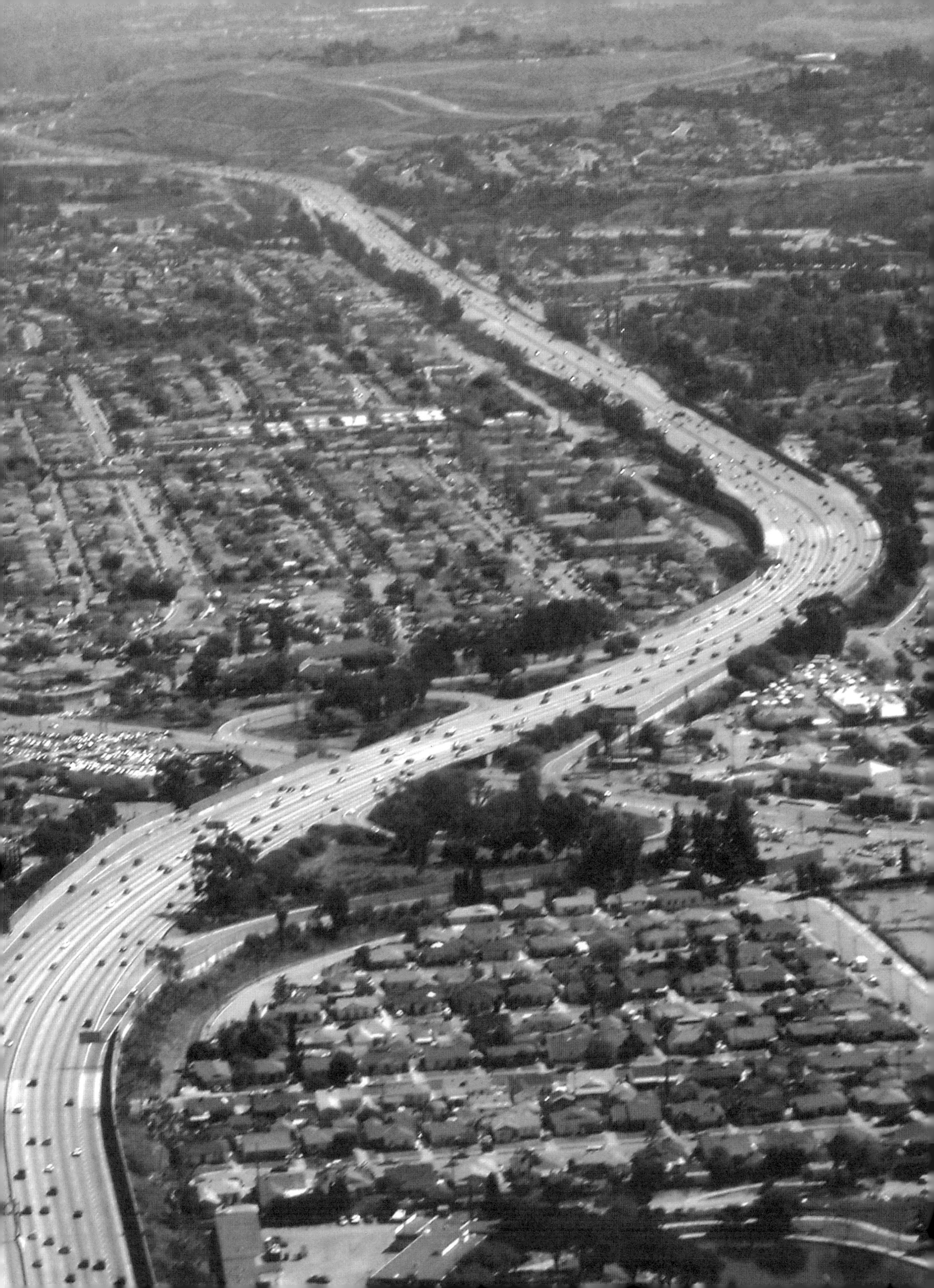

YOU'RE EVERYWHERE

Words by
EDWARD HEYMAN

Music by
VINCENT YOUMANS

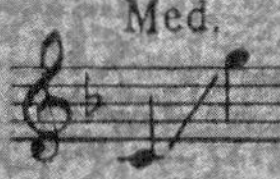

PRICE **60c** IN U.S.A.

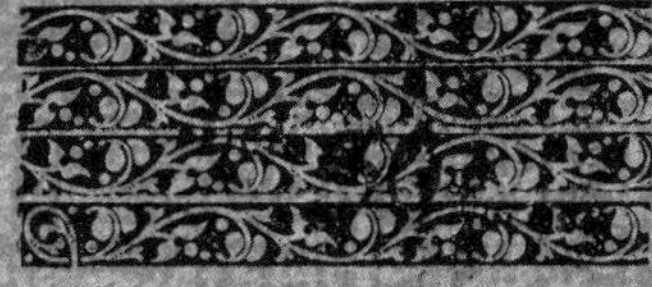

MILLER MUSIC CORPORATION
1619 BROADWAY · NEW YORK

BY ARRANGEMENT WITH
VINCENT YOUMANS, Inc.

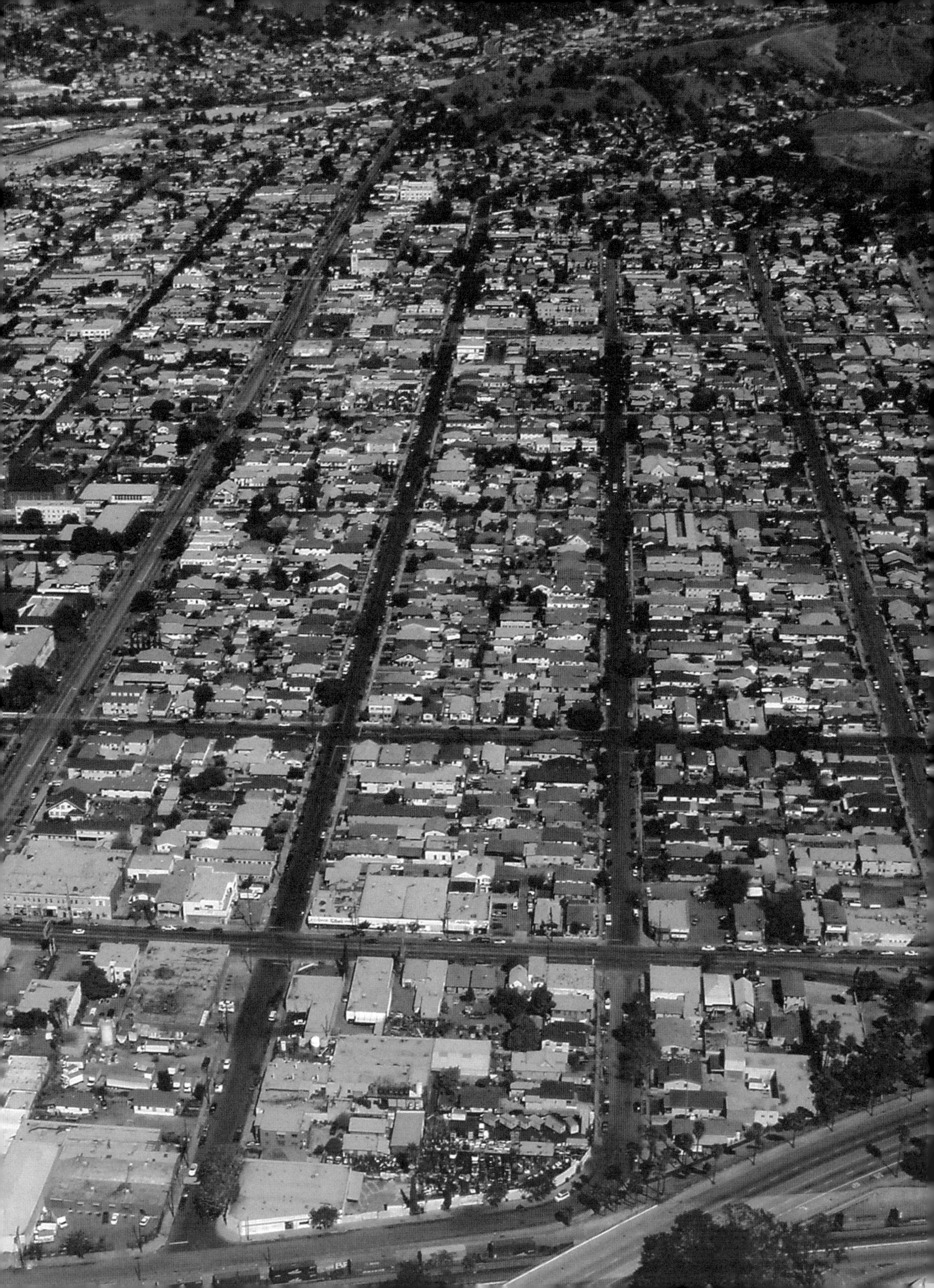

MORE THAN YOU KNOW

Lyrics by
WILLIAM ROSE
and
EDWARD ELISCU

Music by
VINCENT YOUMANS

PRICE **60¢** IN U.S.A.

MILLER MUSIC CORPORATION
799 SEVENTH AVENUE • NEW YORK 19, N. Y.
By arrangement with VINCENT YOUMANS, INC.

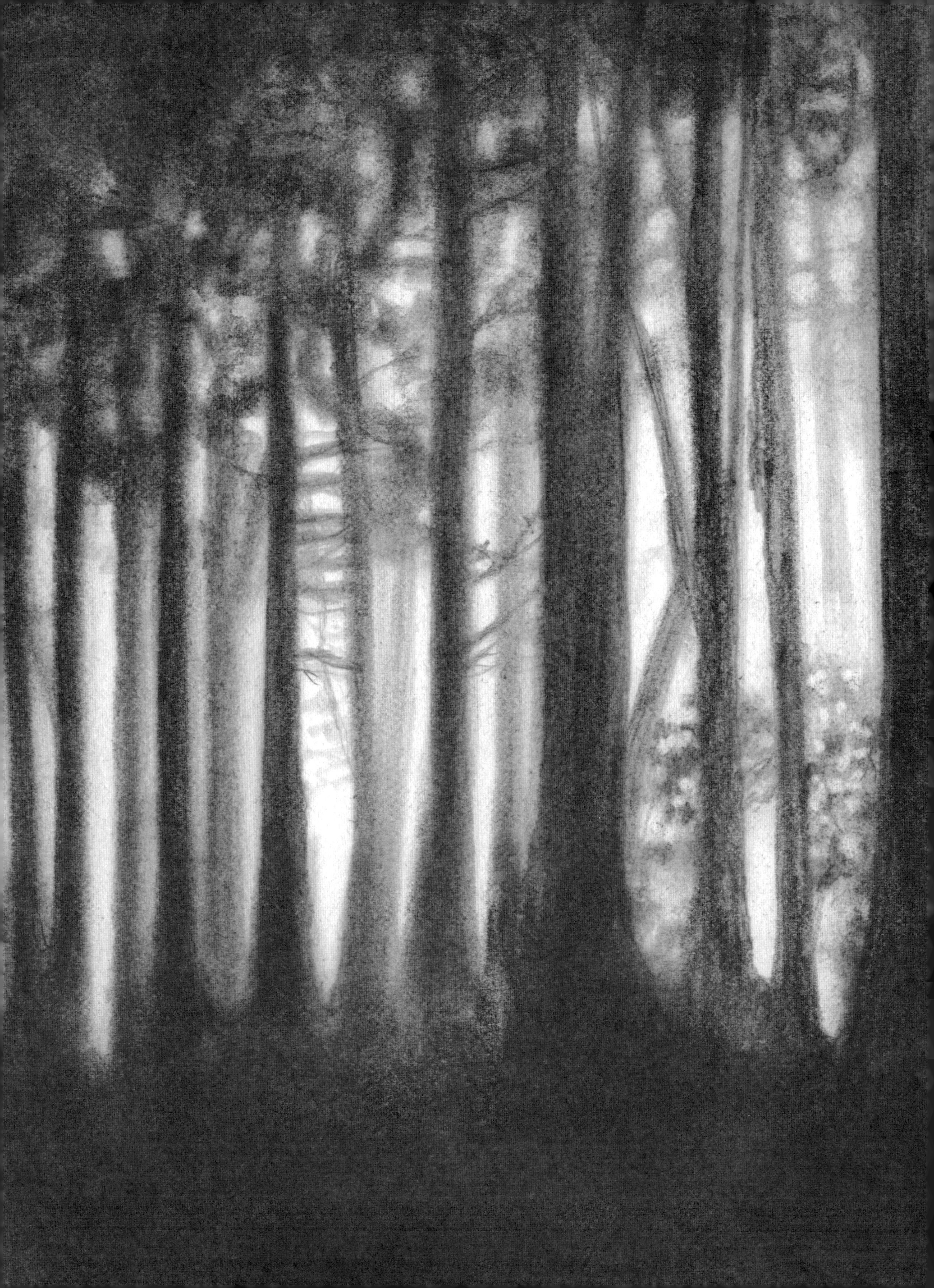

CALL ME

Key of C (E♭–E♮)

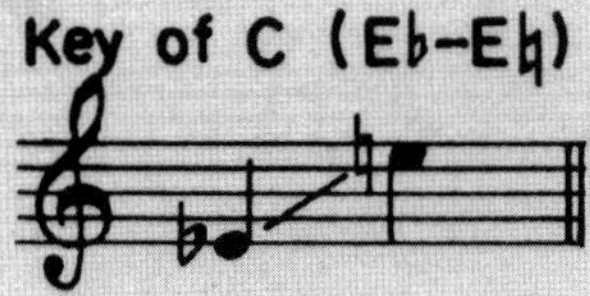

Words and Music by
TONY HATCH

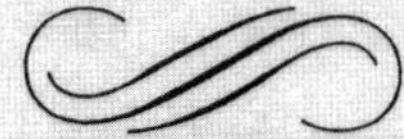

Price
Seventy Five cents
in U.S.A.

DUCHESS MUSIC CORPORATION

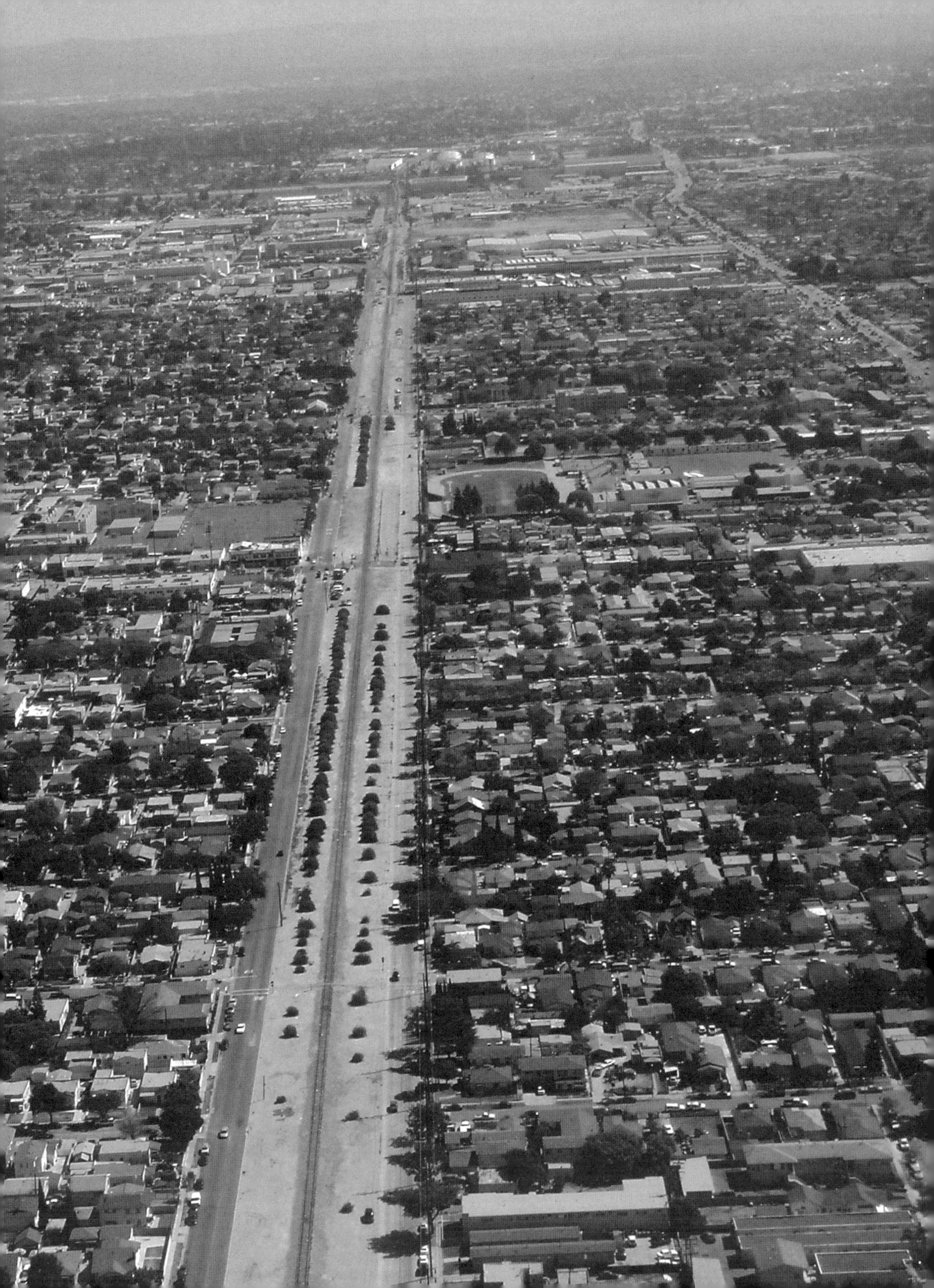

TENDERLY

Lyric by JACK LAWRENCE   Music by WALTER GROSS

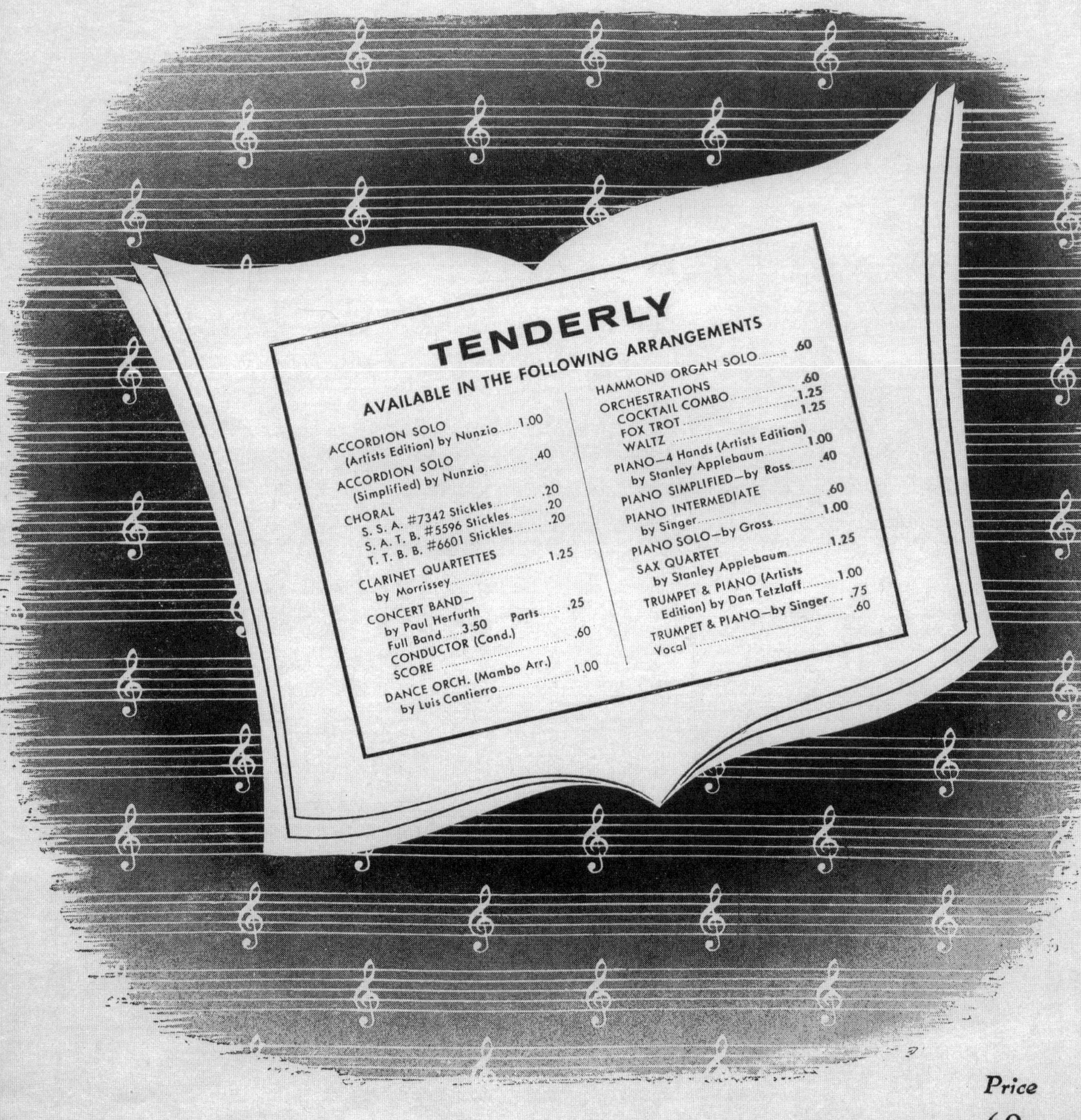

Price

60c
IN U. S. A.

EDWIN H. MORRIS & COMPANY, INC.
35 W. 51st ST.   •   NEW YORK, N. Y.

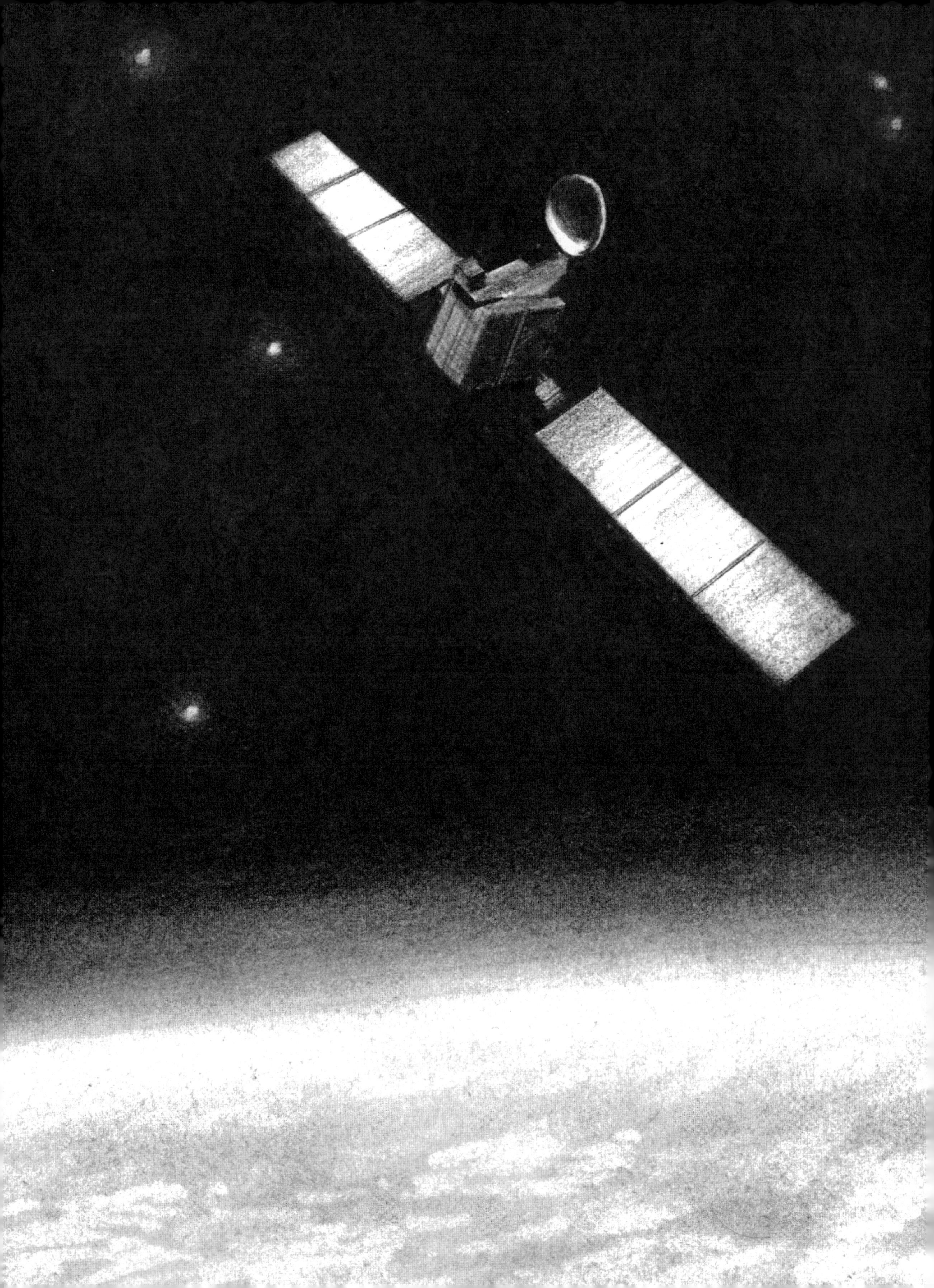

AS YEARS GO BY

BASED ON BRAHMS' HUNGARIAN DANCE No. 4

★

BY
CHARLES TOBIAS
AND
PETER DE ROSE

PRICE 50¢ IN USA

MILLER MUSIC CORPORATION
799 SEVENTH AVENUE • NEW YORK 19, N. Y.

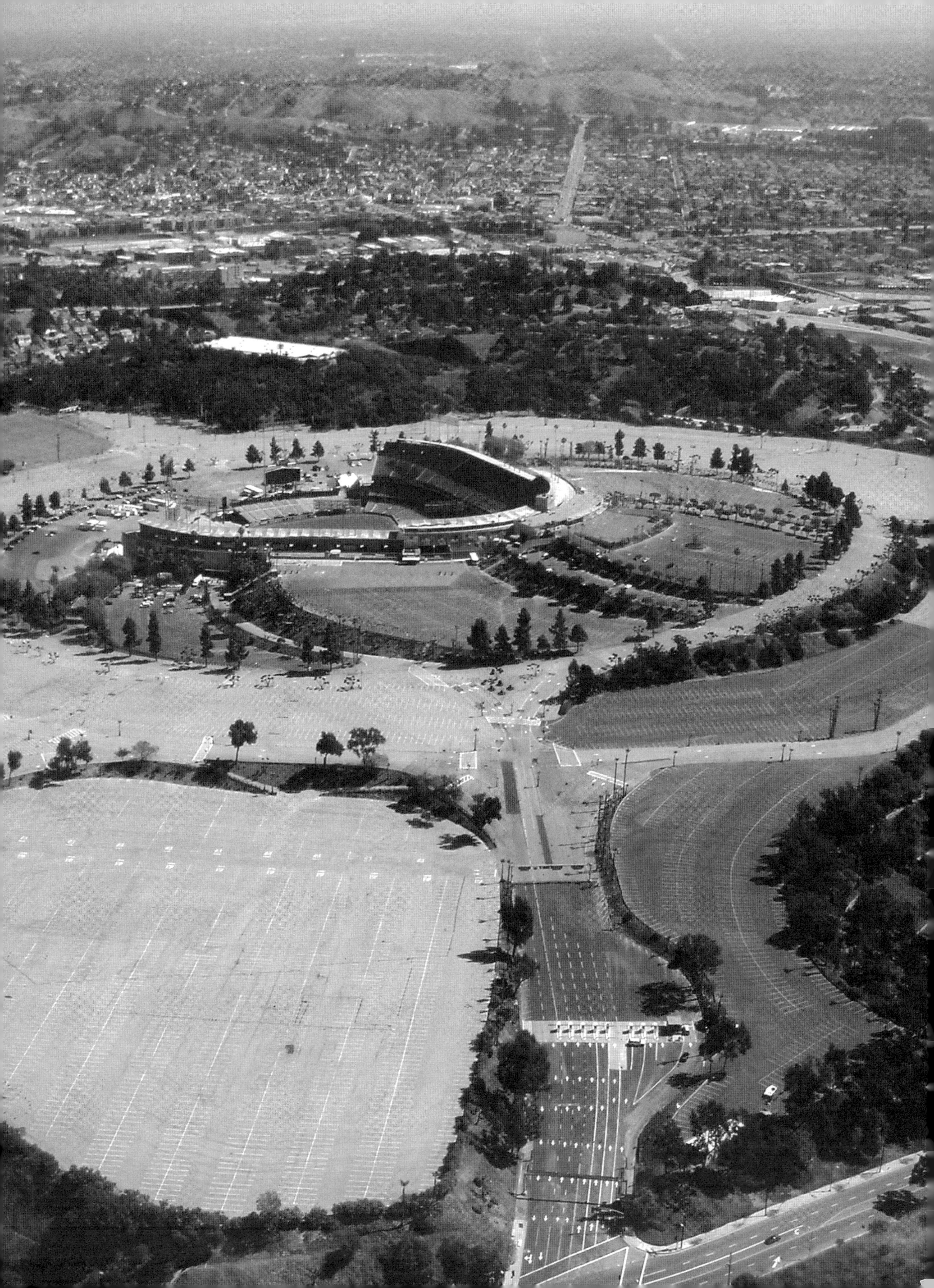

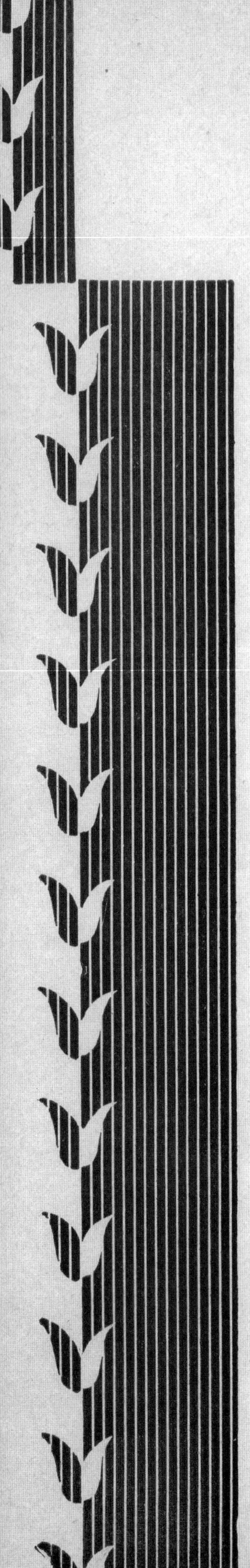

LOVE

Words and Music by

RALPH BLANE
HUGH MARTIN

PRICE **60¢** IN U.S.A.

Leo Feist inc.
799 SEVENTH AVENUE • NEW YORK 19, N. Y.

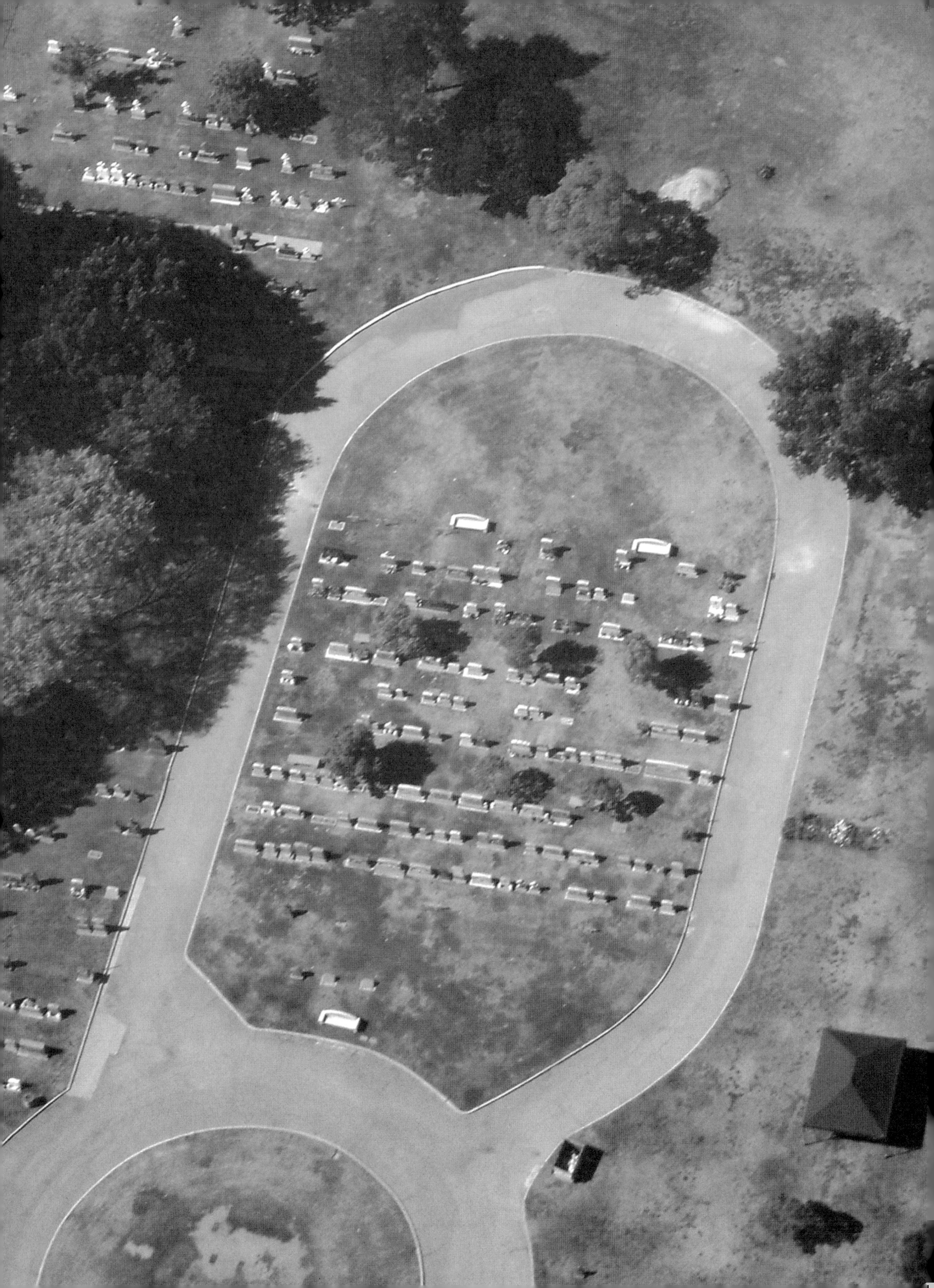

That Tired Routine Called Love

Lyric by
TED STEELE

Music by
MATT DENNIS

Price 60 cents

DORSEY BROTHERS MUSIC, INC.
33 West 60th Street
New York, N. Y. 10023
EVERGREEN MUSIC CORPORATION

340 North Camden Drive, Beverly Hills, California

NEW YORK: 240 West 55th Street, New York 19.

YOU ONLY WANT IT 'COS YOU HAVEN'T GOT IT

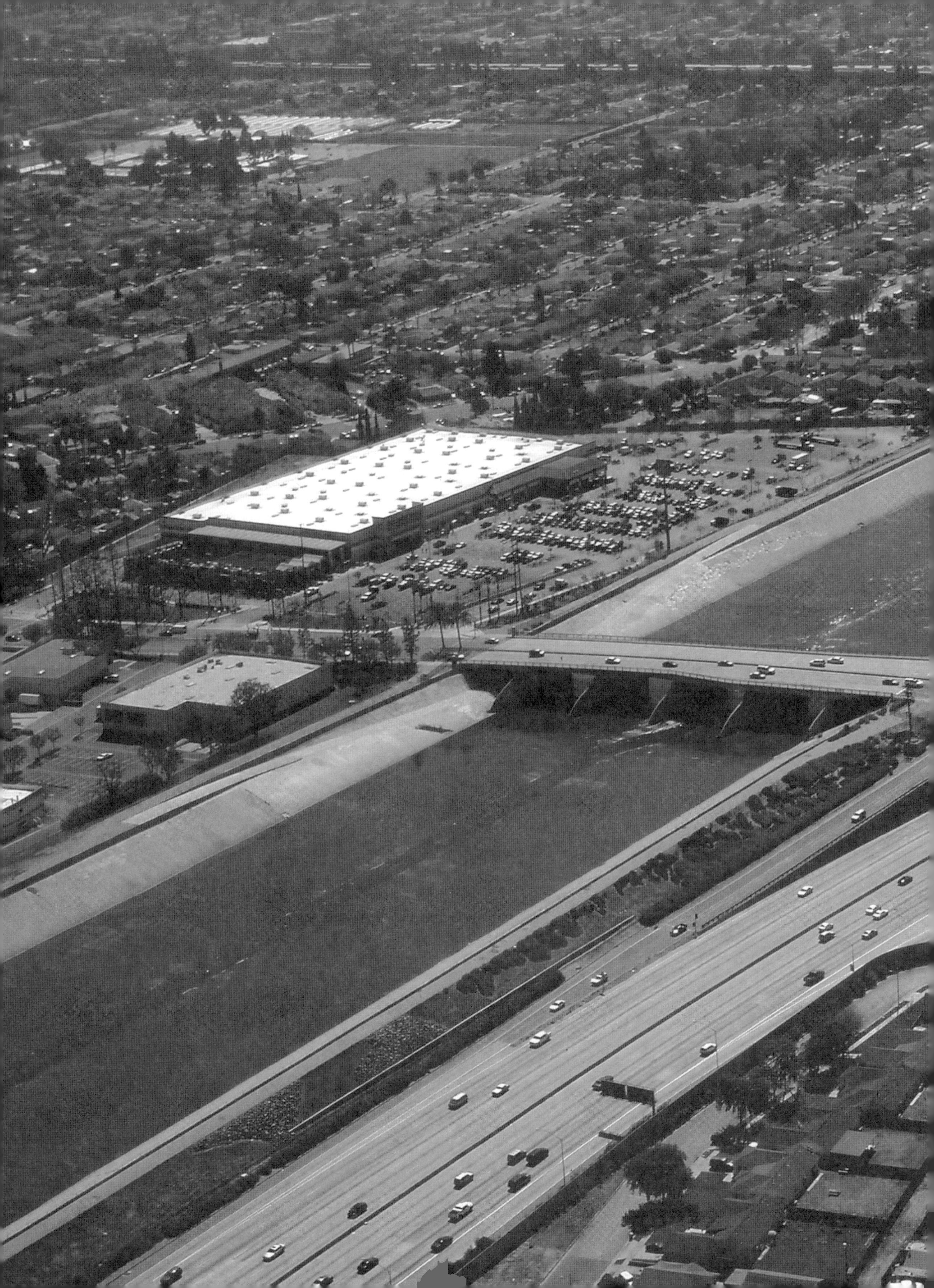

LOVE FOR SALE

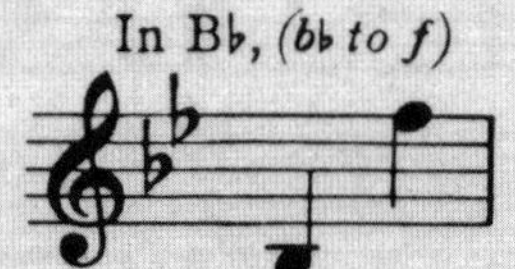

FROM

"THE NEW YORKERS"

WORDS AND MUSIC
BY

COLE PORTER

PUBLISHED IN THE FOLLOWING ARRANGEMENTS

Vocal Solo, B♭ 60
Dance Orchestration (Fox Trot) 1.25

WHEN PERFORMING THIS COMPOSITION KINDLY GIVE ALL
PROGRAM CREDITS TO

HARMS
INCORPORATED
NEW YORK

PRINTED IN U. S. A.

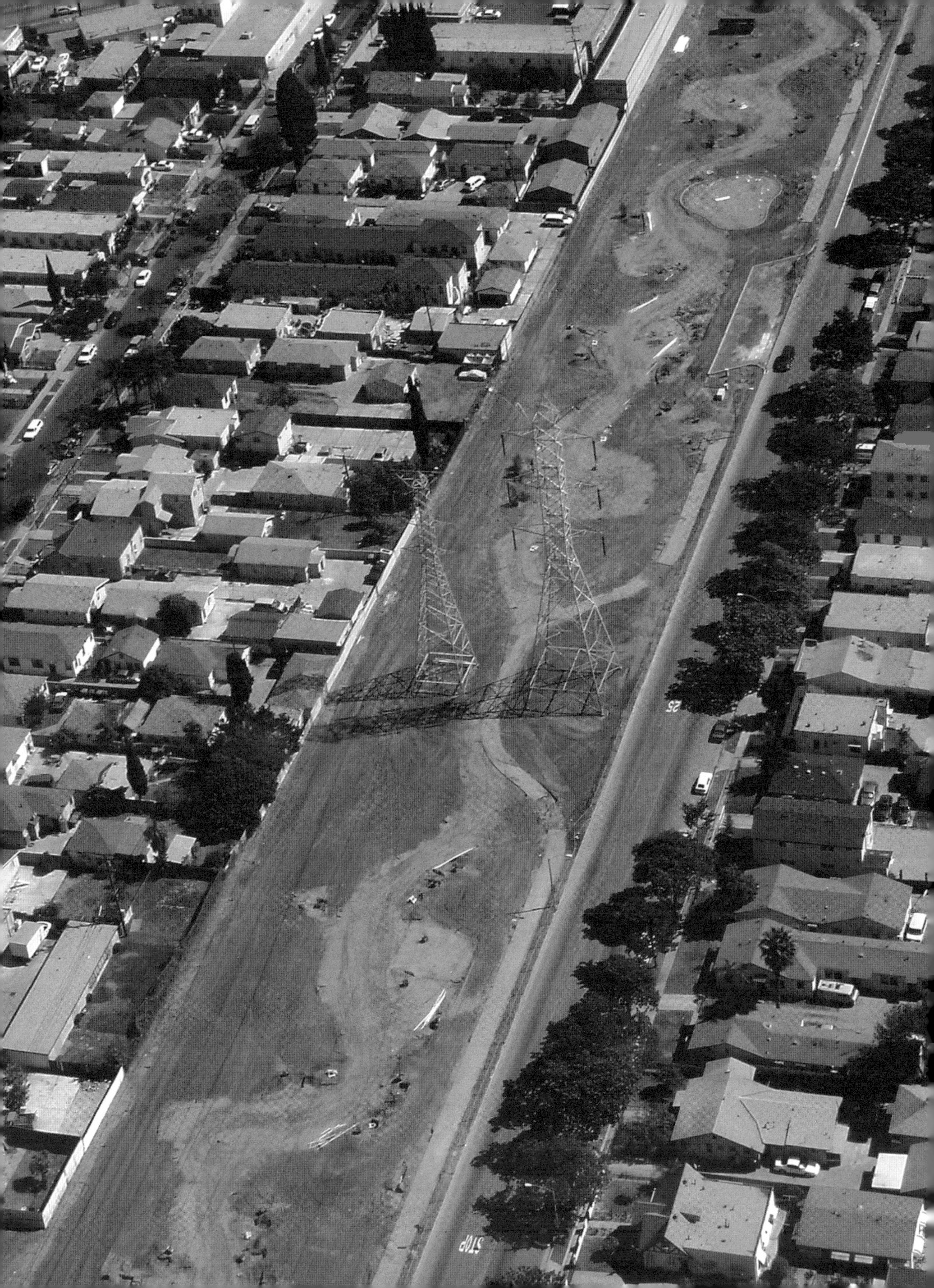

LET'S TAKE A WALK AROUND THE BLOCK

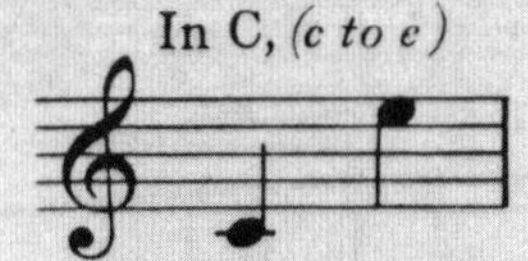

FROM THE MUSICAL PRODUCTION

"LIFE BEGINS AT 8:40"

WORDS BY

IRA GERSHWIN and E. Y. HARBURG

MUSIC BY

HAROLD ARLEN

Price 60 Cents

IN U.S.A.

WHEN PERFORMING THIS COMPOSITION KINDLY GIVE ALL
PROGRAM CREDITS TO

NEW WORLD MUSIC CORPORATION

HARMS, Inc., Sole Selling Agent

NEW YORK

PRINTED IN U. S. A.

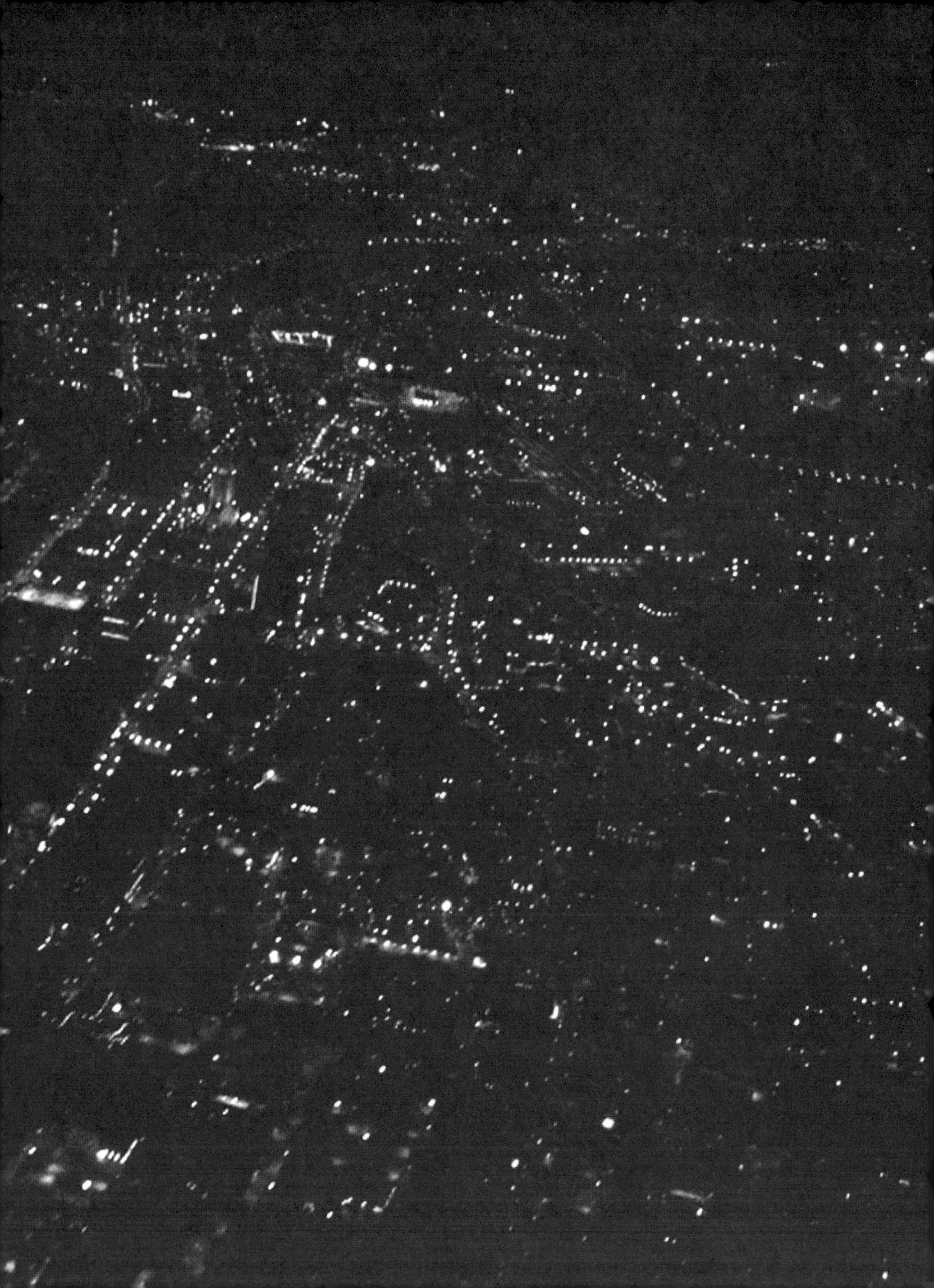

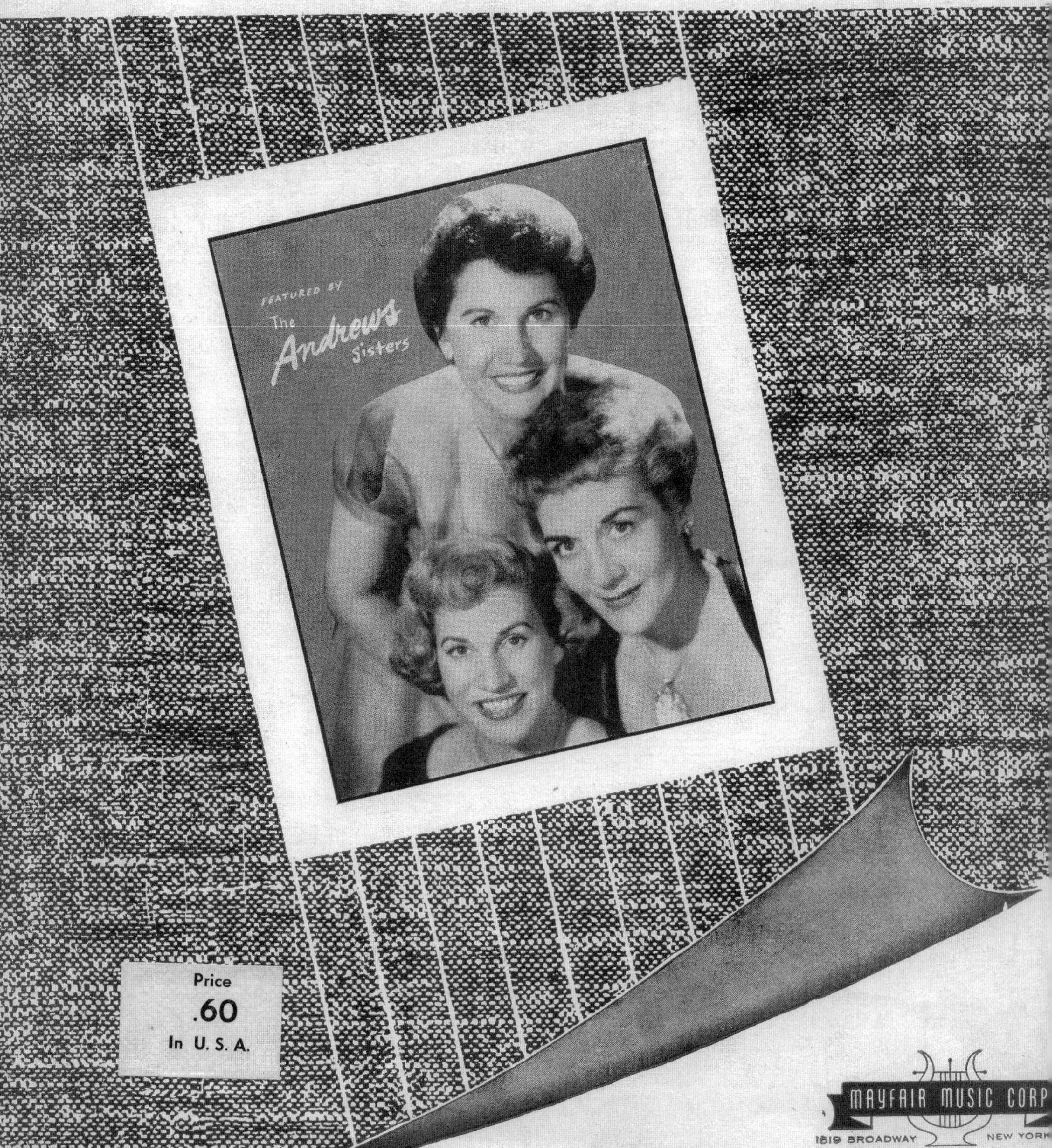

THERE WILL NEVER BE ANOTHER YOU
Words by MACK GORDON
Music by HARRY WARREN
FEATURED BY
The Andrews Sisters
Price
.60
In U.S.A.
MAYFAIR MUSIC CORP.
1619 BROADWAY   NEW YORK

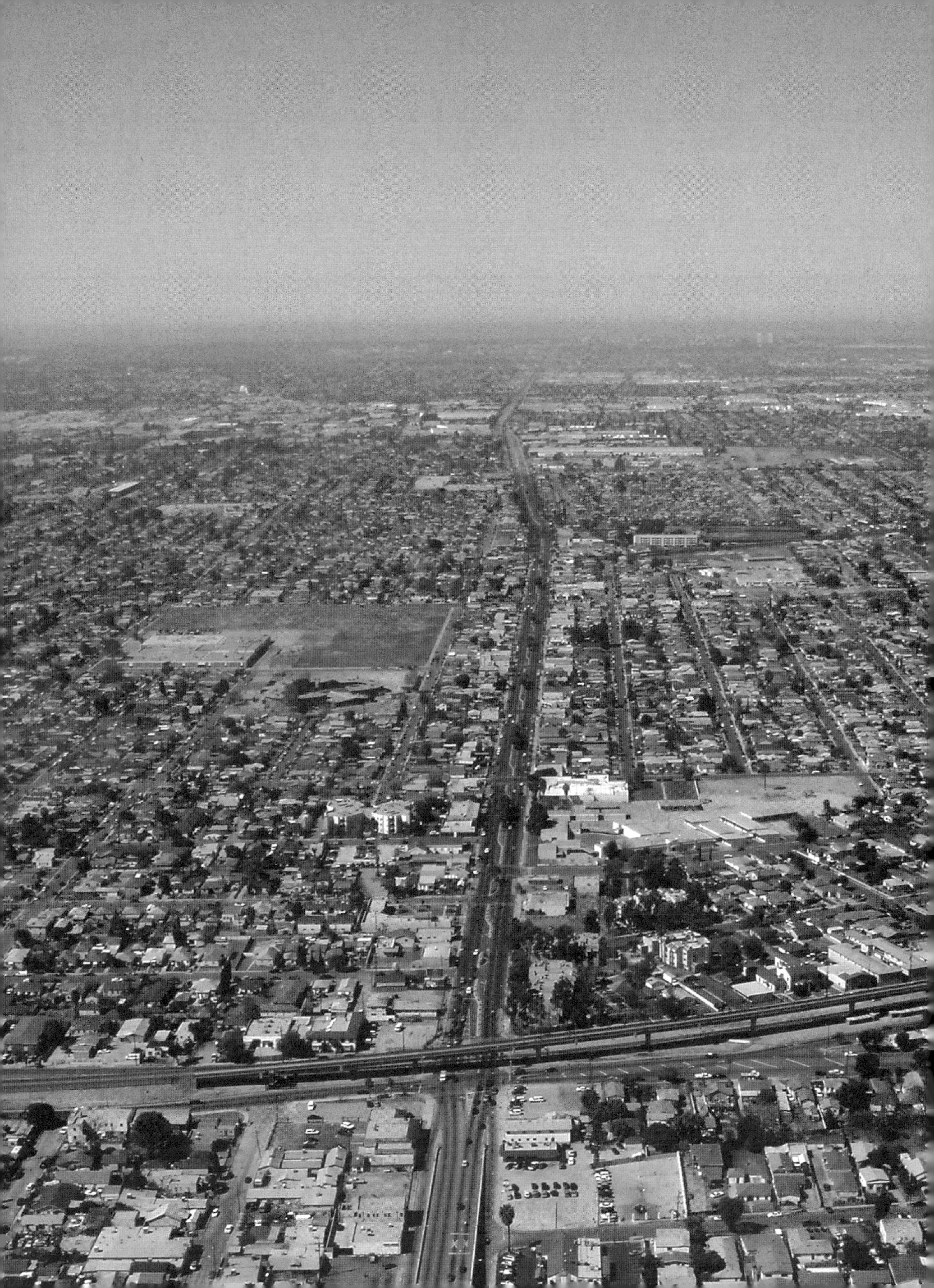

GHOST OF YESTERDAY

Lyric by
ARTHUR HERZOG, Jr.

Music by
IRENE WILSON

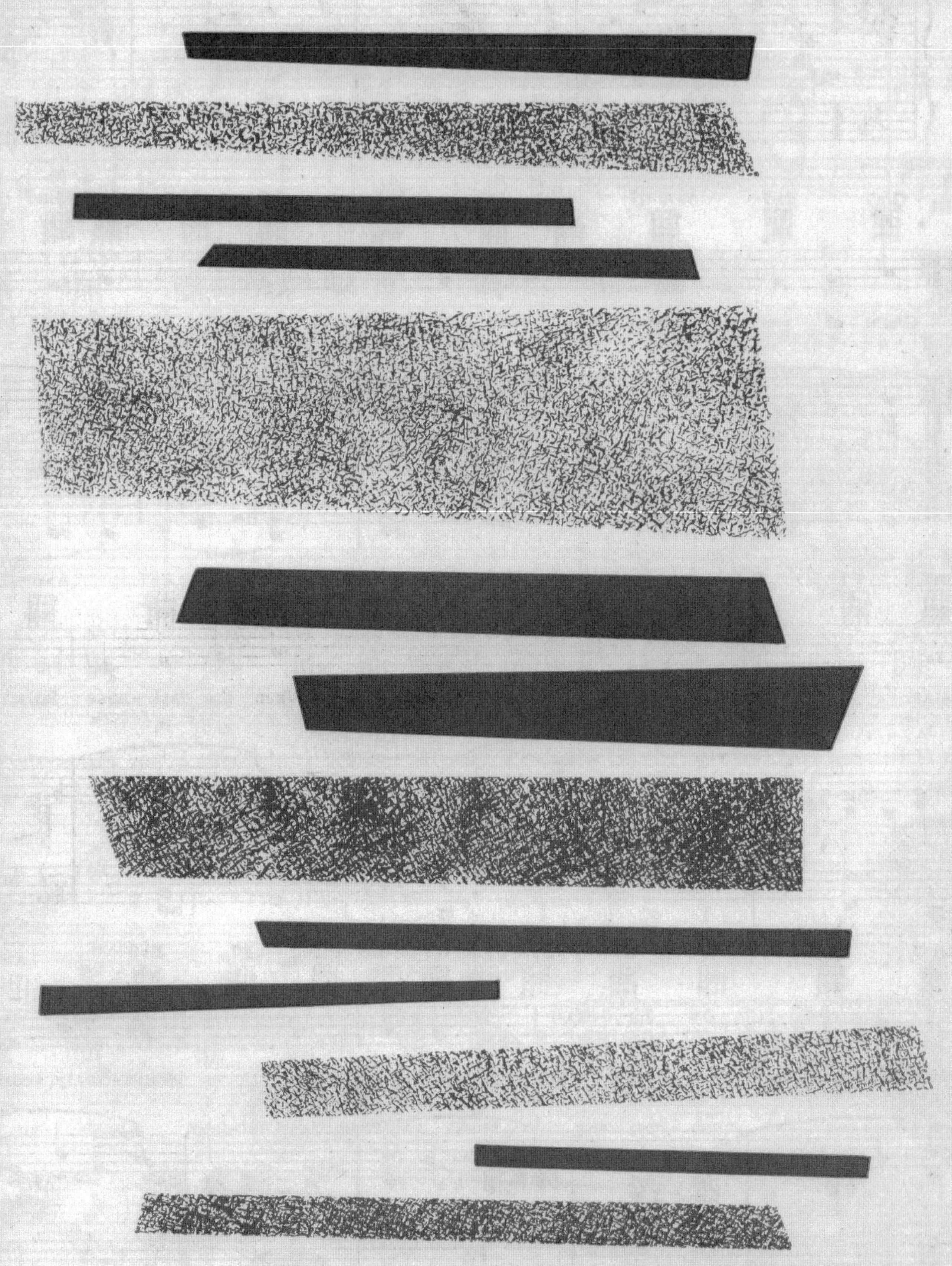

EDWARD B. MARKS MUSIC CORPORATION
136 West 52nd Street   •   New York 19, N. Y.

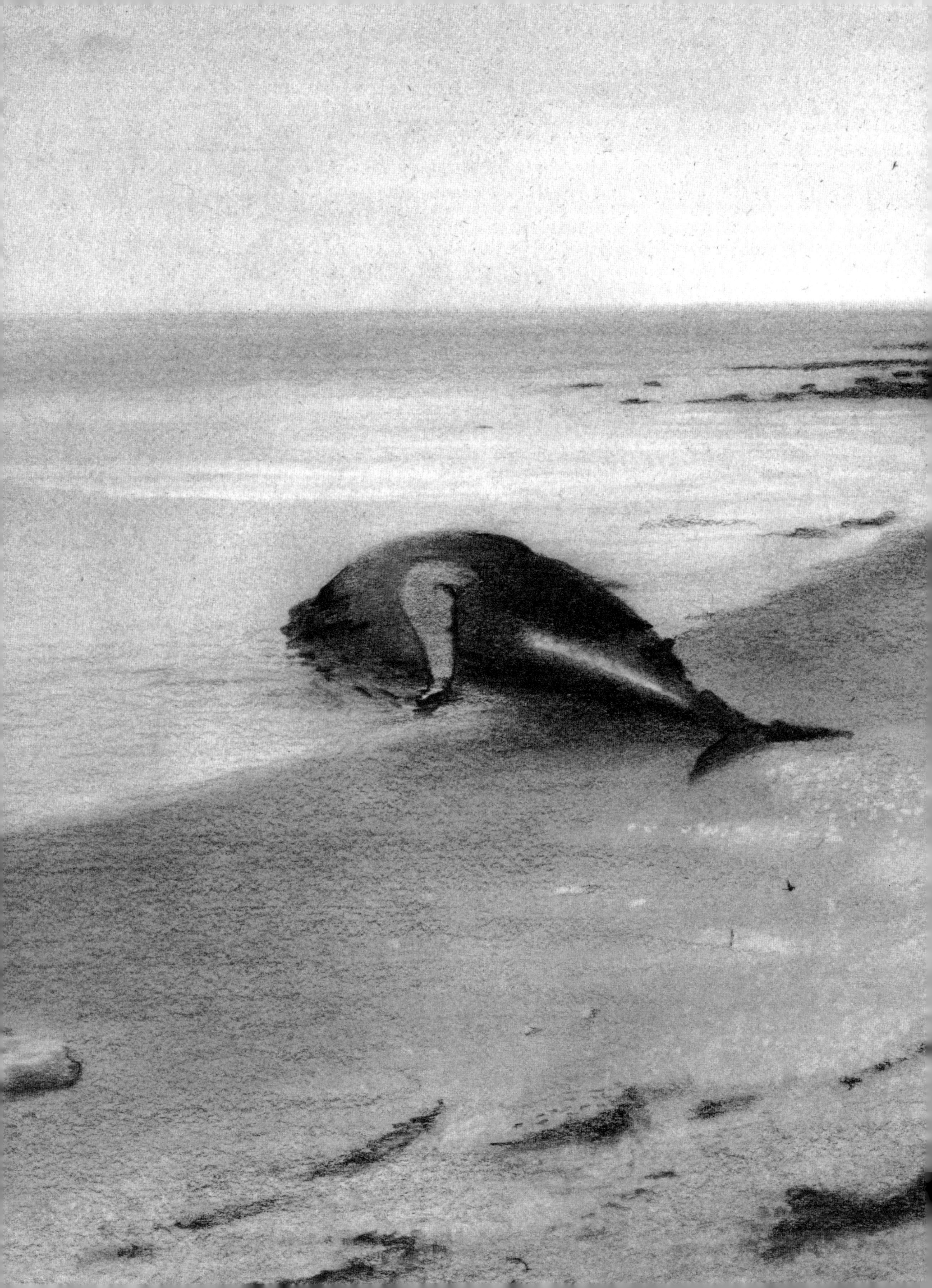

A HUNDRED YEARS FROM TO-DAY

lyric by
JOSEPH YOUNG
and
NED WASHINGTON

music by
VICTOR YOUNG

PRICE **60¢** IN U.S.A.

ROBBINS MUSIC CORPORATION
799 SEVENTH AVENUE • NEW YORK 19, N. Y.

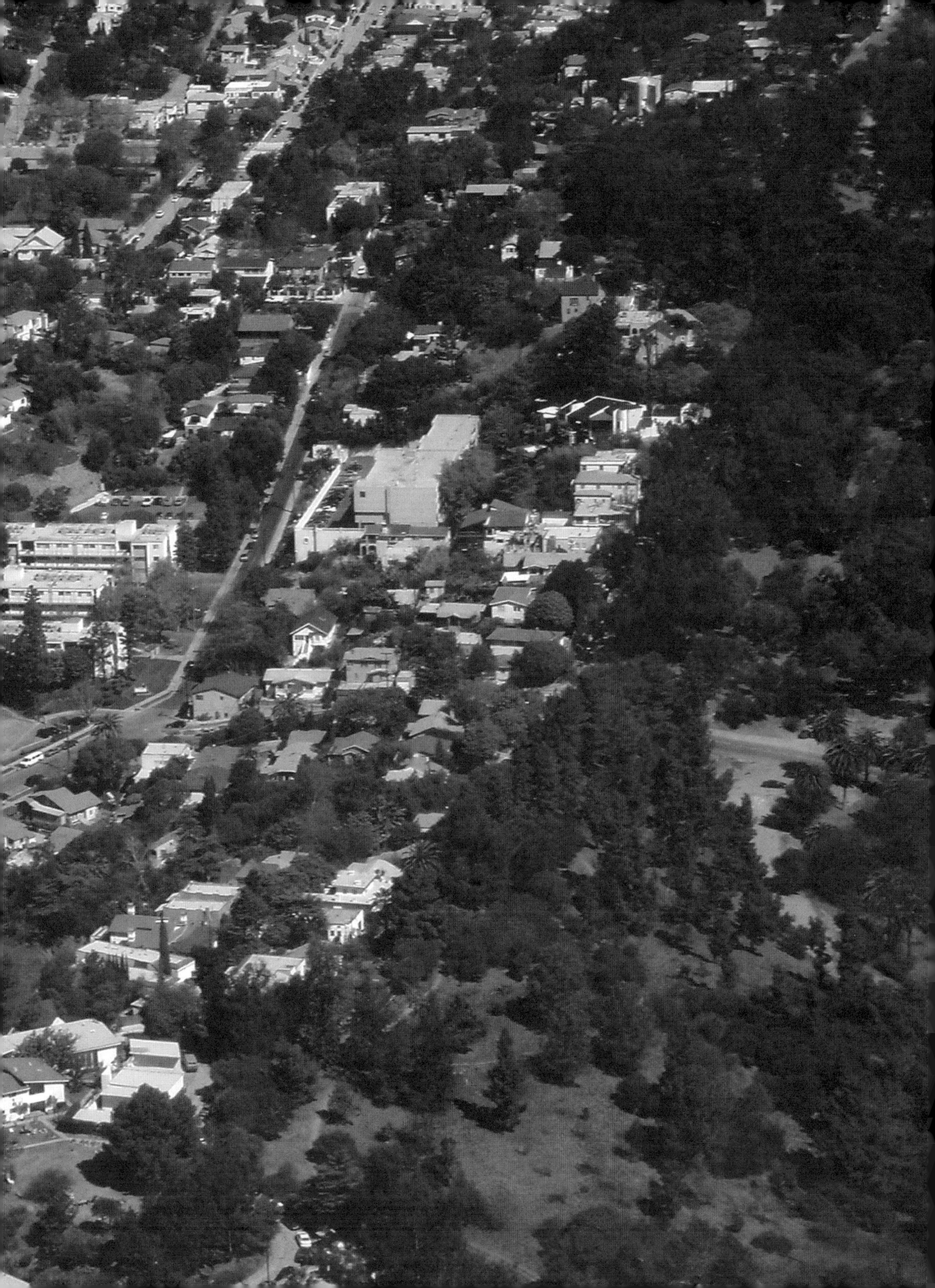

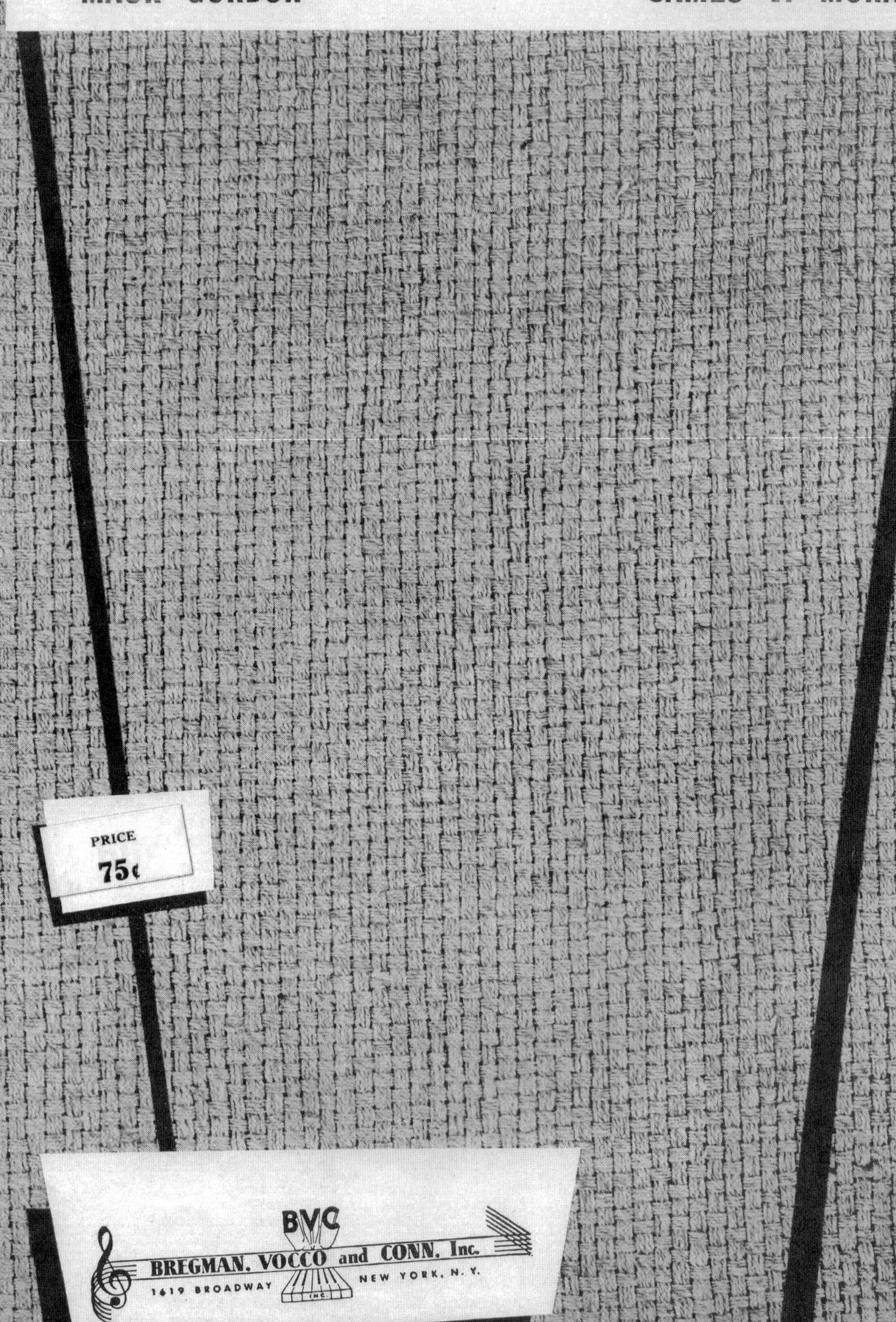

STANDARD BVC EDITION
TIME ALONE WILL TELL
LYRIC BY
MACK GORDON
MUSIC BY
JAMES V. MONACO
PRICE
75¢
BVC
BREGMAN, VOCCO and CONN, Inc.
1619 BROADWAY   NEW YORK, N.Y.

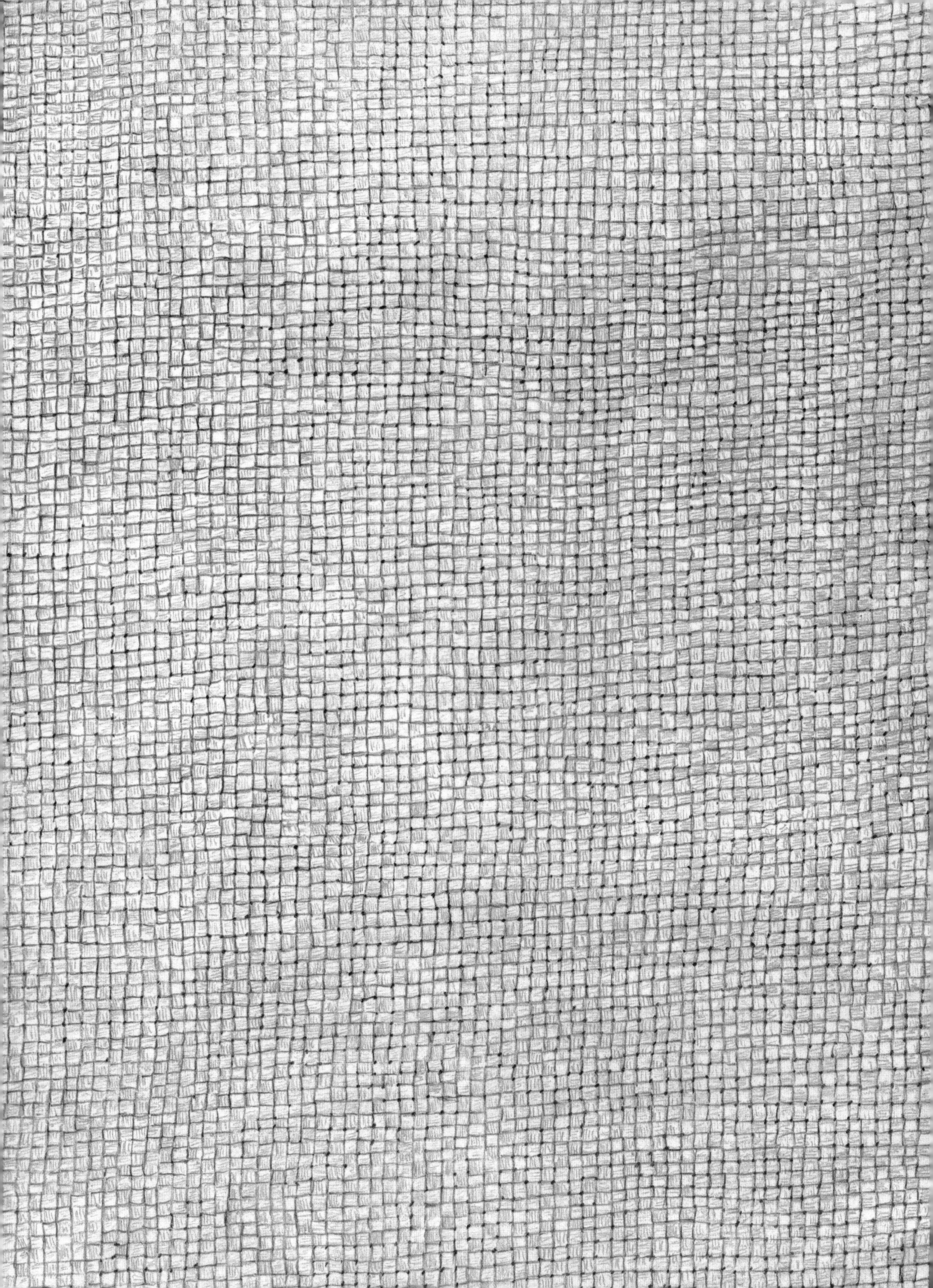

Show Me The Way To Get Out Of This World

('Cause That's Where Everything Is)

Lyric by
LES CLARK

Music by
MATT DENNIS

Price 60 cents

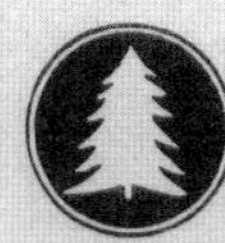

DORSEY BROTHERS MUSIC, INC.
33 West 60th Street
New York, N. Y. 10023
EVERGREEN MUSIC CORPORATION

19710 Henshaw Street, Woodland Hills, California

NEW YORK: 240 West 55th Street, New York 19.

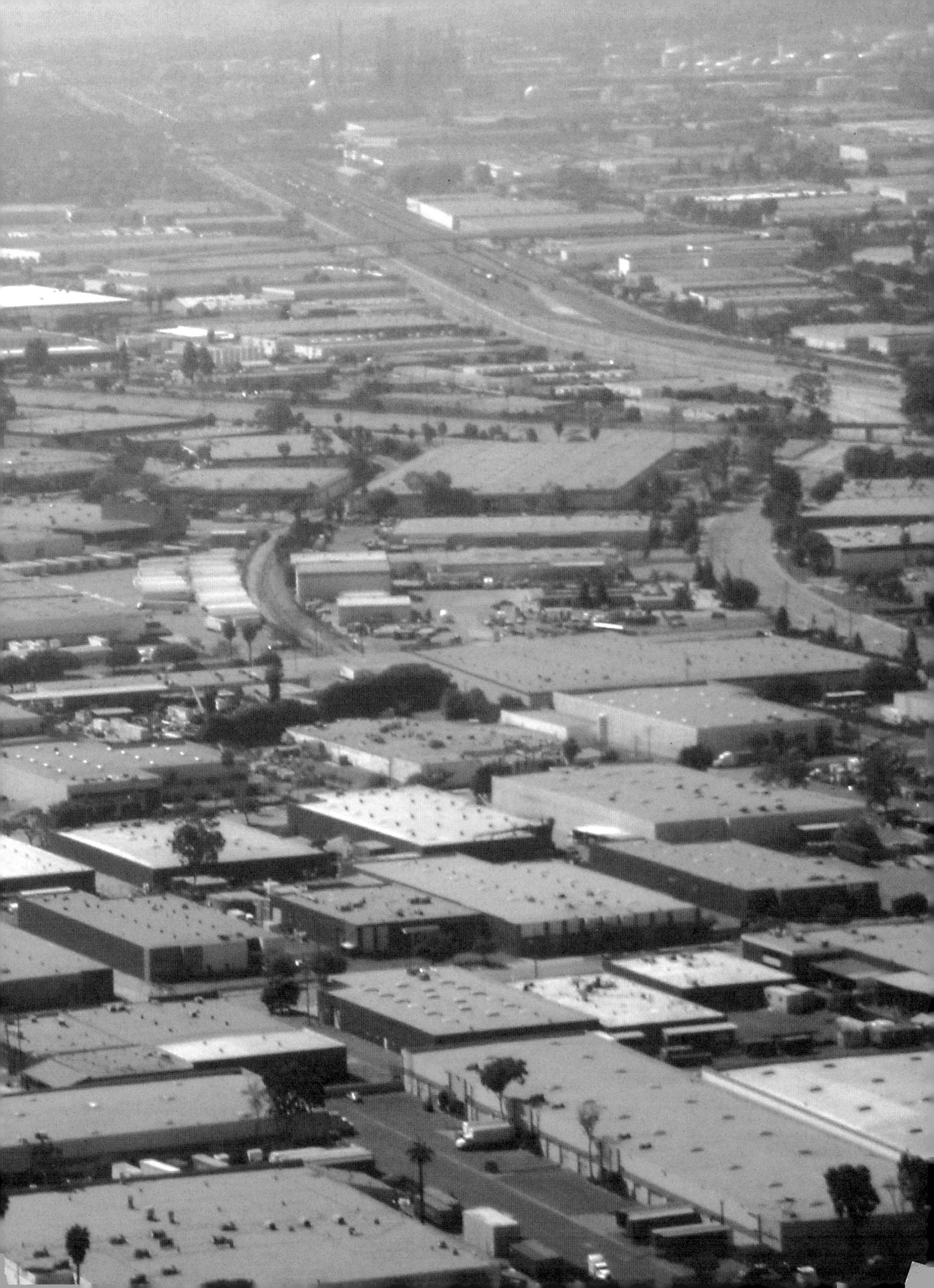

EV'RYTHING'S BEEN DONE BEFORE

by

HAROLD ADAMSON
EDWIN KNOPF
JACK KING

PRICE 60c IN U.S.A.

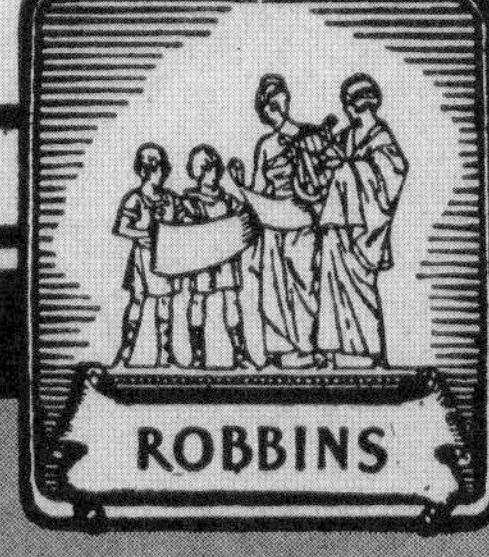

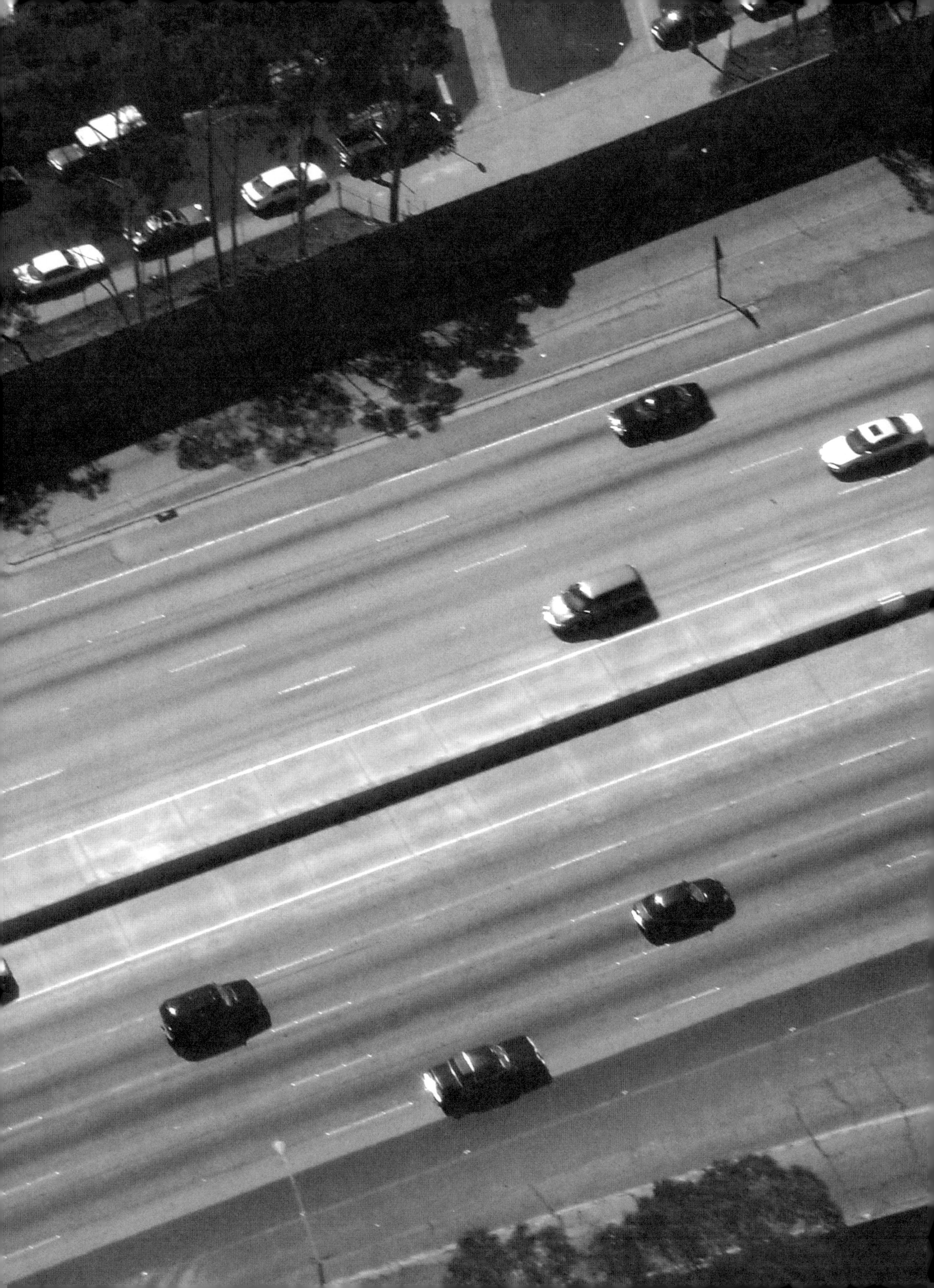

EV'RYBODY HAS THE RIGHT TO BE WRONG!

(At Least Once)

Lyric by
SAMMY CAHN

Music by
JAMES VAN HEUSEN

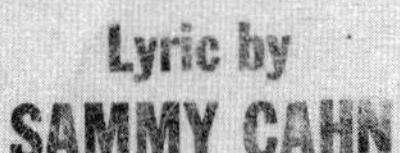

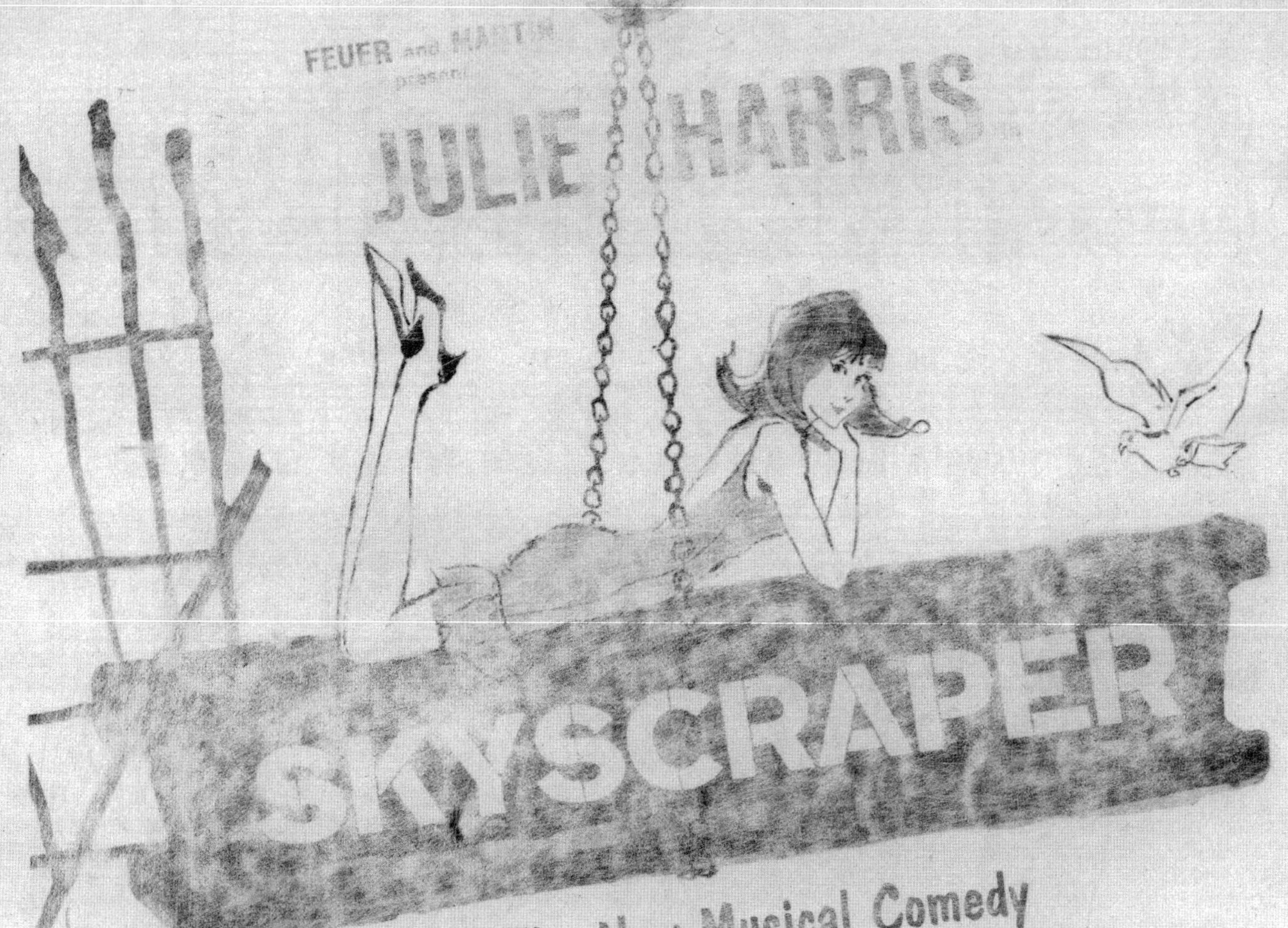

MORE THAN ONE WAY
(Theme from "SKYSCRAPER")
RUN FOR YOUR LIFE!
AN OCCASIONAL FLIGHT OF FANCY
I'LL ONLY MISS HER WHEN I THINK OF HER
EV'RYBODY HAS THE RIGHT TO BE WRONG!
(At Least Once)
OPPOSITES

Printed in U.S.A.

Price **75¢** in U.S.A.

Harms, Inc. New York, N.Y.

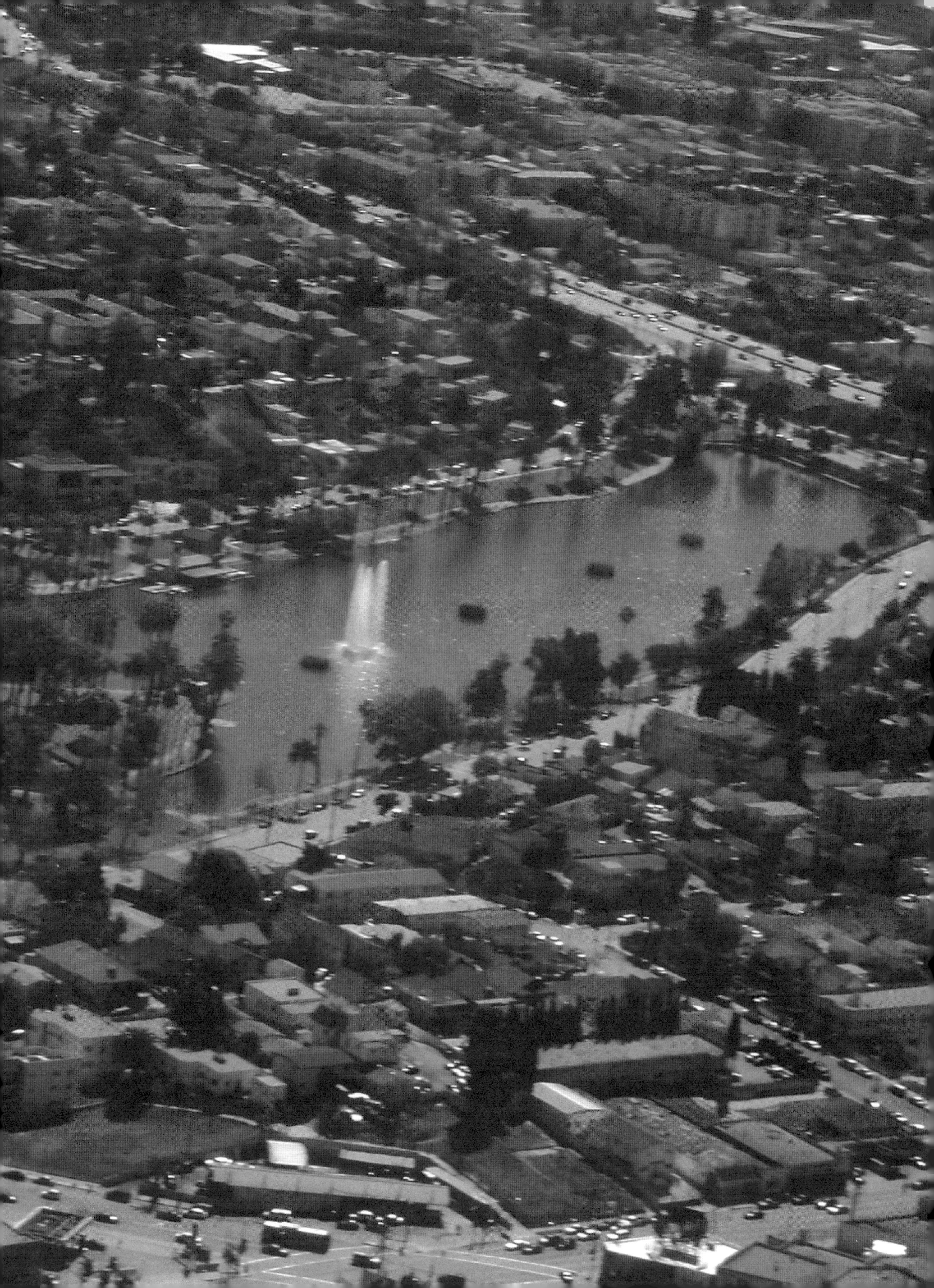

ADIOS

English Lyric by
EDDIE WOODS

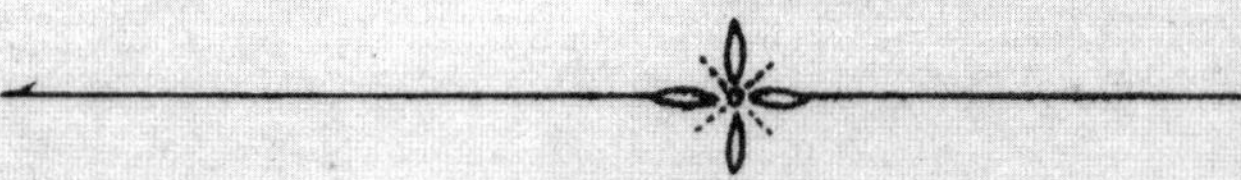

Music and Spanish Translation by
ENRIC MADRIGUERA

Sole Selling Agent

SOUTHERN MUSIC PUBLISHING CO., INC.

1619 BROADWAY   NEW YORK, N. Y.

PRINTED IN U.S.A.

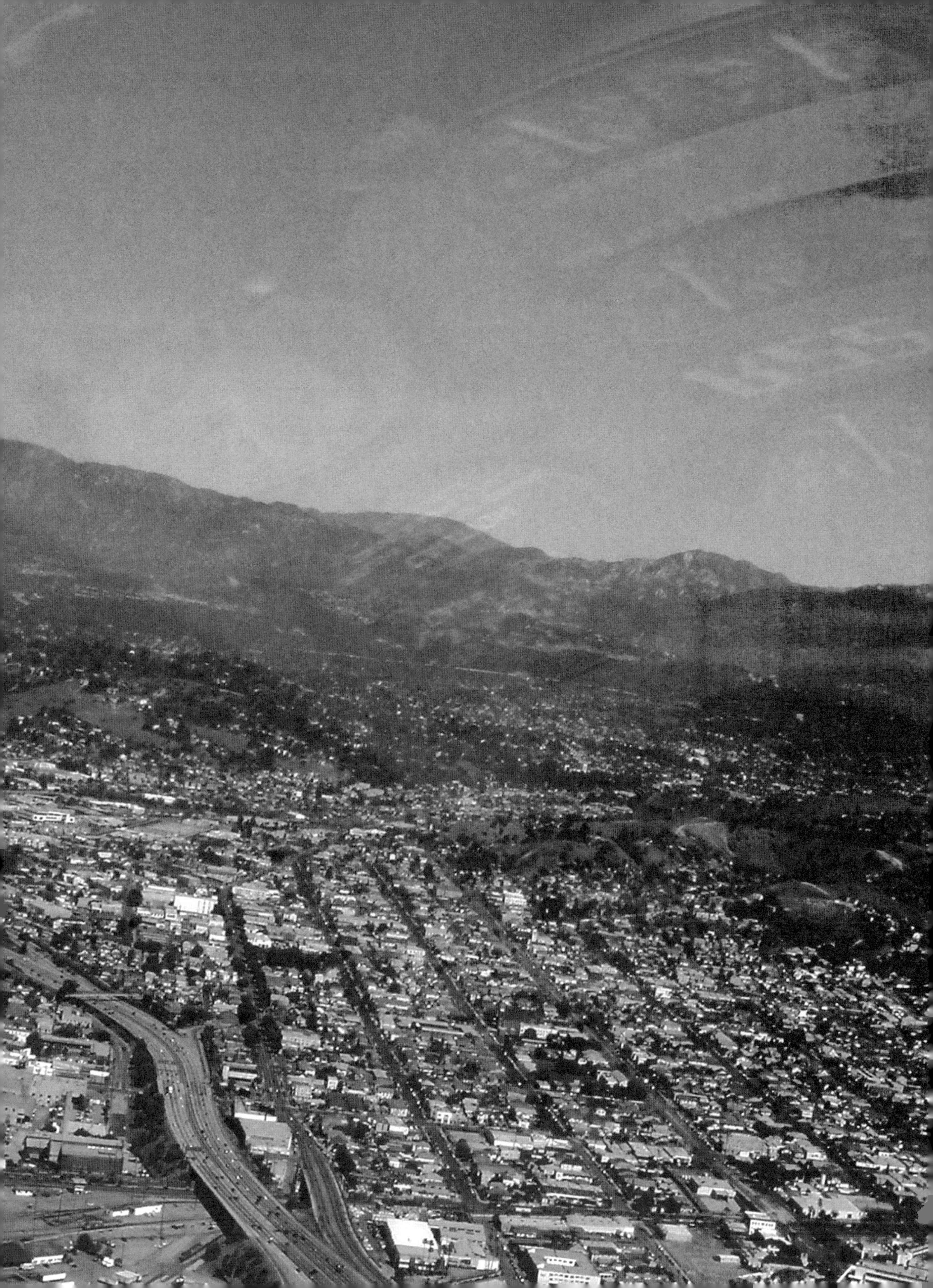

WE'LL BE TOGETHER AGAIN

Lyric by

FRANKIE LAINE

Music by

CARL FISCHER

Price, 60c
(In U.S.A.)

MARMOR MUSIC INC.
224 WEST 49th STREET • NEW YORK 19, N. Y.

SOLE SELLING AGENT

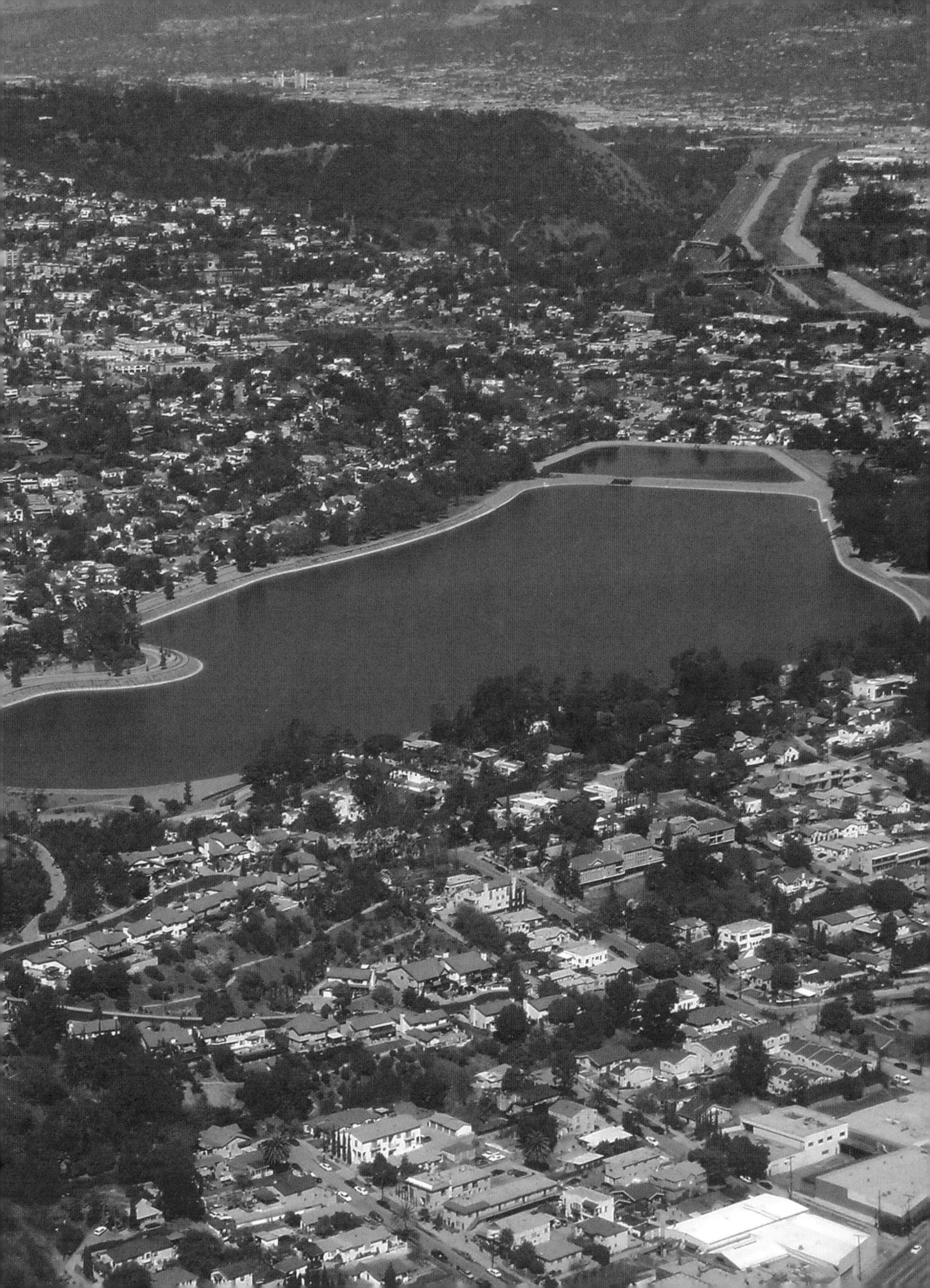

SOON

by
GEORGE GERSHWIN

Paraphrased for Piano by
MAURICE C. WHITNEY

Price 75¢ net
in USA

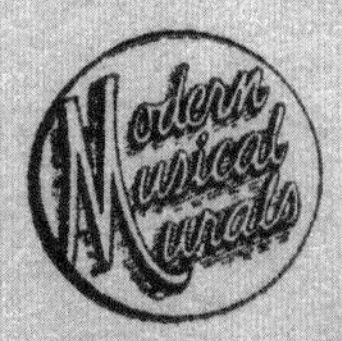

Printed in U.S.A.

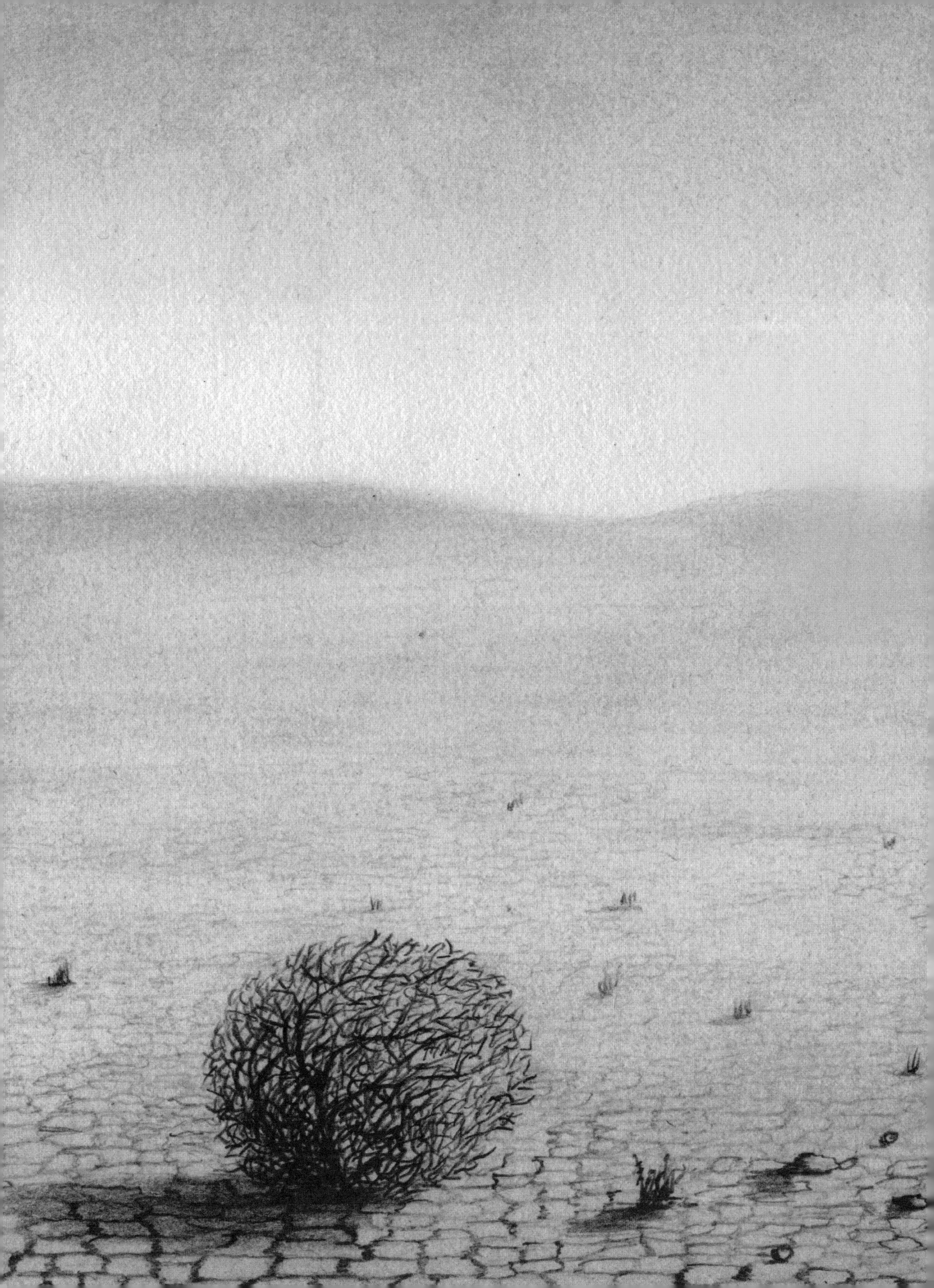

LIVE FOR LIFE

(VIVRE POUR VIVRE)

MUSIC BY FRANCIS LAI

TRANSCRIBED FOR PIANO SOLO BY JOHN BRIMHALL
FROM THE FERRANTE & TEICHER RECORDING

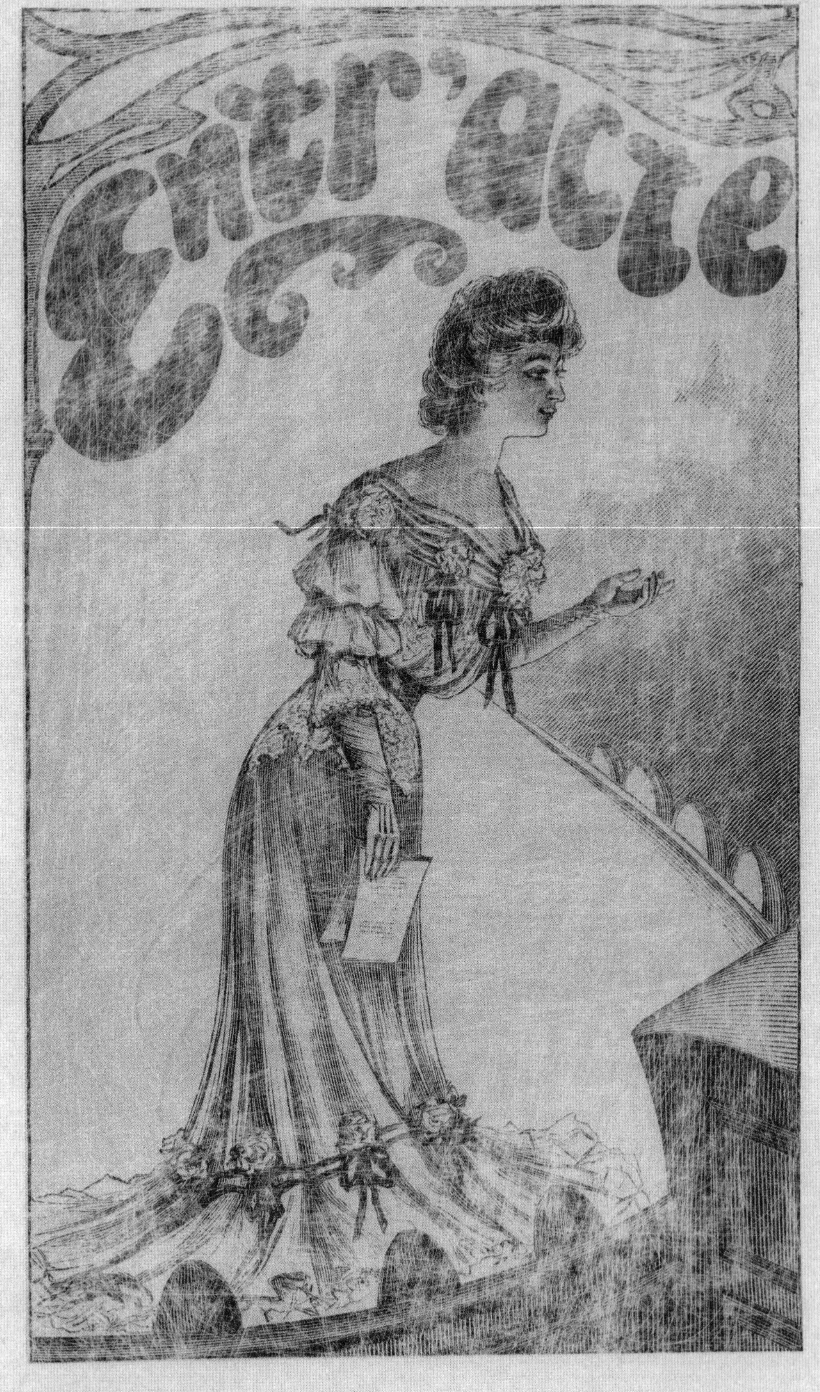

FROM THE UNITED ARTISTS MOTION PICTURE "LIVE FOR LIFE"

MUSIC BY FRANCIS LAI

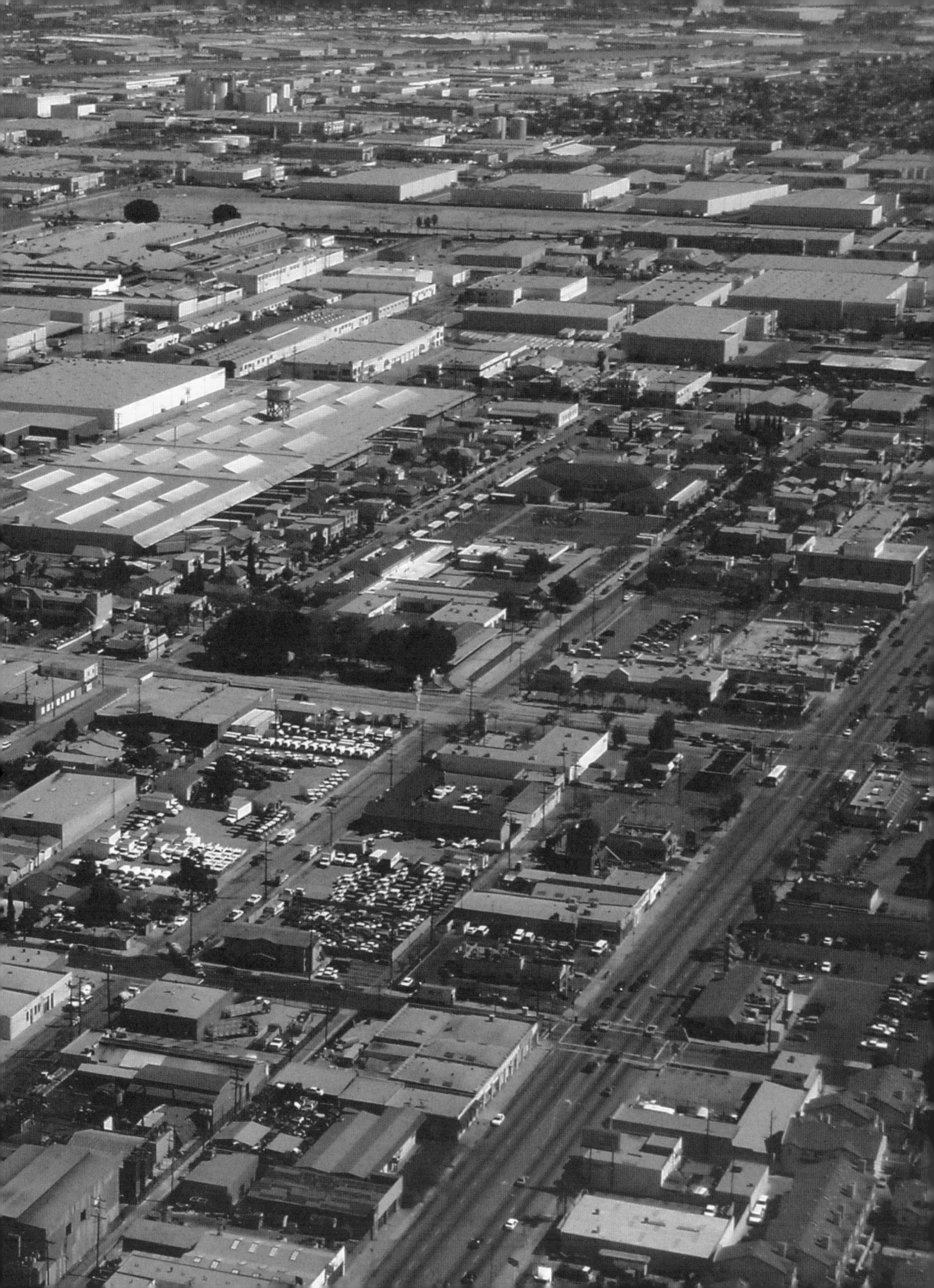

NEVER LESS THAN YESTERDAY

Words and Music by

RICHARD AHLERT and LARRY KUSIK

PRICE
60¢

APRIL MUSIC, INC.

Sole Selling Agents:
Cimino Publications Incorporated
479 Maple Avenue • Westbury, L. I., N. Y.

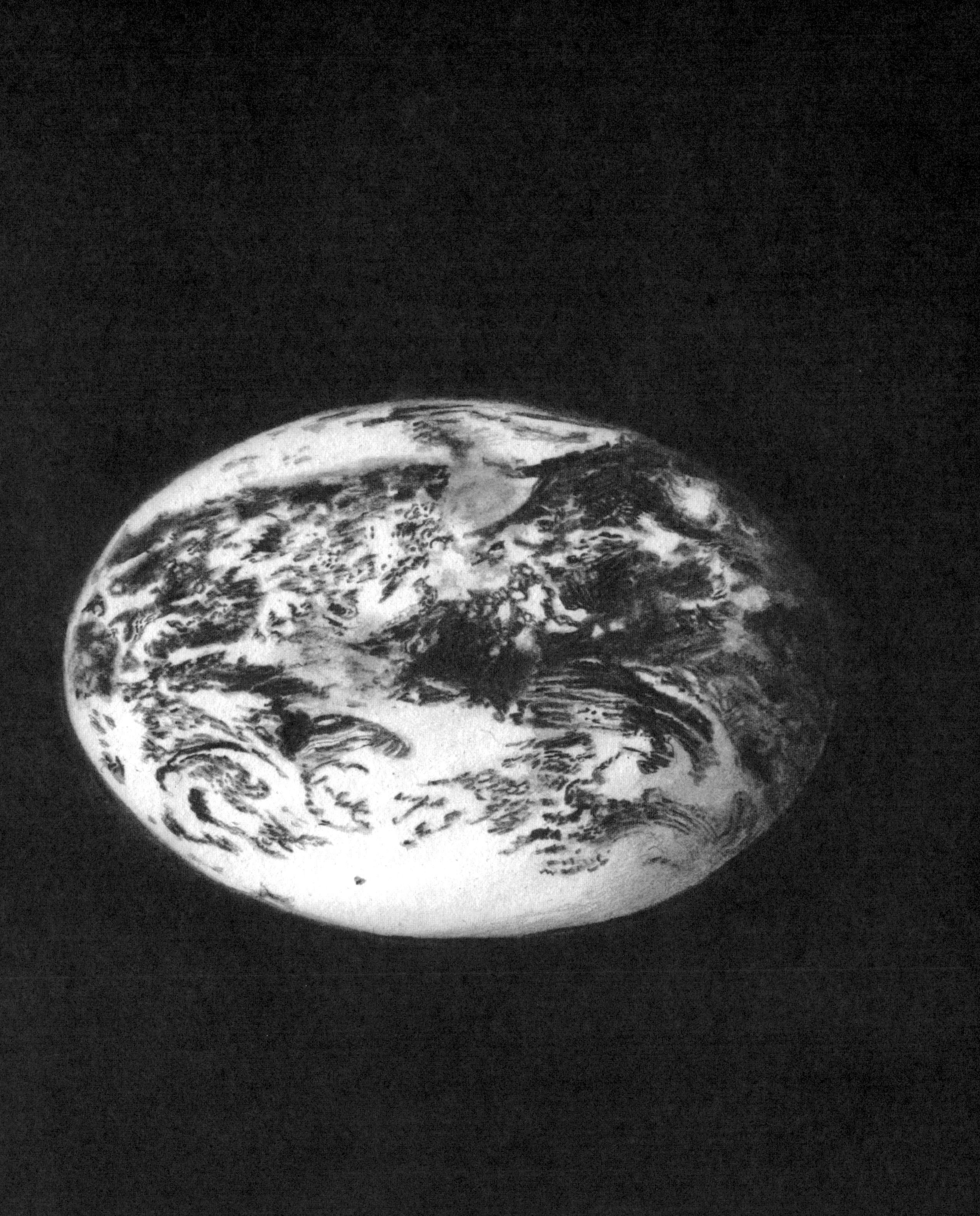

AGAIN

lyric by

DORCAS COCHRAN

music by

LIONEL NEWMAN

PRICE **60¢** IN U.S.A.

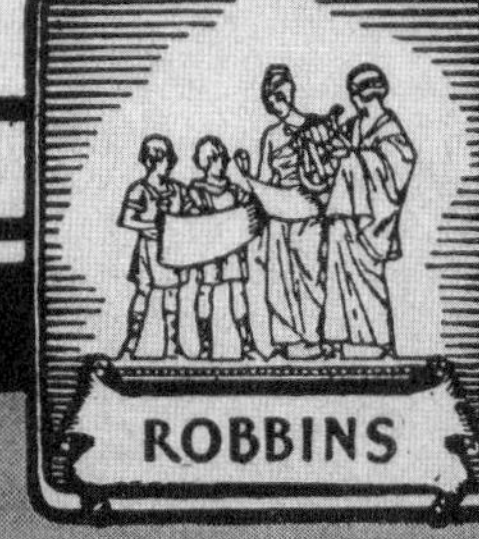

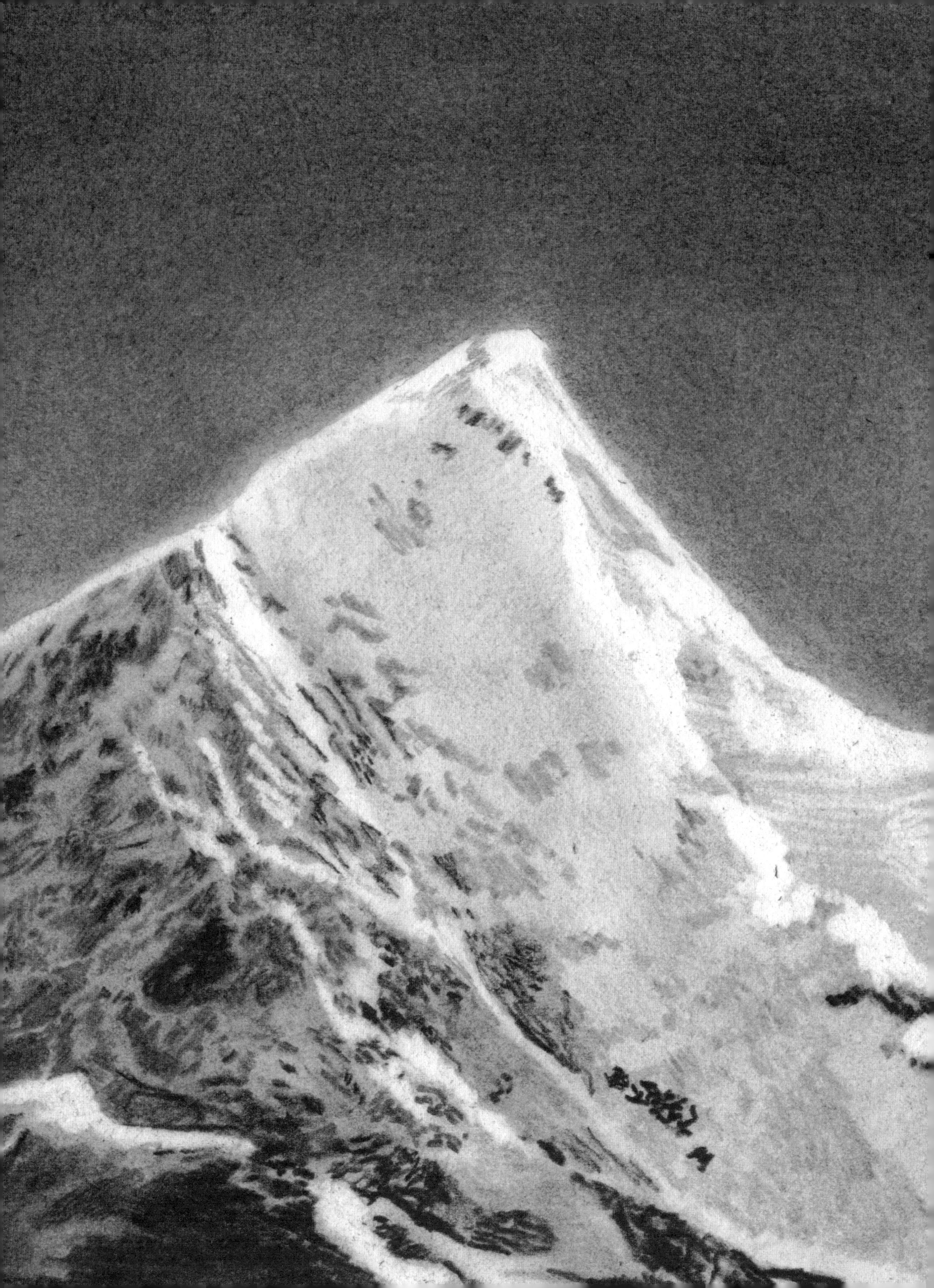

new in town
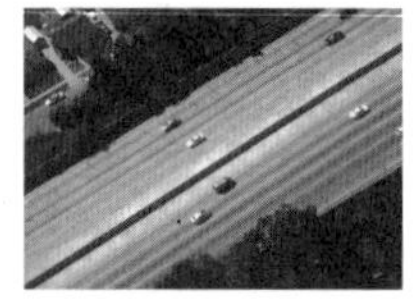

coffee time
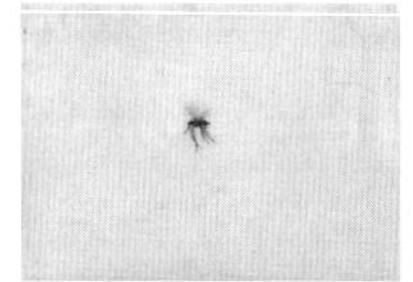

the friendliest thing
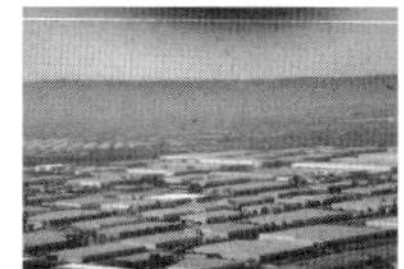

new sun in the sky
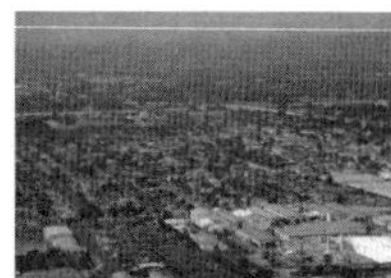

fine and dandy
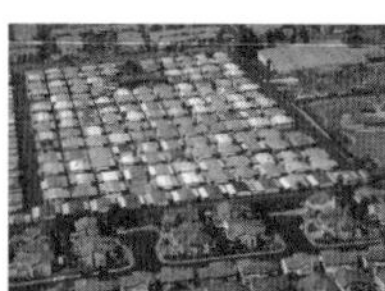

love is wonderful ev'rywhere
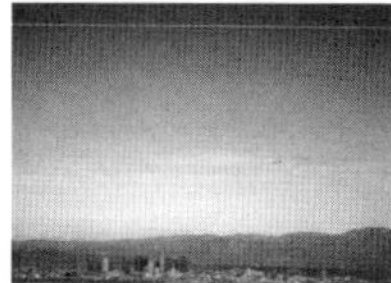

my silent love
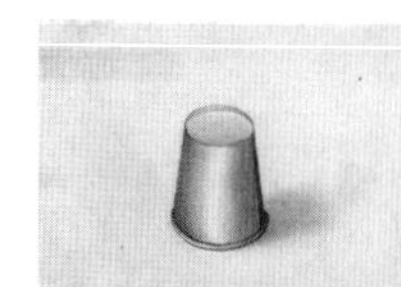

soft as spring
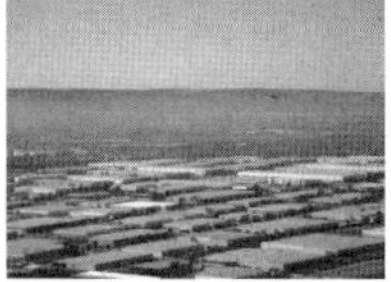

l'affaire
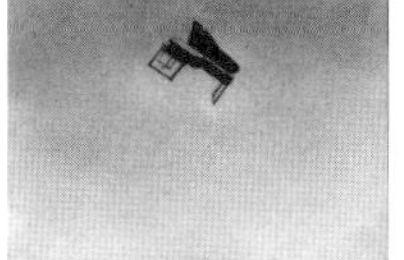

I know that you know
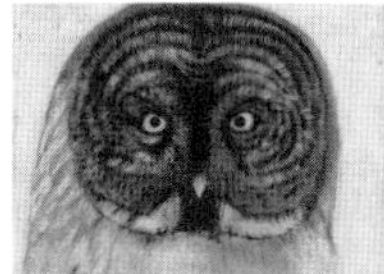

I understand
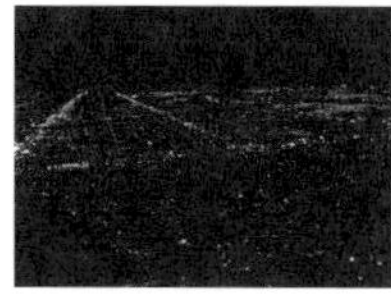

you are my sunshine
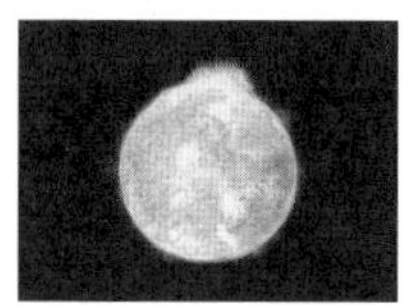

cocoanut sweet
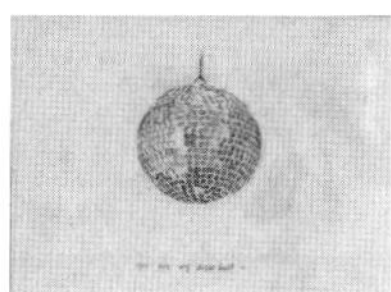

summer in your eyes
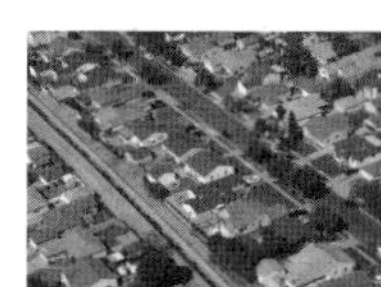

everything I have is yours
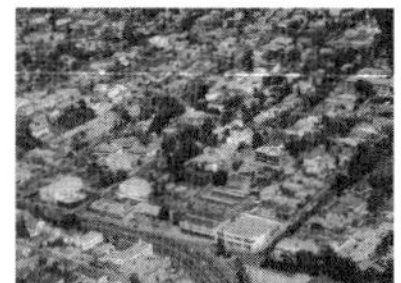

let's get away from it all
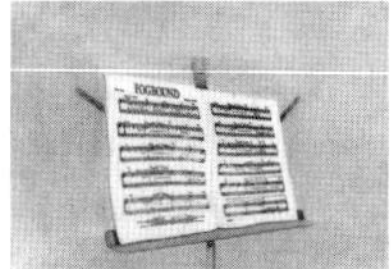

you smell so good
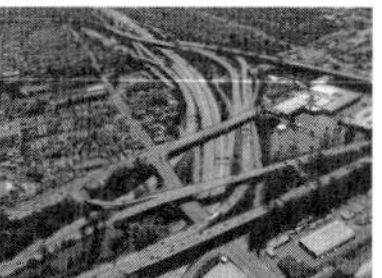

I'll always be with you
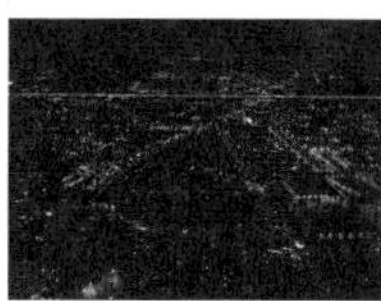

little bird
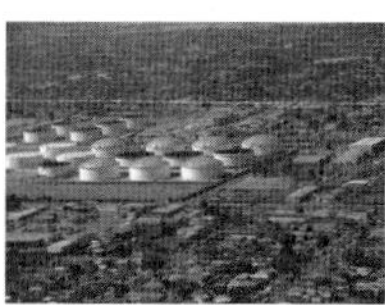

make love to me
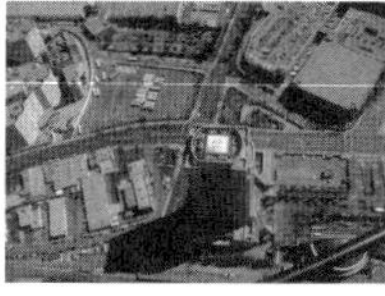

face to face
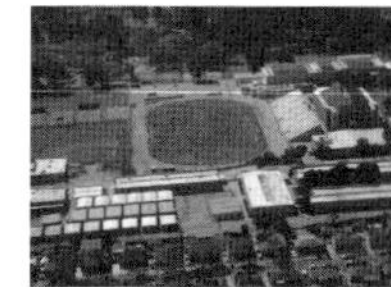

back in your own back yard
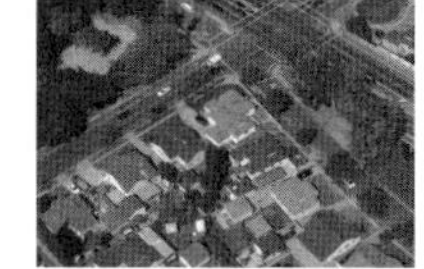

just for now

draw me a circle
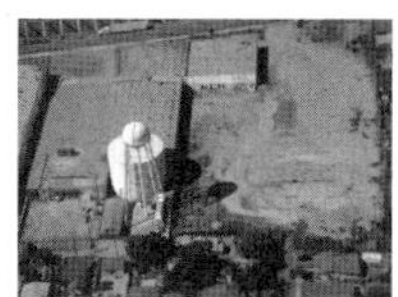

always in my heart
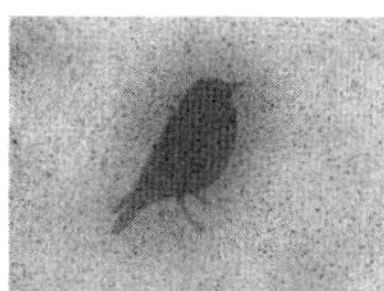

it's a good day
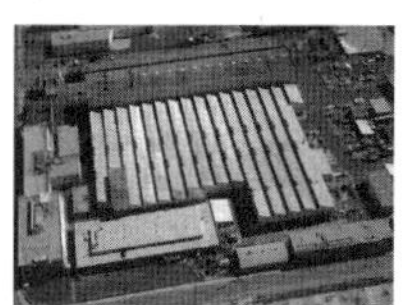

it's a big wide wonderful world
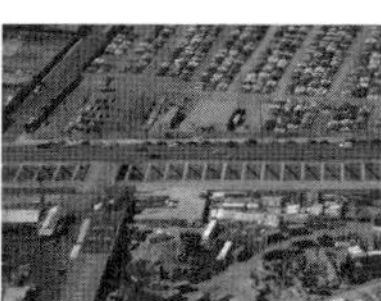

falling leaves
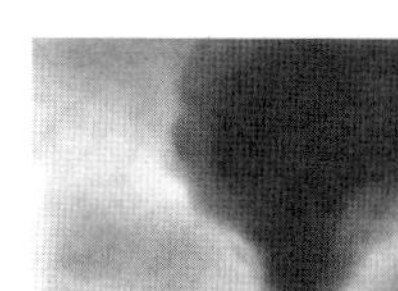

december
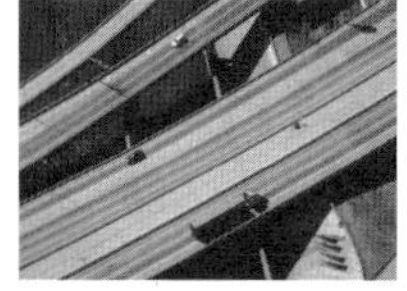

snowfall
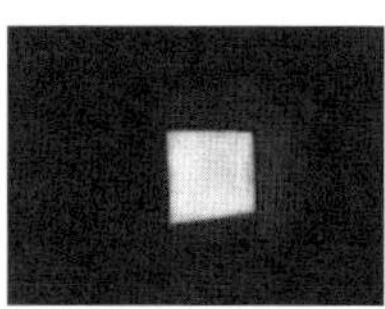

through a long and sleepless night
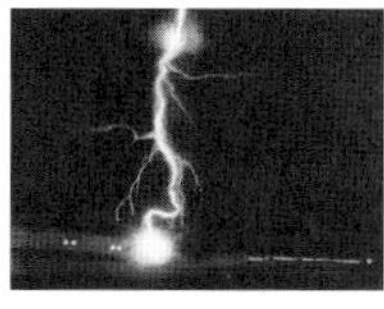

the starlit hour
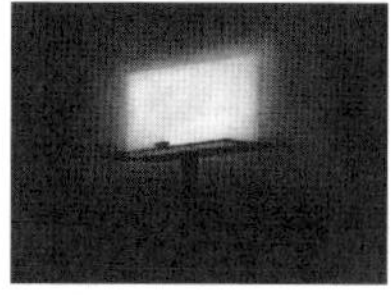

moonlight mood
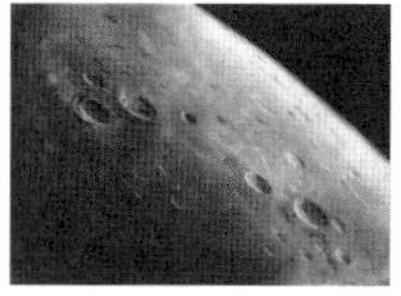

how beautiful is night
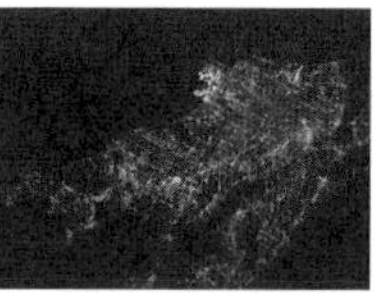

there are such things
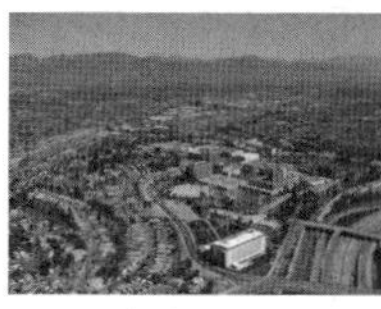

I never knew
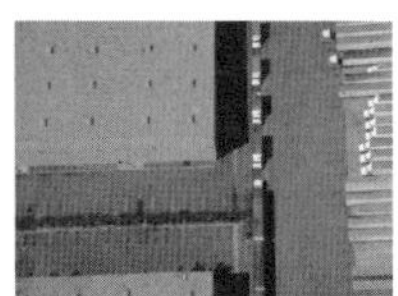

all through the night
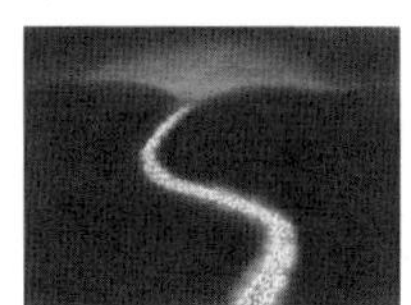

deep night
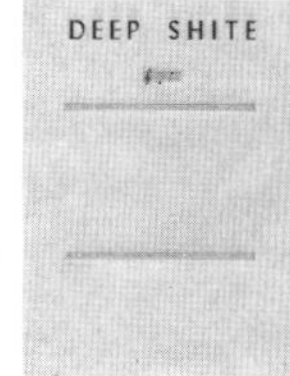
DEEP SHITE

the bad and the beautiful
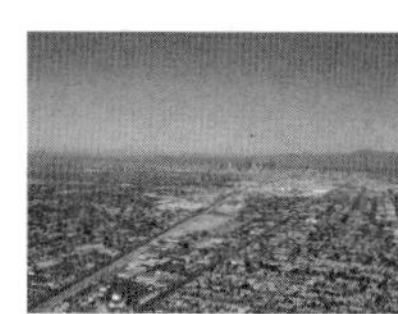

please be kind
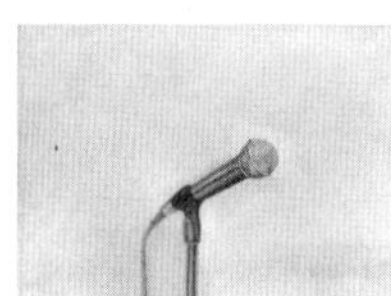

where, I wonder
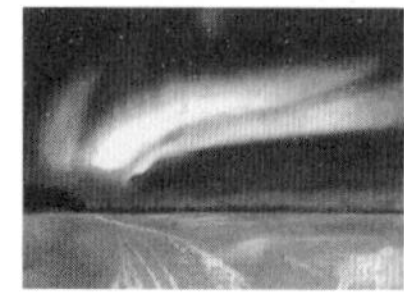

where are you?
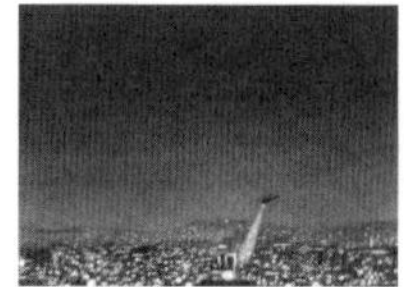

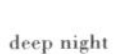

deep night   where are you now   there's no you   easy come, easy go lover   if I should lose you   that's the beginning of the end   possesion

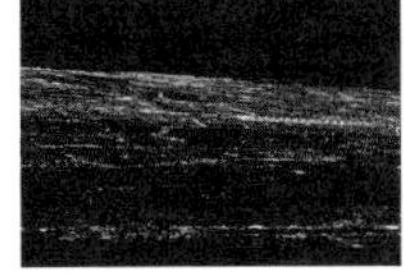 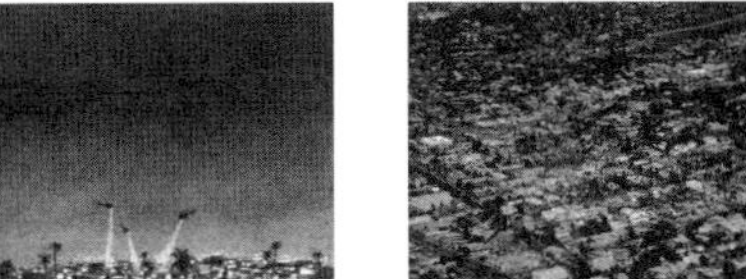 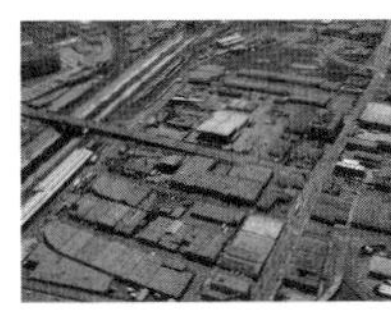 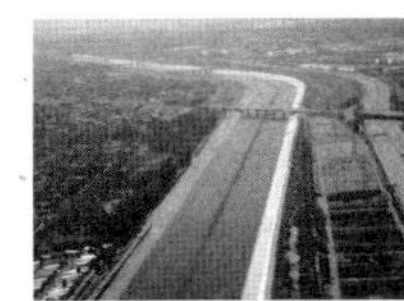 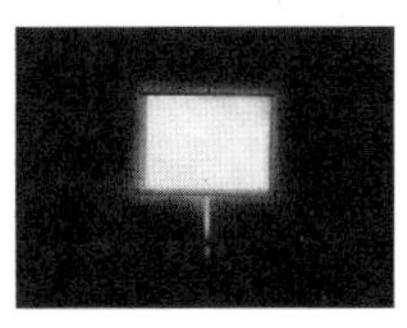 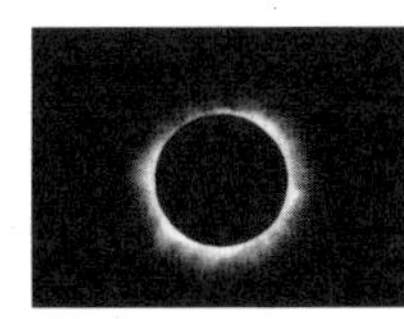

everything happens to me   deep in a dream   land of dreams   far away places   almost paradise   where flamingos fly   blue orchids

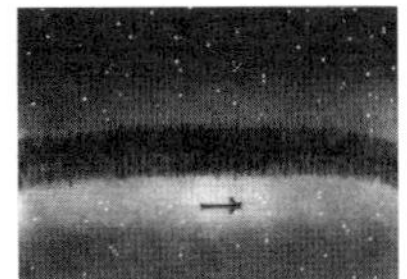 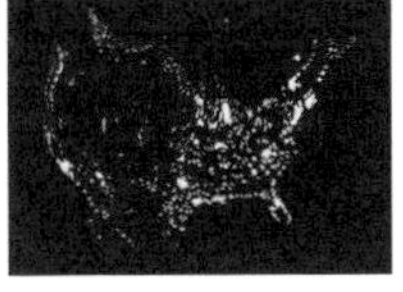 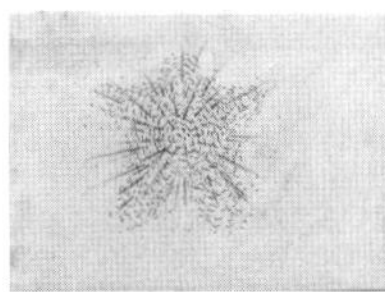 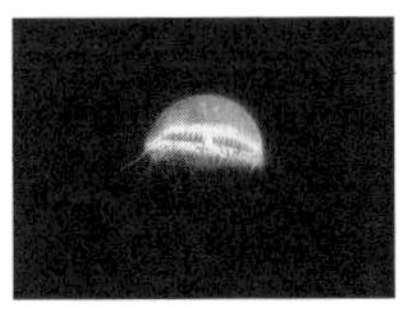 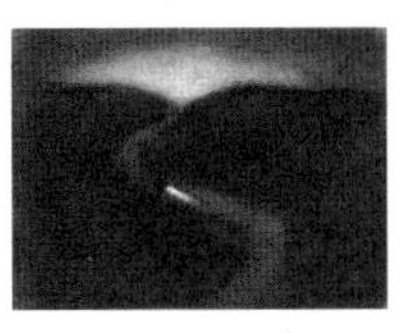 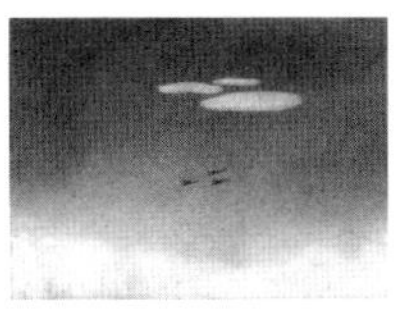 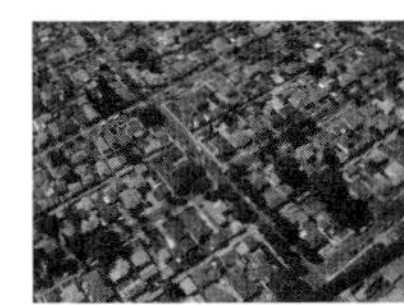

compared to you   imagination   ev'rywhere   all of me   fogbound   you're everywhere   more then you know

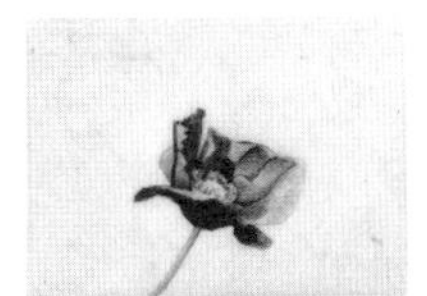 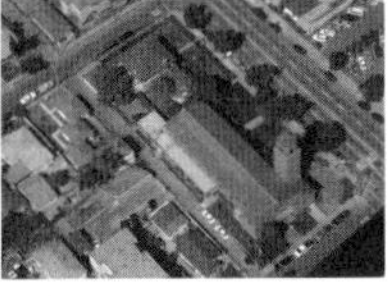 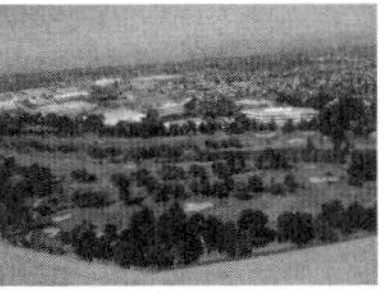 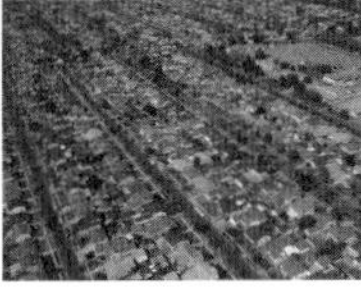 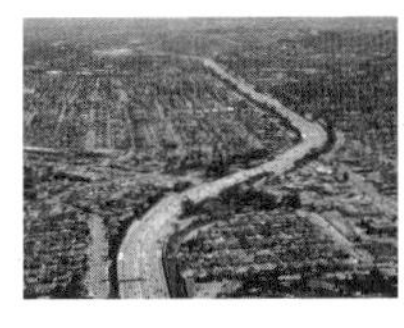 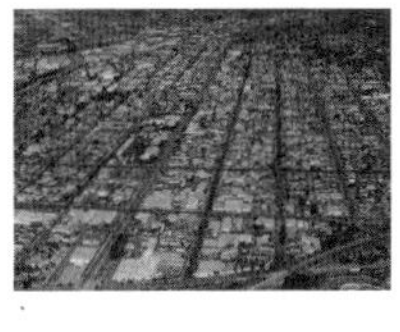 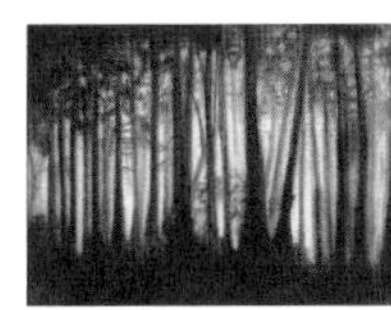

call me   tenderly   as years go by   love   that tired routine called love   you only want it 'cos you haven't got it   love for sale

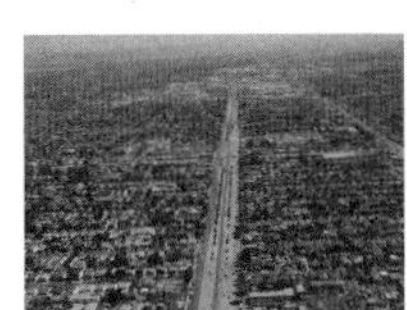 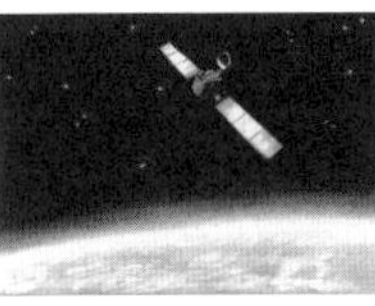 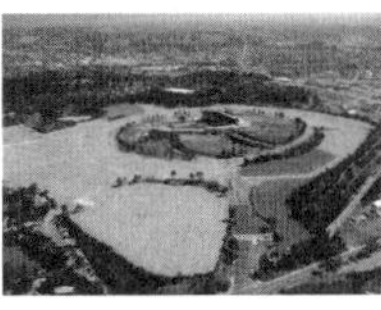 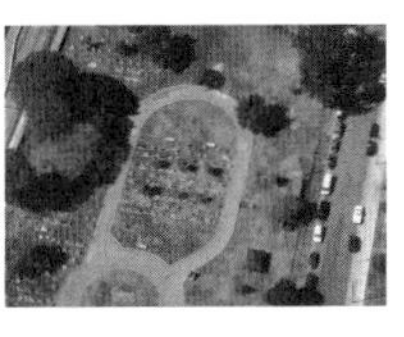 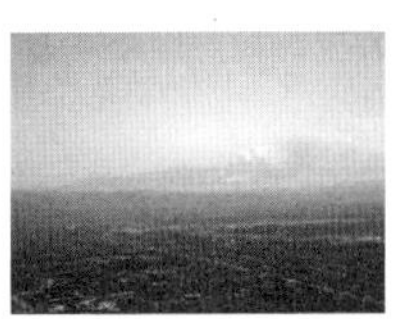 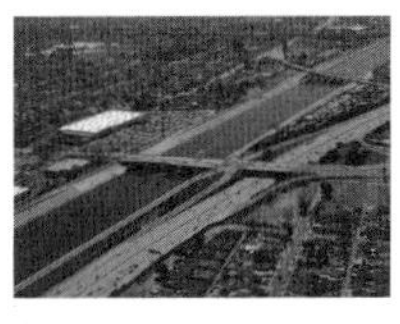 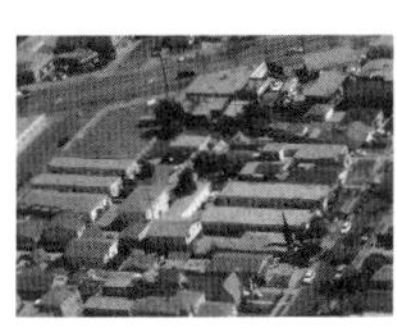

let's take a walk around the block   there will never be another you   ghost of yesterday   a hundred years from to-day   time alone will tell   show me the way to get out of this world   ev'rything's been done before

 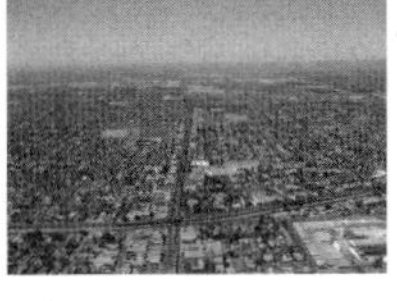 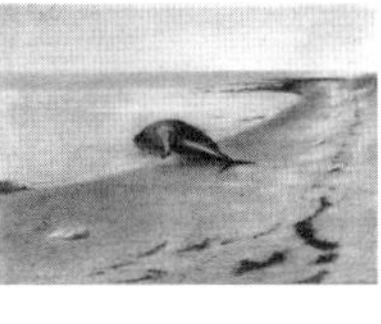 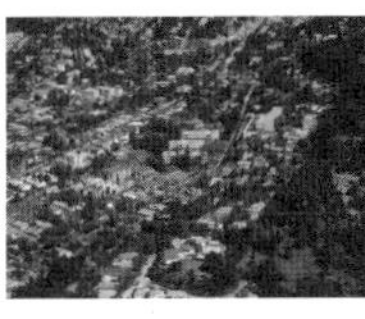  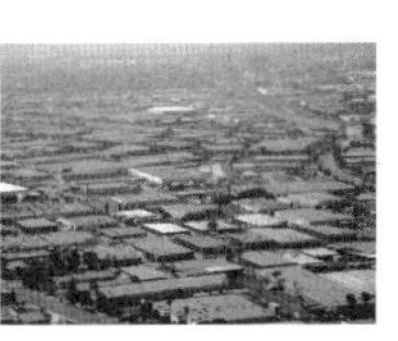 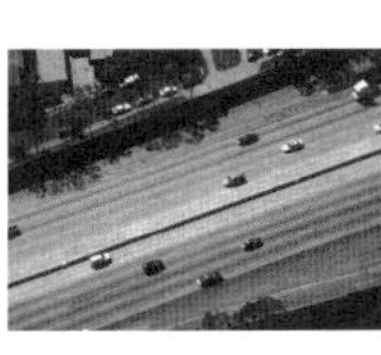

ev'rybody has the right to be wrong!   adios   we'll be together again   soon   live for life   never less then yesterday   again

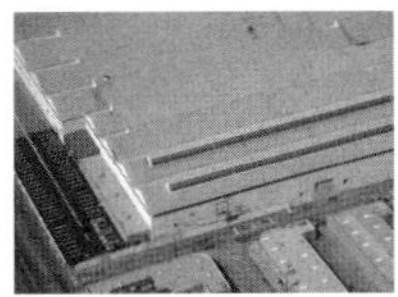

Editor: Euan Macdonald

Design: Henri Lucas for WILLEM AUGUSTUS, Los Angeles

Printed by: Friesens

Printed in Canada

Supported by:

GALLERIA S.A.L.E.S. - ROMA

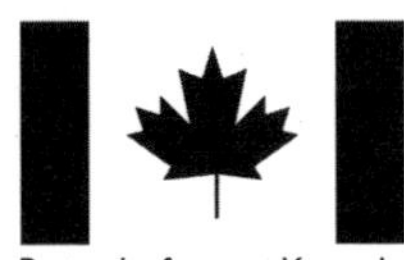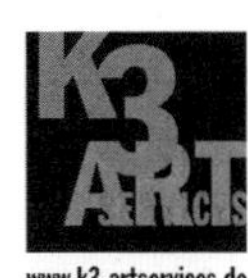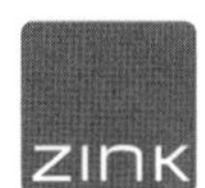

Botschaft von Kanada   www.k3-artservices.de   www.galeriezink.de

Published by:

Städtische Galerie Waldkraiburg

Braunauer Str. 10

D-84478 Waldkraiburg, Deutschland

galerie@kultur-waldkraiburg.de

&

Emily Carr Institute Press

1399 Johnston Street, Vancouver

BC, Canada V6H 3R9

scottgal@eciad.ca

Distributed by:

JRP | Ringier AG

Letzigraben 134

CH-8047 Zurich, Switzerland

T +41 (0) 43 311 27 50

F +41 (0) 43 311 27 51

info@jrp-ringier.com

www.jrp-ringier.com

ISBN 978-3-905770-80-3 (JRP | Ringier)

ISBN 978-3-935356-12-1 (Städtische Galerie Waldkraiburg)

Canadian Cataloguing in Publication Data: A catalogue record for this publication is available from the National Library of Canada.

Available internationally at selected bookstores and from the following distribution partners:

Canada: READ Books, www.eciad.ca/chscott

Switzerland: buch 2000, www.ava.ch

Germany and Austria: Vice Versa Vertrieb, www.vice-versa-vertrieb.de

France: Les presses du réel, www.lespressesdureel.com

UK: Cornerhouse Publications, www.cornerhouse.org/books

USA: D.A.P./Distributed Art Publishers, www.artbook.com

Other countries: IDEA Books, www.ideabooks.nl

For a list of our partner bookshops or for any general questions, please contact JRP | Ringier directly at info@jrp-ringier.com, or visit our homepage www.jrp-ringier.com for further information about our program.